Love's Greatest Joy

A closer walk with God

ISBN 978-1-105-35020-7

Published by Deposits of Faith, Barrie, ON, Canada
Printed by Lulu.com

For resources visit: www.lovesgreatestjoy.com

To Judi

TABLE OF CONTENTS

Preface

If you have an earnest desire to draw near to God, this book is for you. It is designed to lead you into a greater love for God, to delight in His goodness and to stimulate you to live for Him. It is also designed to provide a solid theological understanding of the character of God, His purposes and desires for all people. It seeks to provide an occasion for personal transformation by teaching, asking questions and providing spiritual exercises that will allow God's Spirit to move you closer to Him. It suggests spiritual disciplines that will lead to godly habits and enhance the quality of your soul-life with God. It seeks to move you to go out into the world to actively love others, by being a blessing and a witness to the God of love. It aspires to help you delight in God, His people and His purposes so as to live a life of supernatural joy.

Many in this life seek happiness. Yet happiness is a transitory, temporary state that is conditional on circumstances. I am happy when I am healthy, well fed, comfortable, doing the things that I enjoy, with people that I like, in circumstances that bring me pleasure. But what happens to happiness when the world crashes in around me? What happens when my health is gone, when my friends abandon me, when I am uncomfortable, hungry, lonely and miserable? Happiness can evaporate quickly leaving me in a sullen state of anxious discontent.

Unlike happiness, joy is of a different nature. It is fuller, deeper, profound and dense. Joy is of a fundamentally different origin and substance. It is a supernatural delight that comes from above and is independent of circumstances. Even if I am hungry, lonely, cold and miserable, in great pain and distress, joy can still be mine. The basis of my joy is something external and eternal, something that comes from my union with the source of all joy, God Himself. Joy as a supernatural delight, comes from outside of me.[1] It comes from Him. That joy can only be had if the Holy One, the source of true joy bestows Himself upon me and teaches me to savor Him, the fountain of joy. To receive it, I must be born from above. A legitimate reception of such joy presupposes being recreated, that is being born of the Holy Spirit,

---

[1] Latin: *extra nos* – outside of us: a key phrase of the Protestant Reformation

the third person of the triune God, who is the sole source of this kind of joy.

And because that joy is from God, it throbs with God's own heart. What God rejoices in, I rejoice in. What God delights in, I delight in. What pleases God, pleases me. Supernatural joy unites me with God, even in the midst of great suffering, for He suffers with me.

Biblical joy is a supernatural delight in God, His purposes and His people. Jesus rejoiced in the Holy Spirit when His disciples returned from being sent out two by two to bless, heal and proclaim the Kingdom. His joy was not only in God, but in His confidence that God's plan for salvation through His people was being made effective and that Satan was finally being defeated (Luke 10:18). Likewise God rejoices in you when you participate in His purpose together with His people.

God is Love. (1 John 4:8). He cannot help but love because He is love. And His love is not tainted with sentimentality or selfishness because He is Holy. His love is a spiritual love, a holy love. And this God, who is Love (1 John 4:16) rejoices greatly when you walk closely with Him, hand in hand, together with His people. The title of this book comes from this thought. *Love's Greatest Joy* is God finding His children walking in truth with Him. The Apostle John writes:

> *"I rejoiced greatly to find some of your children walking in the truth, just as we were commanded by the Father." 2 John 1 :4*

The theme of walking with God or before God occurs over 50 times in scripture. Enoch is described simply as walking with God, and startlingly we read "and God took him for he was not" (Gen. 5:24). Noah walked with God (Gen. 6:9). Abraham, Isaac, Jacob and Moses are all described as walking with God. God's people are continually exhorted to walk with God or walk in His ways (Lev. 26:12, Deut. 5:33, 19:9, 30:16, 1 Ki. 2:3, Ps. 56:13, Eze. 20:19, Eph. 2:10 ,5:2, Col. 1:10, 1 Thess. 2:12).

Walking is simply a metaphor for living, for the normal course of a person's life requires them to walk. But walking also brings to mind fellowship with another of like mind through the normal course of life. To walk with someone else, implies a fellowship and an agreement that both are headed in the same direction. It is possible to walk alone, but walking with God implies that one is united in purpose and moving in the same direction.

In Micah 6:8, the prophet rhetorically asks the question "And what does the LORD require of you?" The answer is simple yet profound: *"...do justice, love kindness and walk humbly with your God".*

Adam and Eve walked with God in the garden and they enjoyed a harmony with God, with each other, with themselves and with the created order. Eden, portrayed in Genesis 1 and 2, was a peaceful paradise. We all yearn for such a peaceful state. But paradise was shattered when they trusted in their own judgment and disregarded the command of God. The harmony and peace of Eden dissolved into a consequential state of disharmony that shattered their own self-esteem, their relationship with God, with each other, and with the created order. Enmity, inner turmoil and conflict entered the human experience. As a result, every person born has that inner predisposition to rebellion. If you observe a two-year old child respond to instruction from a loving parent, you will not have to wait long to see, in that child, the same rebellion that lurks in every human soul.

Yet God has created each of us in His image and has placed eternity in our soul. The initial rebellion, which we call "the fall" did not destroy the image of God in us. But that image is only marred, corrupted, and twisted, yet not eradicated. And so we long for a restoration of something lost. We long to once again walk with God. And the scriptures exhort us to walk with God. But we need a change of heart that is only possible through the divine initiative of God. For in our sinful state, we do not naturally turn to God, but rather we flee God. Adam and Eve's initial inclination after the fall was to hide from God. We hide, because we are ashamed of our sin, our spiritual nakedness. We also hide because we want no part of God's demands on us. Over time, our hearts become cold and calcified and we abuse others and ourselves. Every sort of addictive destructive behavior overtakes us. It is not possible to renew ourselves. We cannot give ourselves new life. Only God can save us.

And God has indeed done what no human could ever do. He has taken our punishment upon Himself. His only Son, Jesus Christ, willingly and obediently surrendered His life on the cross for us. Jesus is "the Lamb of God who takes away the sins of the world" (John 1:29). And it is only in Him that we have new life, a Spiritual life that comes from God. He supernaturally regenerates us and gives us the gift of faith. But that faith must be personally appropriated and exercised to be real. It results in a transformed life, lived in the power of God's Holy Spirit.

This book together with the study guides at the end of each chapter is designed to help you appropriate that faith and grow in your relationship with God. It will help you understand the character of God and His heart for you. It will help you establish habits that will progressively draw you closer to Him, give you His heart for those around you and help you to discover *"Love's Greatest Joy"*.

How to Use This Book

Each chapter of this book is designed to be read meditatively with a prayerful attitude. If you find that you don't understand or disagree with a particular section, you should ask God to guide you into all truth. Have your Bible near and look up scripture references whenever you feel led or that God is speaking directly to you. If you are convicted at certain points, you should pause and enter into a time of prayer, asking God to forgive, restore and cleanse you. We know that as we confess our sins, He is faithful and just to forgive us our sins and cleanse us from all unrighteousness (1 John 1:9).

The questions and exercises at the end of each section are the heart of this book. *Your personal growth as you go through this study will be five to ten times greater if you actually do the exercises than if you do not.* This is because the exercises are designed to connect you with God in prayer and meditation. If you simply read the chapters without doing the exercises, you will know what you ought to do, but you may not encounter God directly. It is like trying to teach someone how to ride a bicycle just by reading a book. That is not possible. At some point the person must get on the bicycle and try it himself.

You should use this book and the study guide exercises to give shape to your personal devotional times for the next eight weeks as you go through the material. One chapter should be read each week and you should allocate 30-60 minutes each day to do the exercises. There is sufficient material for five devotional sessions each week. You should pick a time of day when there are no distractions and you are fresh and settled. See this as your appointment with God each day for the next eight weeks.

The answers to the questions and exercises are designed to be recorded in a personal journal. There is insufficient space in the pages of the study guides to write down the answers and do the written exercises.

A journal is a blank notebook in which you will write down the answers to the questions. In your journal, you can take as much space as you wish to do the written exercises.

If you find the exercises uncomfortable, because you have never done this sort of thing before, persevere through it. People are different and some will get much out of some exercises and little out of others. You should write down your personal reflections on the exercises so that you can build an understanding of what works well for you and what doesn't. In addition, you should use your journal as a way of communicating with God. Write down your feelings, thoughts, anxieties and questions. Write letters to God, poetry and anything else that comes to mind. If you are not a verbal person, you can use your journal to draw pictures or map out concepts that come to you. Your journal will be a valuable touchstone for you as you look back on the time you spent in this study. It will also help you develop some habits and patterns and to record any convictions and resolutions that you may make as you go through the book.

Finally, you should dedicate this as a spiritual journey with God over the next eight weeks. Take a moment and ask God to be with you and to help you as you embark on this journey. If you are going through this study with a group, take some time to pray for each member of your group and encourage them to do the same.

May God richly bless you as you devote this time to growing in your love for Him and His people..

Study Guide for Preface

1. Read Chapter 1, *God's Amazing Love*. This chapter introduces the concept of God and what He is like. If you are a seasoned believer, this chapter will be a refreshing review. It will help you get back to the basics of the faith and help you share that faith with others. As you read, have a pen ready. Highlight words, make notes in the margins, and identify any concepts that you find intriguing, baffling or disturbing. These notes will help as you discuss the chapter in your study group.

2. Spend 10-20 minutes in prayer each day, reflecting on God's love and the ways in which you see it manifest in the world. Write down your reflections in a personal journal.

3. Answer the Study Guide *Questions for Personal Reflection* on pages 29-30. It is helpful to preview these questions before you read the chapter, so that you can answer them as you work your way through it. Write the answers in your journal. Do one question each day, rather than leave them all for the end of the week.

1. God's Amazing Love

"The heavens declare the glory of God, and the sky above proclaims His handiwork." Psalm 19:1

No one gazing into a clear nighttime sky can fail to be in awe at the splendor of the universe. The heavens do indeed declare the glory of God. The existence of creation demands that there must be a *creator*, just as the existence of a painting demands that there must be a *painter*. Incredible beauty, complexity and intelligent design testify that God exists. Only "a fool" would deny it (Psalm 14:1). And indeed, most people acknowledge that there must be a God. But for many, *the* question of the day is *"What is God like?"*

Many of the world's religions see God in somewhat vague terms. God is perceived as either a force or cosmic energy or a principle or a capricious deity who does as He pleases. Biblical faith, however, understands God as a *particular* God who reveals Himself to *particular* people and acts in history in ways that He alone explains. The God of Abraham, Isaac, Jacob and Moses identifies Himself as the one true creator God and discloses Himself to a people who experience Him in concrete ways and stand in awe of what He has done.

Often when we read the Biblical stories of God in action, we tend to see Him as one who acts in and for others but not for us. Yet God shows no partiality (Eph. 6:9). He is near and He loves you just as much as He loves anyone else. He desires above all that you experience Him, get to know Him and fall in love with Him. As He revealed Himself to people in all ages, so He is continually seeking to show Himself in a fresh way to you. But that requires a step of faith on your part. You must believe that He exists and that He does reward those who seek Him (Heb. 11:6). It is my hope that as you consider what God has done, the Holy Spirit will testify to your spirit that He is the One true God who loves you and calls you to experience Him in ways that are beyond anything that you might imagine.

Among those who have experienced God through eyes of faith, none can compare to Abraham. Abraham perceived God directing him and responded in obedience. On account of that obedience, God promised Abraham that through him all the families of the earth would be blessed (Gen. 12:1-3). It was through Abraham's son Isaac and then

Isaac's son Jacob, that God chose a people for Himself, Israel, among whom His visible glory dwelt while He guided them through a wilderness to a land of promise. He established a covenant with them testifying to His character and His will in the law given through Moses. He supplied them with prophets to chastise and rebuke them when they strayed. He promised them a new covenant (Jer. 31:31) through which He would write His laws on their hearts and on the hearts of Gentiles as well. When the time had fully come he prepared a people made ready to see His Glory (Gal. 4:4-5).

God then became flesh in the person of Jesus Christ, who lived and walked among us, fully God yet fully human. Jesus lived a perfect sinless life and then, in obedience to the Father, gave Himself up to death on a cross for the sin of the world. He rose from the dead defeating death and imparting new life to those who cling to Him in faith. He, together with the Father, bestows the Holy Spirit on those who are His new creations. He builds His body, the Church, that eternal community of faithful ones who live for Him. He promises to come again to judge the living and the dead, to establish justice and righteousness and to reign forever with His people.

The God of the Bible is not the same god as Allah, for Allah has no son. He is not the Brahman of Hinduism who manifests himself in multiple deities. He is not the pantheistic essence of New Age thought. He is unique. He is real, the one true God. He is Love manifesting Himself in action, action that creates something out of nothing and displays His glory, His holiness and absolute magnificence.

When Moses first meets God at Mount Horeb, he asks His name (Exodus 3:13). God's answer: "I AM WHO I AM". The Hebrew verb tense can also be read as future, I WILL BE WHO I WILL BE. Here also the personal name of God is revealed in the Hebrew *Tetragrammaton*, the four consonants *YHWH*. It is translated LORD in English versions of the Bible. This word is unpronounceable in Hebrew, because the vowels have been omitted. It has always been considered too holy to utter. Even today Israelis refrain from saying or writing the name of God, lest it be defaced. In their newspapers they publish it as G_d, or they use the circumlocution *The Name.* A name that is unpronounceable cannot be translated. And that which cannot be translated cannot be substituted.[i] There is no substitute for *YHWH*. He is the Holy One of Israel, the great "I AM". He is the God who redeems Israel from slavery in Egypt with ten mighty acts. Subsequently, He reveals Himself through Moses as the God of creation. He is also the God who raises Jesus Christ from the dead and, through the power of the Holy Spirit, redeems a people for Himself.

The "I AM WHO I AM" defines Himself by Himself and by His actions, which are a manifestation of who He is. In other words, *He is what He does and He does what He is*. There is no inconsistency in Him, but He always acts in accordance with His nature. Because His actions might be misinterpreted, we must rely on Him telling us the significance of these actions through His prophets, apostles, and of course through His Son. That is why we need the scriptures, which, when read by the illumination of the Holy Spirit, are normative to our perception of Him. If we did not have the Holy Scriptures, we would never know the significance of any of His acts, nor would we know Him.

The scriptures tell us that God is Love (1 John 4:16). And because God is Love, any act of God is an act of love. Love is not an abstract concept but is an action word, a verb. And love in action always has an object for that action. Within the triune Godhead, the Father loves the Son in the unity of the Holy Spirit. Because God is infinite, the expression of love within the Godhead is an infinite expression. This infinite expression of love bestows infinite value on the objects of that love. In creating us, God bestows such value on us. In creating you, He has bestowed such infinite value on you. You are worth more than anything to Him, for He withheld not even His own Son, for you. He loves *you*.

The God Who Creates

When one reads the creation accounts in Genesis chapters 1 and 2, one cannot help but be gripped by a sense of the absolute transcendence of God and, at the same time, His hands-on personal intimacy as He works with the dust of the earth to create the first human beings. Here we do not have an impersonal God who works at a distance. Rather, like a master workman (Prov. 8:30), He orchestrates each step in creation and speaks all things into existence with a logic that leaves one breathless. As each day of creation builds on the day before, the goodness of all creation is affirmed several times (Gen.1:4,10, 12,18,21,25,31). God provides for us an incredibly good, beautifully complex and intricately woven world. The climax of the creation account is humankind. In creating humans, God does not merely speak them into existence but forms them Himself, breathing the breath of life into them personally (Gen. 2:7). In creation, God provides a magnificent setting within which human beings will dwell and flourish, and over which He gives them dominion. Humankind is the crown jewel of God's creation.

We should note also that creation is a completely voluntary act of God. There is in God no inner compulsion to create. If there were, then God would have to be subject to some sort of compulsion, which would negate His absolute autonomy. Loneliness could not be a motive, for He is eternally Father, Son and Holy Spirit, three Persons, one God. He would have still remained God in all His glory had He decided not to create. Because God has existed in a state in which He was *not yet* creator, creation is *a novum* (a new thing) in God's life. And so, God's decision to create is purely an act of selfless love for in it He bestows existence on that which is not. Had God not chosen to create, we would simply not exist. In addition, God creates *ex nihilo* (out of nothing). His love expressed brings into existence that which is not. Out of the great nothingness, He causes everything to be. His love expressed is the creative energy that causes you and I to be, to continue to be and to flourish.

Moreover God creates us in His own image, endowing the created order with autonomous beings, who are like Him and who will represent Him and rule over the animals and world. We humans are the highest of His created order for we alone are made in His own image (Latin: *Imago Dei*). We are also the only earthly beings to whom God speaks. Adam and Eve heard His voice and experienced Him firsthand. He held them responsible for responding appropriately to Him. So also He hold us.

Creating autonomous creatures, who bear God's image is a step of faith. In the decision to create us with free will there is risk. What happens if such freedom results in rebellion, a creation gone wrong? To think that God was somehow unaware that it could all go wrong is surely naïve. The very act of creating humankind in His image manifests God's amazing love, for in it He bestows His *likeness* upon the objects of His love, for which there exists the very real possibility, perhaps even a certainty, that love will be spurned and that rebellion will follow. It is a cosmic drama that has no parallel. And in this drama, we see the supreme act of God's guiding yet releasing love.

AGAPE LOVE

As there are many meanings of the English word *love*, we should perhaps amplify what we mean by it. The Greek word used in the original language is *agape.* This is love characterized by a deliberate conscious commitment to the well being of another, even at great personal cost. The fact that Jesus died for us, demonstrates that He loves us in that way. It makes us incredibly valuable to the Father for He withheld not even His own Son to express it. It is an act of pure grace. A true apprehension of this love calls us to also respond similarly in love, laying down our lives for the One who first loved us. Such love redeems, recreates, and quickens fresh love. It makes worshippers out of rebels.

And such love always entails the willingness to suffer. For a person to truly love another, there is a giving of one's heart and spirit that requires acceptance to be complete. Just as gift given in love must be accepted to be complete, God's love seeks to create a receptor that responds with quickened love returned. When such love is rejected it causes great pain to the lover, for the gift is One with the God who gives it. God is the supreme Lover. We are the intended receptors of His love. It is this love accepted that unites us to Him as we are recreated and called to reciprocate that love.

There is a definite Trinitarian pattern here. Just as God is Father, Son and Holy Spirit, so the Father is Lover, the Son is the Beloved and the Holy Spirit is the Love itself, the *between* that unites them together. When any one of the three suffers, all suffer for they are one God. When God created us, His love for us was such that He gave us the freedom to receive that love or to reject it. In rejecting it, we reject Him for He is Love. Our rejection and rebellion towards God causes Him great pain for He loves us with an infinite and eternal love which, when spurned, kindles His righteous wrath, His love burning hot. Yet He withholds nothing to win back our love, not even His own Son.

Oh the marvelous love of God for us! The very fact that I am alive at this moment, drawing breath and aware of my surroundings, conscious of myself and those around me and aware of the God who created it all and continues to provide life and breath to all living creatures is a testimony to His amazing act of ongoing love. The Apostle Paul, in His address to the Greeks in Athens credits God as the One who *"gives to all mankind life and breath and everything." (Acts 17:25).* He goes on to say that "*he is actually not far from each one of us, for "'In him we live and move and have our being'; as even some of your own poets have said, "' For we are indeed His offspring.' (Acts 17:27b-28).*

Unlike human love, which springs up by attraction to what pleases it, God's love flows to all both lovely and unlovely. When Jesus walked this earth, He was not attracted to those that the world considered lovely, but rather spent His time with sinners, lepers, tax collectors and lowly fishermen. Yet, in His loving, He bestowed value on the objects of His love, lifting them up and transporting them into the Kingdom of God. And to those of us who believe in His name, His love makes us children of God, of infinite value for we belong to Him, the infinite God.

Do we appreciate this on a daily basis? He is very near us and His presence fills the universe. And He loves us. His love is not a sentimental love, nor a manipulating, controlling love, but His love is free of all that is impure, for He loves us with a holy love that desires above all else that *we flourish*. Even God's injunction to humankind to *"be fruitful and multiply and fill the earth"* (Gen 1:28), the same injunction that He also gave the animals, is a testimony to His love in giving life and breath to every living creature.

Unlike the animals, who relate to God through instinct, we are able to reflect on His love and we are able to express and return that love, through words of prayer, worship and obedience. While we ought to be filled with gratitude and thanksgiving for every waking moment, we most often are not. Rather, like ungrateful children, we grumble and complain about every little trial as if God were somehow personally responsible for all of our dysfunction.

Moreover, God has delegated to us humans, *dominion* over all the animals both in the seas, on the earth and in the air (Gen. 1:28). In fact, we could say that one aspect of being made in the image of God is to represent God in a physical way on earth. For this, also we ought to be exceedingly thankful and deeply reflective. The animals have been entrusted to our care that we might also allow them to flourish. Wanton cruelty to animals must be avoided and our using them for our pleasures must be done with much sensitivity to their pain and suffering. Even our use of meat for food has been given to us as a concession, after the flood, (Gen. 9:3) and was not the case in the beginning. Yet, such is God's love for us, that despite the exceeding wickedness that led to the flood, God has not withheld anything from us by way of food, and we are free to kill and eat. God's love continues to be lavished on us as God provides everything that we need to live and flourish.

Creation Spoiled – Dying, We Die

The creation accounts in Genesis 1 and 2 portray a harmonious world as Adam and Eve, the regents of creation, walk with God in the garden of Eden, enjoying a four-fold harmony.[ii] This harmony was with God, with self ("naked and not ashamed" Gen. 2:25), with each other and with the earth, which provides food for them with little effort. God in His gracious love has provided everything that they need. However, there is also a restriction given. They are not to eat of the *"tree of the knowledge of good and evil"* for they are told *"in the day that you eat of it, you shall surely die."* (Gen. 2:17).

The Hebrew word for *"knowledge"* has the connotation of intimate experience. *"Good and evil"* is a reference to the whole range of possible experiences. Therefore, the *"knowledge of good and evil"* is the unbridled partaking of every human possibility under the sun. People were never designed to have freedom without limits. There are some things that are destructive, and there is a huge spiritual world that we hardly perceive. We must remember that we are contingent beings. Our very existence is contingent on the continuing providence and love of God. As such, we must look to Him for direction for what is good or not, what will cause us to flourish or wither and what will leads us to life and what will lead to death. The whole point of the injunction, not to eat of the forbidden tree, is that we must not decide what is good for us apart from God. We are dependent creatures to whom God has given freedom and autonomy. Our continued flourishing depends upon our willing submission to God, our Creator.

The drama in Genesis escalates quickly as the serpent comes on the scene in chapter three. The narrator does not explain the origin of the tempter, who appears in the form of a serpent, however, scripture makes it clear that he is Satan, the devil (Rev. 12:9). We can also infer from this passage as well as others such as Isaiah 14:12-15, that there was an angelic rebellion led by Satan that resulted in Satan and his demonic hosts being cast out of heaven and thrown to the earth. In any case, in Genesis 3, he is described as a crafty serpent, enticing the first woman with a sweetly deceptive subtlety.

Satan begins his assault by casting doubt on the words of God. *"Did God actually say 'You shall not eat of any tree in the Garden?'"*

(Gen. 3:1b) The subtlety is apparent, as no specific tree is mentioned, inviting Eve herself to name the forbidden tree. Her addition of "touch" to the prohibition (verse 3b) is an indicator of the work of her imagination, or perhaps an overly zealous rendition of the command by Adam, to whom the injunction was originally given. In any case, Satan comes back with a direct denial of the consequences as stated by God *"You will not surely die."* (verse 4a) Satan then goes on the offensive suggesting that God is not completely "for them" but is keeping them from experiencing all the range of possibilities that would make them fully "like God". This sly suggestion implies that God is not looking after their best interests and that they must take matters into their own hands. They are told that, in doing this, they will realize their full potential (Gen. 3:5). So the original temptation invites a severe breech of faith, a distrust of God and disobedience. At this point they have a choice. They can trust in the words of God, their Creator, or they can launch out on an independent and rebellious path. Denial of the consequences almost always accompanies sin.

Their eating results in a cataclysmic shattering of the harmony of the created order, their own souls and their relationship with God and one other. They suddenly perceive their nakedness, in which they walked unashamedly a few moments earlier. They hide from God, who was once their intimate companion. The inner self-harmony is destroyed ushering a shameful self-consciousness that requires covering themselves. Adam blames Eve for leading him astray and God for giving Eve to him. Eve blames the serpent. Blame shifting is a natural consequence of sin. Relational conflict has begun. Moreover, the ground is cursed on account of their sin and now produces thorns and thistles. A five-fold state of enmity now exists between self, God, one another, the ground and Satan.

The source of every human tragedy can be traced right back to this event which we call "the fall". It would better be termed "the great rebellion". No one can ever understand the human psyche without an appreciation of the devastation that was wrought right here. The Christian doctrine of "*Total Depravity*" is grounded in the consequences of the fall. *Total Depravity* simply means that there is no aspect of our humanity that is unaffected by the original rebellion. Be it our intellect, our sexuality, our self-understanding, our view of others, our relational acumen, all of these have been absolutely corrupted by the fall. Even our resolve to do good is corrupted with selfish motives.

But the fall (this great rebellion) is not just the ancient story of our ancestors. It is also our story. Every human being born of man has inherited the depravity of soul that makes us sinners, not only by nature but also by our thoughts and actions. We each confirm the effects of the fall by acting out our depraved nature and so appropriating by our actions the sentence of death. We become slaves of sin because that is now our inherited nature. And dying, we all die. Post fall, to be human is to be internally self-contradicted and in a continual state of dying.

Yet, we do not forfeit our identity as divine image bearers and remarkably God still loves us. Our own rebellion does not negate the love of God, but it does cause Him great pain. Just like a rebellious son is still loved by his parents, God loves us with a perfect Fatherly and everlasting love. Yet because God is just, justice must be upheld. The consequences for sin must unfold. The sentence of death is not executed immediately, but does become our inevitable fate. In our rebelliously sinful state, we too will share Satan's fate in the lake of fire at the end of the age, the second death (Rev. 20:15). What an absolute catastrophe! All heaven gasps and all eyes turn to God, for unless He acts, humankind is doomed to destruction.

A New Promise Given

Mercifully, however, a new promise is given. In Genesis 3:15 (*the protoevangelium*), God announces that one day, an offspring of Eve, will crush Satan's head, although that offspring (*male and singular in Hebrew*) will himself be deeply bruised. So desperate is the human condition after the fall, that unless God takes the initiative, all people will die an eternal death.

God then foreshadows the ultimate sacrifice by slaying an animal and making skins to cover the nakedness of Adam and Eve. Imagine, their reaction as they watched for the first time, the death of a living being. Imagine as they watched the blood being poured out onto the ground and the first cessation of a life ever seen. The death of a living creature is required in order to cover their shame. God is setting a precedent. An innocent must die in order to take away their newfound nakedness, their guilt and their shame. God will not allow them to live eternally in their fallen state, so the *Tree of Life*, to which they had open access, is now forbidden. They are thrust out of the garden and prevented from reentering by a divine act of God. It is important to note that they do not merely wander out of the garden and cannot find their way back. They are thrust out of the garden and actively prevented from returning (Gen 3:24). There is now a hostility between God and fallen humanity. The teenage son who is thrust out of the home for insubordination and rebellion cannot pretend that he has a good relationship with his parents. While that state of rebellion exists, he is not allowed home. So too, we are not allowed home until we are reconciled to God. This is the thrust of the gospel message *"Be reconciled to God"* (2 Cor. 5:20). This is only possible through faith in the Son, Jesus Christ, "*the Lamb of God who takes away the sins of the world*" (John 1:29).

The God Who Redeems

God's love for us is such that He will not abandon His image bearers, even when they rebel against Him. Yet God loathes rebellion, is repulsed by evil and cannot tolerate the unrepentant sinner. And so, in our natural state, we are thrust out of the garden and out of communion with Him. We are exiled rebels in a shattered land. We have become slaves to sin. It is all that we can do, because inner corruption now characterizes all humanity. And so in the first generation, Cain, slays his brother in jealousy (Gen. 4). Likewise we all become murderers. For Jesus said that anyone who is viciously angry with his brother in his heart is a murderer (Matt. 5:22). And so also we hide from God, we flee from Him. We try to live without Him. We deny He exists.

The concept of sin is not a popular one in today's society. Many people prefer to talk about shortcomings or mistakes, yet these are mere circumlocutions for what the Bible describes as sin. Sin is essentially a refusal to acknowledge God as God. It is rebellion. God's commands are for our own good, because He loves us. A mother tells her child not to go onto the street for the child's own protection, not to spoil the child's fun. The child who disobeys deliberately is rebelling against the mother, thinking that he or she knows better than the parent. The consequences of such behavior if allowed to continue are disrespect for the parent and a wild, out-of-control child whose inner corruption has been intensified through expression. In the same way, when we ignore God, we set ourselves up as rebels and thumb our noses at a perfect and Holy God who loves us. In addition, our attempts to do good, apart from faith in God are merely our own man made barricade against what God really requires. He requires faith, a heartfelt trust in Him. He requires that we believe in Him and His words.

Without faith, it is impossible to please God (Heb. 11:6). And anything done apart from faith is sin, our shallow attempts to prove that we are not really all that bad.

In exercising faith, I surrender any attempt at self-justification and acknowledge that I am a sinner who deserves death. At the same time I acknowledge what God has done in Christ Jesus, that which I could never do for myself. In exercising faith, I believe the gospel and trust exclusively in the One given up for Sin.

What About You?

Have you ever told a lie? Have you ever stolen anything, even something small? Have you ever been so angry with someone that you wanted them dead? Jesus said that whoever is angry with his brother is a murderer at heart. Have you ever used God's name as a curse? That is called blasphemy, defiling the name of the God that gives you life and breath and all good things. Have you ever looked at another person with lust? Jesus said that whoever does so is an adulterer at heart. These questions are based on the moral law of God given to Israel (Exodus 20). If God were to judge you based on what you have done (Rev. 20:13), would you be innocent or guilty? Be honest and listen to your conscience. How would you fare before the just and Holy God? God's word says that no liar, no thief, no blasphemer, and no adulterer will inherit the Kingdom of God (1 Cor. 6:9-10, Gal. 5:21). So, on judgment day (Rev. 20:12) you would be left to yourself. You would die in your sins and be consigned to eternal punishment. But the good news (the gospel) is that God has made a way for you to be forgiven and to live eternally with Him in heaven. Jesus Christ, in dying on the cross, died in your place and took your punishment upon Himself. You can be released from condemnation, not because of your innocence, but because of His. The innocent, sinless and Holy One, out of an act of supreme love, has taken the penalty for your sin upon Himself. You can be released and set free if you turn away from sin and, by faith, trust in the One who died for you. As you turn, acknowledge Him and surrender yourself, the Holy Spirit gives you new life that is empowered by Him. You become a new creation. The evidence of this is a transformed heart and a love for God and others that is extraordinary. Can you say for certain that you have repented of your sin and embraced Jesus Christ by faith? Perhaps you should pause for a moment now as you read this and have a conversation with God. [iii]

It would seem at this point in the Genesis narrative, that God could have given up on the human experiment and called it quits, justly consigning us all to destruction. Yet, *He is love* (1 John 4:8) and He still loves us. And so He proceeds with a divine plan to redeem us back from our slavery. The price of our redemption is incalculable. For we have sinned against an infinitely holy and perfect God. There is nothing and no one on earth that can suffice for our redemption. Our debt is too great. The price is too high. We can only be bought back if someone of infinite worth and of perfect holiness were to give Himself up as a ransom. And so God's only begotten Son, who is Himself fully God, comes into the world on a divine mission. Jesus Christ comes, born of woman, and of The Holy Spirit, fully God, yet fully human for the sole purpose of giving Himself up for us and showing us beyond a shadow of a doubt that God loves us, every one of us. He comes into the world, not to exalt Himself as God but to humble Himself and to be obedient to death even death on a cross.

At the cross, the Father, the Holy One of Israel gives up His only begotten Son to humiliation, degradation, and death, making Him the object of His own righteous wrath at sin, as an act of supreme selfless love to us. The cross of Jesus Christ shocks every mind and cuts every heart that comprehends the enormity of what transpired there. For there, the righteous and Holy One, God Himself in Himself, presents Himself as a sacrifice, *"the Lamb of God who takes away the sin of the world."* (John 1:29) This supreme act of selfless love causes the Father, the Son and the Spirit great pain, anguish and suffering as the fabric of the Godhead (the three persons-in-one) is torn asunder by the Son becoming Sin for us. The Father turns His face away and the Son cries out *"My God , My God, why has thou forsaken me?"* (Mark 15:34) In the dereliction of the Son, the Father suffers indescribable pain because He is at one with the Son who bears the weight of becoming Sin, the very thing that He finds utterly repugnant. The righteous and Holy One, taking on what is most abhorrent to Him, absorbs in Himself the punishment that we deserve on account of our sin. In doing so, He demonstrates His amazing love for us the beneficiaries of His self-sacrifice and self-abasement. At the cross, every mouth is stopped and every heart shocked at the depth of God's love for us.

Martin Luther saw God as an uncompromisingly stern judge, who knew his own sinfulness and condemned him for it. Luther's medieval view of God as judge and executioner was fuelled by the church's emphasis on sacraments, purgatory and indulgences. The turmoil generated in Luther's heart was tearing him apart. He was almost hit by lightening in a severe storm which confirmed in his own mind that God was after him and was hunting him down to destroy him. In that moment out of desperation, Luther promised that he would become a monk. He was spared but the turmoil did not stop. Overwhelmed by a sense of the presence of Satan and his own depravity, Luther turned to his spiritual mentor, Johannes von Staupitz , for help. *"Look to the cross, meditate on the wounds of Christ"* was the advice that he received. In the cross, God's amazing love is displayed. In the cross, the just God becomes the justifier, the one who declares as righteous those who look to Christ in repentance and faith. As Luther began to meditate on the wounds of Christ and on scripture, it suddenly struck him that the righteous shall live by faith (Romans 1:17). He saw that it was faith in the finished work of Christ that made him acceptable to God. He no longer felt condemned or that he had to work for his salvation. Yet, he still suffered the continued attacks of Satan who sought to make him doubt his salvation. *"I am yours, save me"* (Psalm 119:94) became one of Luther's breath prayers that sustained him in times of great trial. As he began to study and teach, he began to see God, not as a wrathful judge, but as a God of love, whose heart continually goes out to His children, who wants us all to turn from sin and to find our rest in Him.

The God Who Bestows

While the cross is the ultimate expression of His love for us, aspects of God's love run even deeper. Redemption is only the beginning of His amazing love for humankind. He also lavishes upon His redeemed people blessings and honors that are unparalleled. To rescue someone from certain death is grace indeed. But to go beyond that and bestow upon them the rights and privileges of sons and daughters is astounding. To bestow His very own self is mind numbing. To bestow eternity is indescribable. To bestow union with His precious Son is stunning. Let us consider the profound mystery of each.

HIMSELF

First, He has bestowed upon us His very Self. Through faith, we are filled with the Holy Spirit, the Spirit of Truth that unites us with

Jesus Christ and the Father. The Holy Spirit is the third person of the Trinity, God Himself acting upon us and giving us Himself so that the giver and the gift are one. He is the Personal reality within us that convicts of sin and regenerates us creating new life, converting us to a life of faith, justifying and sanctifying us, uniting us with Jesus Christ and the Father, quickening our spirits to respond to God and bestowing upon us a new order of life. He is the Divine Comforter, who comforts us in all our afflictions, testifying within us that we belong to God. He is the Paraclete, who walks beside us and guides us. He quickens us like the wind, giving life and action to our faith. His promptings are deeply mysterious to us, yet we know with an indescribable certainty that we have been visited by God. He continues to dwell within us, giving us divine instincts that direct us. He teaches us and leads us into all Truth. He never contradicts the very nature of God for He is God. He is God's love in action within us. He walks alongside us and guides us. He is God with me and in me.

The psalmist rejoices in the Spirit's presence and writes:

> *"Nevertheless, I am continually with you; you hold my right hand. You guide me with your counsel, and afterward you will receive me to glory. Whom have I in heaven but you? And there is nothing on earth that I desire besides you. My flesh and my heart may fail, but God is the strength of my heart and my portion forever." Psalm 73:23-26*

When we sense a deep abiding presence of God, it is the Holy Spirit that we are sensing. The Apostle Paul enjoins us to be filled with the Spirit and with all the fullness of God (Eph. 5:18, 3:19). It is the Holy Spirit that puts within us a desire to walk with God and to pursue Holiness as a way of life. It is the presence of the Holy Spirit that is our confirmation that we are indeed born from above. And no one born from above keeps on sinning (1 John 3:6). When we do sin, we grieve the Holy Spirit, and He convicts us so that we are immediately driven to our knees in repentance. He is the giver of gifts and He gives Spiritual gifts to His children as He sees fit, equipping us for service in His Kingdom (see 1 Cor. 12). Through Him we are able to bear witness to Christ and to serve His people. Where would any of us be without God's Spirit living in us?

ETERNAL LIFE

Secondly, God bestows upon us eternal life. In our culture, the popular view is that everyone has eternal life naturally. Most people believe that when we die, we will all go to heaven (except perhaps those who have been wicked beyond measure). Yet the Bible does not support this. The Apostle john writes:

> *"And this is the testimony, that God gave us eternal life, and this life is in His Son. Whoever has the Son has life; whoever does not have the Son of God does not have life." 1 John 5:11-12*

It is clear that only the one who *" has the Son"* has eternal life. Those who reject the Son will *"die in their sins"* (John 8:24). The end of those who die in their sins and whose name is excluded from the Lamb's book of life is the second death, the Lake of Fire. (Rev. 21:8). But the scriptures are also clear that those who belong to Christ receive the free gift of eternal life.

Eternal life is not simply life unending, but a new kind of life characterized by union with Christ. Jesus Christ, as God incarnate belongs to that category of transcendence that is reserved for God alone. By virtue of union with Him, we now exist with a new quality of existence that transcends time and space and this world. In a spiritual sense we are now *"seated with Christ in the heavenly places"* (Eph 2:6). Our lives are now "*hidden with Christ in God*" (Col. 3:3). Because of our finite understanding, we cannot now fully comprehend this. But for those doomed to die in their sins, this is incredibly good news. In fact "good news" is a colossal understatement. If only we could fully comprehend what has been given us, and the alternative that we were headed for, we would live our lives in a state of grateful worship. Our God has given us eternal life and elevated us into the realm of living with Him in eternity. The twenty-first chapter of the Book of Revelation gives us a glimmer as to what that might we like. Living in the New Jerusalem, which is adorned like a bride for her husband and is let down from heaven, we have free access to what we lost in the garden, the Tree of Life (Rev. 22:2). We also have access to the water of life. *"bright as crystal"* (Rev. 22:1) and the Lord God as our eternal light. There will be no more tears or pain or sorrow for all the former things will have passed away (Rev. 21:4). Moreover, God will indeed surprise us with blessings unimaginable.

> *"But, as it is written, 'What no eye has seen, nor ear heard, nor the heart of man imagined, what God has prepared for those who love him'" 1 Corinthians 2:9*

Does this not fill you with fresh joy and spur in you a desire to love God with every ounce of your being? Does this not make you yearn for that Day when He returns to bring it about? It should!

AN ETERNAL INHERITANCE

Thirdly, God adopts us as His own children and bestows on us an eternal inheritance. Think of it. Those of us who are Gentiles (non Jews) were all once outside the family of God, spiritual orphans looking in through the windows of the house seeing God dwelling with His chosen people Israel. We were excluded from the family of God. But, God being rich in love has always had in His plans our inclusion into His family. The promises made to Abraham (Gen. 12:3) and confirmed in His test of obedience (Gen. 22:18) were that through him, all the families of the earth would be blessed and included as fellow heirs of the promises and of an eternal inheritance kept in heaven for those who through faith, also became children of Abraham (Eph. 3:6, Rom. 9:8). There is indeed an eternal inheritance that awaits us. It is not one that we deserve. It is not one that we worked for. It is not one that we have even inherited because of our parent's wealth. It is a completely free gift of pure grace that God has bestowed upon those who love Him and are called through faith to be children of the living God and members of God's own household (Eph. 2:19).

Moreover, Jesus has gone before us as the first fruits of the resurrection from the dead, to prepare a place for us. In comforting His disciples before He was to give Himself over to death, Jesus told them that in His father's house were many rooms and that He was going to prepare a place for them (John 14:2). And He will return for us on *The Day* and take us to be with Him forever. Can you imagine, the God who created all the incredible beauty of the universe preparing a special place for His beloved children? Can you imagine how amazingly incredible will be this inheritance? How can we be enthralled with the temporal things of this present world, when an eternal inheritance awaits us? Surely, we ought to lift our hearts and set our minds on the things to come.

HIS ETERNAL BRIDE

Finally, God bestows on us an honor, which shows us His heart. He gives us to His only Son as His eternal bride.

Frank Viola in his book *From Eternity to Here*[iv] marvels that God's ultimate passion is to provide a bride for His Son. Rightly, he sees the entire bible as a love story. This love story is a divine mystery unfolding over the ages. The patriarchs, prophets and kings were custodians of the mystery, but did not understand the mystery. Israel did not know the mystery. Jesus' own disciples did not see the mystery. Finally, the mystery was revealed to Saul of Tarsus who became the Apostle Paul. This mystery is that the church, the body of believers that Jesus came to redeem for Himself is the one eternal bride that God the Father betrothed to His Son before the beginning of time (Eph. 5:30-32, Rev. 19:7, 21:9).

The human story begins with a man who is alone. That is not good. Neither is it good that the eternal Son is without one to pour His passion upon. So God creates Eve, the first woman, taking her from the side of Adam. And Christ brings from inside Him, the bride whom He cleanses and perfects with His own blood, the universal church, that body of saints throughout the ages of whom believers are a part.

> *"Then came one of the seven angels ……… and spoke to me, saying, "Come, I will show you the Bride, the wife of the Lamb." And he carried me away in the Spirit to a great, high mountain, and showed me the holy city Jerusalem coming down out of heaven from God, having the glory of God, its radiance like a most rare jewel, like a jasper, clear as crystal." Revelation 21:9-11*

The human adventure begins with a wedding and culminates with a wedding celebrated at the marriage supper of the Lamb. From that point on the dwelling of men is with God. The greatest honor that any man can bestow upon a woman is to invite her to be His beloved bride. In doing so, he covenants to not only share his goods but to share his very self with his bride. As the scripture says "they shall become one" (Gen. 2:24). God's plan throughout the ages has been to provide a bride for His Son. And that bride, fellow Christian is that universal assembly of which you are a part. It is the body of Christ whom He redeemed from among the sons and daughters of Adam, the human race. John the Baptist described himself as a friend of the Bridegroom.

The bride, he said, belongs to the Bridegroom and that he (John) rejoices at the Bridegroom's voice. (John 3:29). Jesus, as long as He lives on earth remains alone, but once He dies, he gives birth to the bride from within Himself. In John's gospel Jesus says:

> *"Unless a grain of wheat falls to the ground and dies, it remains alone, but if it dies, it produces much fruit." John 12:24*

Just as Eve was created by God putting Adam to sleep and taking a rib from His side, so too is Jesus put to sleep in death so that in resurrection, He brings forth the bride, that body of faithful followers who cling to Him in faith.

We as believers now live in that age when Christ has betrothed us to Himself, but the wedding is not yet consummated. And He is still adding to His bride those who come to faith. We are now collectively a betrothed bride awaiting the appearing of her Bridegroom. In this metaphor, Jesus Christ our Bridegroom is masculine, but we all are feminine *to Him.* And He is the One who has called us individually and personally to belong to Him. As our Bridegroom looks deep into the eyes of His bride and says "I am yours" so we are look back into His eyes and answer: "And I am Yours". In this giving of ourselves to Him, there can be no holding back. There can be no partial commitment. There can be no conditions. The King of Kings is calling us to be His bride. He is calling *you.* Will you accept the call? There can be no future self-centered; independent plans for the bride of the King. There can be only complete surrender, a complete giving of oneself without reservation, no holding back.

Will you, dear friend, say yes to the King of Kings? Will you then spend the rest of your life preparing yourself to be the bride of the King of the universe? Will you love unselfishly as He has loved you? Will you love also those others who are together with you His bride? Will you devote yourself, as you wait to learning and doing His will? Will your heart pulsate in unity with His? The Apostle Paul's prayer sums it all up well.

> *"[May] Christ .... dwell in your hearts through faith- that you, being rooted and grounded in love, may have strength to comprehend with all the saints what is the breadth and length and height and depth, and to know the love of Christ that surpasses knowledge, that you may be filled with all the fullness of God." Ephesians 3:17-19*

Study Guide for Chapter One

A. Questions for Personal Reflection:

Write your thoughts on each of the questions below in your journal.

1. One characteristic of God is consistency. God is what He does and does what He is. Reflect on the Biblical story from Genesis to Revelation. Write down ten things that God has done. It may help you to flip through your Bible to refresh your memory. Opposite each item, write down what this act tells us about God.

2. Reflect on some of the things that God has done in your own life. How have you experienced Him personally? Those who are in Christ, He has clothed with His righteousness and made His own (see Isaiah 43:1, 1 Cor. 3:21-23, Phil. 3:12). Reflect upon the fact that by faith you belong to Him. Preface you prayers for this week by the affirmation *"My chief comfort in life and in death is that I belong to my faithful Savior Jesus Christ"* or you may use the short prayer *"Jesus, my Savior, I am Yours"*.

3. Are God's promises a valid indicator of His nature? Why or why not? (See Deut. 11:13-15, Psalm 37:4, Psalm 146:8, Isaiah 62:5, Rev. 21:3-4)

4. Many people see the evil in the world and conclude that God cannot be good. How does the fall of humanity in Genesis 3 explain the existence of suffering and pain in the world? When God gives people up to their own depravity, is this hard hearted or is it an aspect of His love? (see Romans 1:21-25) (see also pages 17-19)

5. What does the death of Jesus Christ on the cross tell us about God? What does it say about us as He sees us? (See John 3:16, Romans 5:6-8, 6:3-6)

6. God not only redeems but also bestows on those who trust in Him the four things outlined on pages 23-28. What are those four things? How do you respond to what God has in store for those who trust in Him? Will you be a part of this? If so, on what basis? (see Hebrews 11) What is your assurance of this? (see 1 John 5:12)

B. **Exercises** (Individual or Large Group)

Our objective in this first chapter is to practice being still before God. Solitude and silence are disciplines, which are of great value. God tells us to *"Be still and know that I am God"* (Psalm 46:10). Jesus often withdrew to quiet places to pray (Mark 1:35). He instructed us to pray in secret (Matt. 6:6). He spent much time with His disciples off in a boat where they could escape the crowds. Our lives are so crowded that we often feel guilty taking an hour or even half an hour to be still before God. Yet, no one who has a deep spiritual centeredness neglects these disciplines. So, during the course of these sessions, resolve to create some space in your life to be alone with God. The exercises for each day will give you things to reflect upon while you do. We will start by identifying a general template for a quiet time. This can be adjusted later but for now, try it out. The template consists of four parts. You should allow 30-45 minutes.

Formula For a Quiet Time

1. **Relaxation and Breath Prayer:** (3-5 minutes)

Find a quiet place where you will be alone and not be disturbed. Sit in a comfortable chair and place you hands on your legs or in your lap. Relax your entire body starting from your neck down to your feet. Take several deep breaths breathing in with your nose and exhaling with your mouth. Feel the tension leave your body as you exhale. Imagine that you are breathing in the Spirit of God. Then as you exhale say the following as a breath prayer *"Oh Lord, open my lips that my mouth may declare thy praise." (Psalm 51:15).* Say this three times slowly with a pause in between each time. Say it as a sincere prayer to God.

2. **Opening Prayer for your quiet time** (2-3 minutes)

Begin to praise God for His goodness, love, mercy and faithfulness. Lift up your voice in adoration. Confess your unworthiness and any sins that come to mind. Thank Him for His forgiveness and His blessings upon you. Ask Him to open your heart and spirit to hear from Him. Ask Him to speak to you today. *"Speak for your servant is listening."* (1 Sam 3:10) This prayer pattern is known as the *ACTS* formula. (Adoration, Confession, Thanksgiving, Supplication.)

3. **Holy Reading** (15-30 minutes)

There are two ways of reading your Bible. The first way is for *information*, to study. The second way is for *formation*, that is to allow God's word to *form* you. In the first way, you are the subject trying to master the object, the Word of God. In the second way, you become the object and you allow the Word of God to become the subject, operating on you. This second way is sometimes called *Holy Reading.*[v] The idea in Holy Reading is to select a small portion of scripture, that contains a logical unit, a story, parable, prophecy, portion of a letter or Psalm. Usually 5-15 verses would be enough. This one scripture is read several times with different emphasis each time. There are four movements. They have been given Latin names.

i. **Lectio** (listening, reading, attending)

The scripture is read slowly and you are listening for the general sense of what is being said. Allow the scripture to wash over you. Listen for a word or phrase that might stand out to you. Sit in stillness as you let the scripture passage impact you.

ii. **Meditatio** (meditation, pondering)

Read the scripture passage again slowly, this time allow yourself to ponder or meditate on the passage. What is it about the word or phrase that struck you? Hear what God might be saying to you in your mind and in your heart.

iii. **Oratio** (prayer, responding)

Now you respond to God in prayer by speaking back to Him. Prayer is essentially a dialog. God speaks through His Word to our spirit and we respond, expressing what is in our hearts. Be real when you pray, let God know what is really going on in you. Express your fears and frustrations, hopes and dreams. Tell Him if you are confused, angry or fearful. Be open. How are you responding to what He seems to be saying through this passage?

iv. **Comtemplatio** (contemplation, being)

Read the passage one more time slowly. This time simply sit in silence before God. This is often the hardest part, for it requires that we simply *be* in His presence with no agenda. Allow His presence to flood over your soul and experience the joy of just sitting at His feet.

Suggested Holy Reading passages for week 1: (Psalm 145, John 10:7-15, Psalm 103:1-14, Luke 6:27-36, Eph. 2:1-10)

4. **Personal Petition** (5-10 minutes)

Now that you have spent some time alone with God, go ahead and ask Him for things that are on your heart. Use this time to present your requests to Him. James, the brother of Jesus said that we often have not because we ask not and when we do ask, we ask for the wrong things. (James 4:2-3) Having spent some time alone with God, we are in a much better frame of mind to ask for things that really matter to Him. Pray especially for others, for family members, friends and enemies (Matt. 5:44).

C. Small Group Exercises

1. In small groups of two or three, share your experience with Holy Reading.
2. Talk over your plan for the coming week to integrate this devotional formula into your life. What obstacles do you think you will encounter? How can they be overcome?
3. Take some time to share and pray for one another.

D. Assignment for this Week

1. As you go through this week, meditate on the amazing love of God as evidenced in creation, redemption and the bestowal of God's promises. Write down reflections in your journal to share with others.

2. Engage in five quiet times this week of 30-45 minutes. Use the template provided above with breath prayers, holy reading, etc. Use the passages suggested or others that you may be lead to. Write down reflections in your journal.

3. Find a spiritual friend (same gender or your spouse) that you can share this experience with. Meet with them once this week for sharing and prayer. Share your experiences throughout the course of this study.

4. Read chapter 2. Answer the questions for personal reflection at the end of that chapter (page 52).

2. Transformation – The Purpose of Love

"Be holy for I am holy." Lev. 11:44

If we were allowed only one word to describe God, that word would have to be *Holy*. Holiness is that overarching characteristic of God that encapsulates all His attributes and summarizes His absolute magnificence. God's love, goodness, wisdom, righteousness, justice, mercy, glory, power, beauty and moral perfection are all attributes of His holiness. It is the grand theme of scripture that God is Holy. This word in Hebrew implies absolute brilliance and distinct separateness.[vi] YHWH dwells in unapproachable light (1 Tim 6:16). He is absolutely transcendent, so far above us that it requires a super-superlative word to describe Him. The closest that we can come is that word *Holy*. The holiness word group occurs over seven hundred times in scripture, over seventy times in the book of Leviticus alone. God is referred to as the *Holy One of Israel* thirty-two times.

God's holiness is a *communicable* attribute for He also exhorts His people to "be holy". He sanctifies those whom He calls and imparts His holiness through the Holy Spirit. However, there is also a sense in which God's holiness is uniquely His and is absolute Holiness. This Holiness is so breathtaking that the prophet Isaiah, upon seeing a vision of God in the temple, falls on his face completely undone. The doorposts of the temple tremble and the earth shudders. Two mighty angels, the seraphim at God's throne, call out continuously in a thunderous roar:

> *"Holy, Holy, Holy is the Lord God of hosts. The whole earth is full of his glory." Isa. 6:3*

Isaiah is beside himself, face down and overwhelmed at the holiness, the majesty and the glory of God. This word *Holy* reverberates in the heavens and declares the magnificence of God.

It is evident, as Isaiah experienced, that sinful human beings, tainted as we are by our sinfulness, cannot stand in the presence of the Holy One. His absolute moral perfection is so blazingly radiant that we, like an ice cube thrown into the sun, would be instantly vaporized if we approached Him in our carnal state.

So obviously we have a problem. As we saw in chapter one, God's heart and purpose is to redeem us and bestow upon us a place in His family as a bride betrothed to His own Son. Yet, we are corrupted in sin. Even our most righteous deeds are like filthy rags before a holy God (Isa. 64:6). The scriptures are clear that no one living on earth is righteous (Rom. 3:10). So we must be cleansed, transformed and sanctified in order to dwell with God.

In this chapter, we will look at what God does for us in Christ and what must happen in us to accomplish this transformation. We will look at how that transformation changes us and our world.

Paradise Lost

After the fall, Adam and Eve emerge from their first encounter with death, having watched animals be slaughtered to provide skins to cover their newly discovered nakedness. Their eyes certainly have been opened, but not in the way that they had imagined. Their innocence is gone and they are acutely aware of their self-contradiction and brokenness. But that is not all. Now, they are thrust out of the garden. Now, they have lost access to the Tree of Life. (Gen. 3:24) A divine pronouncement of death hangs over them. As their offspring, we too are exiles from paradise and under the same banishment. It is not the case that we somehow wandered out of the garden and couldn't find our way back. No, we have been driven out and there is appointed a flaming sword that guards the way to the Tree of Life. There is now separation between all humankind and God. In Isaiah 59:2, the prophet writes: "*...your iniquities have made a separation between you and your God, and your sins have hidden his face from you so that he does not hear.*"

God turns away from unrepentant sinners and does not hear their prayers. He gives them up to their own depravity in the hope that, once they hit bottom, they will be broken, look up and repent (Rom. 1: 24, 26, 28). All unregenerate[2] humanity is in this state. Our corporate and individual "*sinner-ship*" is what we have inherited from our ancestors Adam and Eve. It is called *original sin*. It is like blood poisoning that runs through our veins. There is absolutely nothing that

---

[2] Unregenerate: not born afresh or from above of the Holy Spirit through faith in Christ (John 3:3-8, 1 John 5:12)

we can do to cure ourselves. And so our very nature, once perfectly "in the image of God" has been corrupted. In theology, this is known as the doctrine of the *Total Depravity of Humankind.* This doctrine is often misunderstood. It is not the case that we are, in our natural state, as bad as we can be. Each one of us is capable of behaving much worse than we do. Thieves, murderers, swindlers and criminals of the worst order are just ordinary people who continually give into their base urges. The doctrine of depravity does not describe humanity's moral condition but rather its spiritual condition.[vii] It is not that we do not know right from wrong, but that we cannot abstain from the wrong. We are poisoned internally. There is no aspect of our human nature that is unaffected by the fall. Absolutely every faculty, be it our mind, our emotions, our will, our sexuality, our inner psyche has been completely corrupted.

For example, let us look at our will, that faculty within us that we call volition. Now, while it is believed that we humans have free will, this is in fact true only in the sense of things that are *"below us"* [viii]. Martin Luther coined this phrase and said that our free will is bound and cannot be extended to things that are *"above us"* but only applies to things *"below us"*. Insofar as we want to make decisions about what to have for supper, where to go on vacation, what to wear, we do as we please. We may even decide to be moral or religious and benevolent to others. All of these things are *"below us"*. However, with respect to things *"above us",* that is with respect the Holy One who is truly *"above us",* we are not free at all. The problem is that in our sinfulness, we can't stand to have someone *"above us"*. We are rebels.

The fall itself was a rebellion against a God who places restrictions, restrictions that are really for our own protection. But, we have succumbed to the temptation to throw off what we perceive to be unfair shackles. As a result of our rebellion, our will is now enslaved to our sinful self. It is bent in on itself and distorted so it can only will its own continuing depravity. It cannot choose "the Good" for it is unable to do so. It is enslaved to sin, not forced to sin, but bound to. We act out by nature what we are by nature. As a result of the fall, we are by nature sinners. Even our most benevolent actions are tainted with self-centeredness. Even our tears of repentance are self-serving. We are slaves to sin. It is all that we can do. Yet we remain fully human. The image of God in us has been severely *defaced*, but it has not been *erased.* There is even in the vilest criminal that spark of divine resemblance that leaves that person made in the image of God. And there is no human being who is beyond God's reach. No person is God forsaken. Human life is sacred. However, in our unregenerate, natural state, we are not fit for heaven nor can we have fellowship with God.

What I have described here is the natural state of humankind, apart from transformation through a divine encounter with the Savior. We will look at that in more detail later. But in order to fully appreciate the depth of our loss, we must follow the human story just a little further.

Soon after the expulsion from the garden in Genesis chapter three, humanity experiences its first murder in Genesis chapter four. Adam and Eve's own son Cain gives vent to his corrupted nature. He slays his brother Abel in jealousy. Before long, vindictiveness is multiplied on the earth. By Genesis chapter seven, the situation is so bad that there is continual evil in people's hearts and violence upon the earth. Humankind has become so vile that God despairs that He ever made them (Gen. 6:7). God resolves to flood the entire world in judgment destroying all flesh except for Noah and his family and those with them in the ark. After sustaining them through the flood, God brings them out safely and life begins again on the earth. God also institutes human government allowing capital punishment to restrain violence (Gen. 9:6). Even after Noah settles on the refreshed earth, it is not long before human pride manifests itself in a joint effort to build a tower that will reach the heavens. At the tower of Babel (Gen. 11), God confuses language to scatter people all over the world so that evil will be further restrained.

And then God sets in motion a plan to redeem the world. He chooses one man Abram and sends him away from his own country and kinsmen to a land that God will show him. Abram is challenged to believe God and he responds in obedience, going out, not knowing where he is going. God promises him a land for his descendants and offspring as numerous as the stars. He promises to be with him and to bless him. He promises that through him all the families of the earth will be blessed (Genesis 12:1-3). Abram is promised a son and God changes his name to Abraham, which means father of many nations. Abraham acts in faith, believing God and taking Him at His word. He is even willing, at God's command, to sacrifice his own son, the heir of the promise (Gen. 22). It is through this line of descent: Abraham, Issac and Jacob that the nation Israel is born. God prepares a people who will guard the deposit of faith that will culminate in the Messiah, the Savior, who is Jesus Christ.

Slaves in Egypt

But first, this particular people must be formed and prepared through trial and suffering. It is suffering and slavery under the Egyptians that God uses to prepare them. Through it, God shows them their own helplessness. The situation is so desperate that the Egyptian Pharaoh orders genocide. Every male baby is to be killed. Israel has become a people facing extinction. They are slaves in Egypt. They groan and cry out to God. And God sees. And God knows (Ex. 2:25).

This is completely analogous to the human condition. We too are slaves, slaves to sin. Jesus said *"everyone who commits sin is a slave to sin"* (John 8:34). And there is no way for us to break free on our own. Just like the Israelites in Egypt, the situation is hopeless and destined to destroy us. We cannot help ourselves.

This reminds me of a situation that my former neighbor Grant faced one morning. We both lived on the shore of Lake Simcoe. Grant's boat, which had been moored just off shore had broken free of its mooring. A strong wind had whipped up four-foot waves, which had driven his boat onto my beach. It was being relentlessly pounded against the stones and rocks on the beach. Grant had tried for an hour to push it off, but there was no use, the wind was too strong, the breakers were too big. In a panic he had knocked on my door for help. As we came down to the beach, we both knew that the situation was hopeless. There is no way we would be able to push the boat off. The wind force and the waves were just too great. We needed the help of someone offshore. We needed something beyond the breakers with enough power to pull the boat off. I came up with an idea. My own boat, a sailboat was moored just off shore beyond the breakers. If I could get out to my boat with a line tied to Grant's boat then I would be in a position to pull it off the beach. So off I went in my little ten-foot dinghy into the four-foot waves. After a few tries, I managed to get the dinghy past the breakers and got the line from Grant's boat to the sailboat. After that it was simple. I quickly pulled the boat off the beach using one of the sailboat's winches. Grant's boat was saved.

The point of this story is that there was no way for us to push the boat off the beach as long as we were on the beach with the boat. We had to get beyond the breakers. Only someone outside of our condition on the beach could help. I was able to get out and be that someone.

In the same way, there is no way that we can solve the hopelessness of human slavery to sin. It requires someone outside of the human condition. God Himself must intervene. If God does not step up, we are done. And that is precisely what God does for Israel in its slavery to Egypt and for us in our slavery to sin. In Israel's situation in Egypt, God sends Moses as a messenger to confront Pharaoh with a message, Let Israel Go! (Ex. 5:1). He refuses and it takes the ten mighty acts of God in the plagues before Pharaoh is finally beaten. The last plague is the one that breaks him, the death of every firstborn in Egypt. God uses this to teach his people a vital truth. The price of redemption is the death of the firstborn. The angel of death will descend on the land and slay every firstborn of man and beast. To spare their own firstborns, God initiates the Passover, a new beginning for Israel (Ex. 12). They are to take a lamb without blemish and slaughter it, applying its blood to the doorposts and lintel of each Hebrew house. It is the death of the substitute, the lamb and its blood that provides the means for their escape. The angel of death "passes over" every house that has the blood of the lamb applied to it.

So too for us sinners, it is the death of God's own firstborn, Jesus Christ, that releases all who have His blood applied to themselves. Jesus Christ is fully human, and hence a fitting substitute, yet also fully divine, God incarnate. For only one of infinite worth can atone for sin against an infinite God. And because human sin is the issue, He must also be fully human. Jesus is *"the Lamb of God who takes away the sin of the world" (John 1:29).* God does for us what we could never do for ourselves. Only, like the Hebrews, we must have the blood of the Lamb, His blood, applied to our situation. We must appropriate by faith through action what God has provided. He Himself provides the sacrifice for us. This is the essence of the Gospel. We are to believe in the One whom He has sent (John 6:29). We are to repent of our sin and receive Him, being baptized in the name of the Father, the Son and the Holy Spirit (Acts 2:38, Matt. 28:19). It is God's gift of faith that allows us to do that. It is not something that we can conjure up on our own, because we are powerless to do so, bound by our sin and unable to grasp the Good. In Ephesians, the Apostle Paul writes:

> *For by grace you have been saved through faith. And this is not your own doing; it is the gift of God, [9] not a result of works, so that no one may boast. Ephesians 2:8-9*

The way God does this; the way He saves and transforms us is what we will call transformation logic.

Transformation Logic

Coming to faith in Christ is a divine encounter between a person and the Person of God, The Holy One of Israel. How it happens is a deep and profound mystery into which, we as humans have limited insight. We know it happens; those of faith have experienced it, yet all we can do is tell our stories and marvel at the change that God has wrought in us. Yet, there is a commonality and a logic in these divine encounters that we can identify and appreciate if we think deeply. While some might ask, why bother, why not just accept it and move on, I believe that we can gain a profound insight into the nature of God and how He works by studying it. We will also be better able to encourage and support others who go through such a transformation. We might also gain some insight into how to share the light of the gospel with people who are experiencing the contradictions of life. The concept of transformation logic has been postulated in James E Loder's *The Transforming Moment – Understanding Convictional Experiences"*[ix].

We have seen that God acts and through His actions reveals Himself (see chapter one). He also speaks and through His self-utterance reveals the significance of what He has done.[x] For example, Jesus is crucified. But so also are two other men along side Him. How does the crucifixion of the man on the center cross result in salvation for the world? No one could understand this naturally. It seems like foolishness. It offends the sensibilities (1 Cor. 1:23). To comprehend its significance, it must be explained to us. Jesus' ministry through His disciples and their apostolic witness, which is the gospel, tells us that Jesus was *the Lamb of God* who takes away the sin of the world (John 1:29). We are told that His death was substitutionary and made atonement for all sin. But knowing that is not enough for faith. There is a divine action of grace that is required in the heart of each one who hears this. In this divine action God transforms not only the person but that person's experience of reality. A new birth is experienced and a transformation occurs. The regenerated person experiences an *ah-ha* moment that releases him or her into a new world that didn't exist a moment earlier. There is a divine transformation, a fundamental change of state, a new creation (2 Cor. 5:17).

In *Transforming Moments* James Loder begins by examining two-dimensional transformation. The elements of the two dimensions are *self* and *the world*. As relational beings, we experience the world around us as that with which we interact. We also run up against problems and frustrations that instill in us what Loder calls a "rupture in the knowing context"[xi]. As problems arise, we are baffled and distressed by our situation, which induces inner turmoil within us.

Take something as simple as a puzzle. Loder uses the popular one below as an example. In this puzzle, the task is *to connect all nine dots with four straight lines, without going through the same dot twice and without removing the pen from the paper*. If you truly want to experience what I am describing, take five minutes and try to solve this puzzle.

What you are experiencing is the inner stress on not being able to solve a simple puzzle. For some, such stress can last for days as they even dream about the problem. What is really going on here is that there is a rupture in the harmony between my world and myself. We experience such tension all the time. A problem suddenly appears that has consequences for me personally. Perhaps I lose my job, or a close friend is angry with me, or I have to solve a problem like getting to a doctor in a strange city. Immediately, I begin casting about looking for a solution. Loder calls this an "interlude for scanning"[xii] (step two of his logic). In this interlude, caring energy is required. If I don't really care about the puzzle, it is easy for me to dismiss it as not my problem and move on. But for personal problems that have great consequences, like the breakdown of a relationship, this interlude causes very much stress and inner turmoil. It can raise our blood pressure, it can lead us into despair or depression.

The third step in the process is what Loder calls "a construction of insight with convincing force that constitutes a turning point"[xiii]. We suddenly have some new insight into the problem that provides a way out, a solution or a new possibility for the future. For the puzzle, recognizing that I am not restricted to drawing lines within the box becomes that insight (For the solution to the puzzle, see page 55).

Loder's Five Point Transformation Logic

1. Conflict, anxiety or tension – the problem
2. Interlude for scanning – looking for solutions
3. A flash of insight from outside, above us
4. The "ah-ha" turning point - our release
5. Interpretation – public verification – a new world

For personal problems such as losing one's job, insight becomes an awareness that there are better jobs out there, that perhaps this is an opportunity to go back to school, or start up a new business. For relational issues, it may be working with a therapist to gain some new insight into myself or the other person that frees me to move forward. This insight that sets up a turning point usually comes from outside of us. It can come from within, but typically external stimulus and the help and love of others is required.

The fourth element that accompanies this is "a release of energy that sustains the conflict"[xiv]. It is the *ah-ha* experience that changes my world. It is the solution to the puzzle. It is finding a better job, or being accepted at a prestigious school, or securing the funding to start a business. It is being able to address the relational conflict and make enough peace to move forward. The point is that it becomes a transforming moment for it changes my world. The problem is no longer a source of stress or turmoil, at least not to the same extent. I can move on into my future with integrity. My burden has been lightened.

The fifth step of the process is interpretation[xv]. This is a public test of the solution that confirms that the problem is truly solved, that my world is really better. It is my testimony to the fact that the tension is released and that I can rest. It is my story. For the puzzle, it is confirmation that my solution is valid. For my new job, it becomes a testimony as to how losing my old job ushered in a new opportunity. For a relational issue, it is a testimony to resilience, coping, learning and perhaps reconciliation. It becomes part of my story.

The above description of two-dimensional transformation is essentially problem solving on a human horizontal plane. It does not take into account the action of God or Satan in the world, the spiritual dimension.

Loder then introduces *The Void and The Holy* as elements that define another dimension to the logic.[xvi] *The Void* is that universal nothingness that haunts us. It takes the form of conflict, absence, loneliness, sickness, destruction and death. Loder gives the example of waiting in a café for someone who never comes. [xvii] "The 'world' composed by the expectancy of the meeting is violated by a third dimension, the absence, the silence, the void" [xviii]. Immediately, I begin casting about "scanning" to try to recompose my world. Perhaps he was in an accident. Perhaps, I was mistaken about the place or the time. As loneliness sets in, there is a sense in which I have been violated by something outside of my control.

Ultimately, the void is death. As unregenerate[3] human beings, we are all stalked by our awareness of it. Death is the 100% statistic that no one can avoid. Unlike the animals, who also die, we humans are able to reflect on what it might be like to cease to be. As we wrestle with our own self-contradiction, we come up against a sense of despair that pulls and draws us into death. This is the ultimate absence, a sense of separation from the God who made us, who composed us in His own image. It is the self-contradiction of *original sin*. It is also reinforced by our own transgressions of law and conscience. We can try to mask it, or explain it away, but ultimately there is no escape. We are being drawn down into that pit that Loder calls *the Void.* On judgment day it becomes the Lake of Fire (Rev. 20:15). It can be diagrammed as follows:

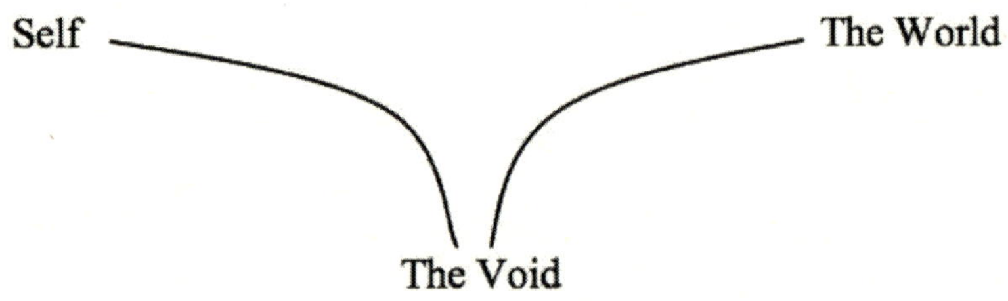

[3] Unregenerate: not born again or born from above (John 3:7)

> *"The cords of death encompassed me; the torrents of destruction assailed me; the cords of Sheol entangled me; the snares of death confronted me." Psalm 18:4-5*

The psalmist describes the desperation of that absolute negation that causes one to despair of life itself. Sickness, illness, broken relationships, depression and despair are all preludes to it. In that time of despair, there seems no way out. Every option is cut off. There is only death and destruction. Why do I continue to live? How can I go on? Some never emerge from it and, in a moment where evil triumphs, take their own life.

Yet, by God's grace, we continue to live. God's invisible help comes and sees us through. There is a divine bestowal that takes place whether we are aware of it or not. Some have called this *common grace*. It is God's providential care over all people whether they acknowledge it or not. Finally, as we come to know Christ, we become aware of all the divine interventions that rescued us all through our lives. It was Him all along. *The Holy One* has come out of nowhere and negates once and for all the desolation of *The Void*. Our world is transformed.

> *"In my distress I called upon the LORD; to my God I cried for help. From his temple he heard my voice, and my cry to him reached his ears……… He bowed the heavens and came down; thick darkness was under his feet. He rode on a cherub and flew; he came swiftly on the wings of the wind". Psalm 18:6-7, 9-10*

The ultimate negation of *the Void* is the cross of Jesus Christ. In the cross, God descends into the void of death, embracing it on our behalf. *The Holy One,* who is the exact antithesis of death, the Source of life and all that is good and true and pure, righteous and just, Himself descends into *the Void,* in order to negate it, to break it's very voidness. The cross is the negation of the great negation, death. In that sense it is a double negation. In it, Jesus Christ, God incarnate, says "No" to sin and death and that which would destroy us. In doing so, He transforms the great Void into new life, union with Christ Himself. Dying, now becomes the way to eternal life. Just as Jesus dies to Himself, descending into the abyss of sin and death, so we too, in order to appropriate life, *must follow and die to ourselves*, descending into

His death by embracing our own. In exercising the faith that God gives us, we must surrender our lives to the One who died for us. Jesus said:

> *"For whoever would save his life will lose it, but whoever loses his life for my sake will save it." Luke 9:24*

Hence, the only way to truly live is to die. We must die to ourselves and embrace the cross that Jesus Christ appoints. This is a highly particular dying. Each of us, in facing the great Void, must surrender that last vestige of self that we cling to in order to justify ourselves. We find it agonizing to surrender self. Satan tempts us to insist that surely there must be something "good" in us that we can offer God. As long as we hold out, we are clinging to self and world, refusing to let ourselves go into the Void. But, it is into the Void that God descends. He will not go part way. We must let go completely. It is an act of faith, imparted and exercised as we surrender ourselves to Him.

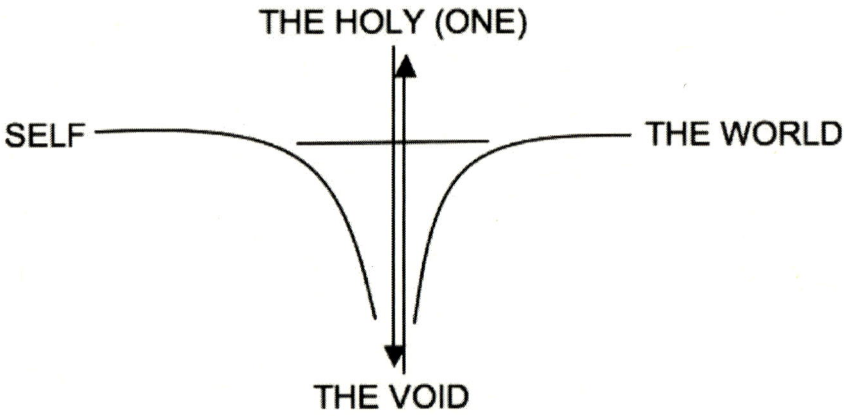

And in that letting go, the Holy One seizes us and lifts us out of the muck and mire of sin and death, washing us whiter than snow and transforming our descent into ascent. We are born afresh, born from above, born again. (John 3:7) As new creations, we rise with Him in newness of life for He becomes our life. It is life born of faith, not in ourselves but, in the Holy One who imparts it. The resurrection power that raised Jesus Christ from the dead transforms us into a mystical union with the Holy One, Jesus Christ, who now becomes our life.

For some, this transformation is a moment of insight from above, an ah-ha moment in which God regenerates us and to which we instantly respond in faith. For others, it is a slow dawning that takes place over time. Our descent into the void can be gradual and our wakening to new life gradual as well. In either case, we can testify beyond a shadow of doubt that there has been a change. We are not the same person, we have been born from above. Our new birth is the result of our experience of that void from which Christ saves us.

This is the symbolism of baptism. In baptism, we descend into the water, symbolizing dying to self. We then rise with newness of life into a new existence that is not our own. It is His. We rise with Him into newness of life. We become a new creation! The Apostle Paul describes this:

> *"We were buried therefore with him by baptism into death, in order that, just as Christ was raised from the dead by the glory of the Father, we too might walk in newness of life.* [5] *For if we have been united with him in a death like his, we shall certainly be united with him in a resurrection like his." Romans 6:4-5*

That union with Him results in a completely new standing with God and a completely new nature from God. These are two benefits of *justification* and *sanctification* that we will describe in the next chapter. All of this comes by faith alone in God's completed work in Jesus Christ. The great transformation is completed. It consists of an astounding exchange. My sin and condemnation is laid upon Christ, and His righteousness is bestowed upon me. But this is not automatically given. I must make it my own as He had made me His own. I must exercise the faith that He gives me and die. Dietrich Bonhoeffer, the German pastor who was executed at the hands of Hitler's regime for his subversive opposition, wrote

> *"When Christ calls a man, He bids him to come and die. It may be a death like that of his first disciples who had to leave home and work to follow him, or it may be a death like Luther's, who had to leave the monastery and go out into the world. But it is the same death every time, death in Jesus Christ, death of the old man at his call." "* [xix] .

And so my life is no longer mine. As the Apostle Paul writes: *"...you have died, and your life is hidden with Christ in God." Colossians 3:3.* The life that I now live is mysteriously intertwined in Him and hidden to the world to which I have died. The world doesn't see it, but I am certain of it, for He dwells within me and His Holy Spirit testifies that I am His.

* * * * * *

We began this chapter describing a dilemma. God is Holy and we as human beings are sinners. Yet God's passion and plan is to form a bride for His Son from among sinful humanity. It is profoundly astonishing that the Bridegroom Himself accomplished that by descending into the abyss of sin and death to redeem His bride from slavery to sin. It is the height of love for a man to die for his bride. It is the height of love to take her shame and disgrace onto Himself and bear it unto death. Jesus was despised and rejected because that was our deserved fate. We are the ones who should have been crucified for our rebellion and sin. In dying for us, He showed us the way to live. A most profound scripture is the Apostle Paul's explicit statement in as to why Jesus died.

> *"..... he died for all, [so] that those who live might no longer live for themselves but for him who for their sake died and was raised." 2 Corinthians 5:15*

In my late twenties, I was heavily involved with a New Age group, that culminated in a personal tragedy. The group that I was involved with practiced a form of meditation that opened me to demonic influences. One night, I was driving back from a weekend seminar with my friend John. After an entire day of meditation cycles, we were both very sleepy and John was asleep beside me. My eyes grew heavy and I too fell asleep. The car went off the road at 70 miles an hour and rolled over multiple times. By God's grace, I managed to stay in the car and emerged without a scratch, but John was thrown from the vehicle and suffered severe head injuries. The next day he died. John's death hit me so hard that it plunged me into a deep abyss. As I wrestled with what my life had become, I was overwhelmed by the sense of responsibility. I had caused John's death.

The next day, while walking the street of Toronto, I fell to my knees in the middle of an afternoon crowd and asked God to forgive me. It was me that should have died that night, not John. In a desperate prayer, I surrendered my life to God and asked Him to do with me what He would. As I rose from my knees, a sudden surge of grace flooded over me. The Holy One had entered into my void and had lifted me up. I rose feeling strangely cleansed and forgiven. Something had changed. I was able to face John's parents and attend the funeral bearing full responsibility yet knowing that my life was now in God's hands. It was a few years later that God showed me that it was Jesus Christ who had met me, had made provision for my release. At that point, I fully acknowledged Him as my Savior. Since then, I have sought to live life as if I had died. After all, for all practical purposes, I should have died that night. The years that God has given me since then have been a glorious bonus.

The Only Way to Live

The only way to really live the Christian life is to die. We consider death to be the ultimate tragedy, because we have such a shallow view of life. But consider yourself for a moment. Suppose that you died this very day. It is possible. A friend of mine was perfectly healthy one day and suffered a brain aneurism and was dead within two days.

Imagine the following scenario: You actually died today. So there you are standing before the LORD. After much rejoicing and a joyous reunion, He says to you:

"Well, what did you think about it, about life?"

Sheepishly you answer: "Well, it was OK, I mean it was good, painful at times but good."

And then God says to you: "You know, there were times when I was frustrated with you. So many times you were in a place where all you had to do was open your mouth and tell people about me, but you just wouldn't do it".

And then you answer quietly: "Yes, I know, I know I could have done better."

Then God says: " Well, it's over. You are dead…., but you know, I am God after all, and ….. I could send you back. That would be interesting. ummm Technically you're already dead. You would have nothing left to lose."

You reply: "Well, yes, I mean you are God, you could send me back, that would be amazing. I really do miss my family".

"Do you think that from now on you could just live entirely for me? After all you are dead, right? Everything from now on is pure bonus."

And so He does send you back, and now here you are back in your body, knowing that He sent you back just so that you would live entirely for Him. How would that change your attitude, your behavior?

The purpose of transforming grace is to free you from trivial selfish pursuits and commission you to a life of holiness and service to Him. So many Christians are happy that they are saved, but their lives are full of things that have nothing to do with the over-arching passion of God. One has to wonder if faith that is void of the passion of the One who gives it, is really real?

How about you? Look at how you spend your time. How much of that activity is engaged in what Jesus would be doing if He were where you are now? He wants you to be holy and to live for Him. He died for you. This is the purpose of love, that you would be continually transformed into a person whose sole purpose in life is to live for Jesus Christ, your redeeming Bridegroom. Your life is no longer your own. You are part of His bride-to-be and He wants to perfect you in holiness that you might be completely ready for that day when He returns for you. As He died, so He bids you die, die to sin, to the world and to self.

> *"For you have died, and your life is hidden with Christ in God. When Christ who is your life appears, then you also will appear with him in glory." Colossians 3:3-4*

This dying is not just a one-time event. This is the pattern of everyday life for the believer. I must die daily, for my inner contradiction, that sinful nature that I wrestle with, daily asserts itself. So each day, I must die to myself and reorient myself to God. This is only possible through the power of the Holy Spirit working in me. Martin Luther, in the first of his famous 95 theses[xx], declared that the Christian life is one of daily lifelong repentance. Repentance is turning away from my own way and reorienting myself back to God. Turning away from my own agenda is dying, dying to myself. As I do this, I am continually transformed. The cycle of entering into the void is the cycle of facing the reality of death in me. I am crucified daily with Christ, and by His grace I daily rise in the power of His resurrection. As a believer, I live in that tension between death and resurrection life. And I rest in the assurance that *"There is therefore now no condemnation for those who are in Christ Jesus"* (Romans 8:1).

Most of us do not think about death. We try to avoid it, even deny it. Yet making peace with our own mortality is a critical element of spiritual life.

Henry Nouwen, in writings published after his own death points out that we need to befriend death. *"In order to become full human beings, we have to claim the totality of our experience; we come to maturity by integrating not only the light, but also the dark side of our story into our selfhood"* [xxi] Befriending death means befriending the Void. We can only do this with integrity if we have faith that the Holy One will meet us there. He has indeed met us there in the cross of Jesus Christ. And He continues to meet us there every time we deny ourselves and live for Him. He calls us to take up our cross and follow. To refuse to do so is to remain alone and to remain incomplete. Jesus said:

> *"....unless a grain of wheat falls into the earth and dies, it remains alone; but if it dies, it bears much fruit. Whoever loves his life loses it, and whoever hates his life in this world will keep it for eternal life." John 12:24-25*

As we die to ourselves each day, we are united to Christ in death and in life. For He did not stay dead. The resurrection power that raised Jesus Christ from the dead is at work in us, so that we live in Him. His continual presence with us through the Holy Spirit is a source of incomparable joy. We live by His power and we move in His strength. We have eternal life and we have it now. So let us live as if nothing on earth could hurt us, for our lives are indeed "hidden in Christ with God" (Col. 3:3).

Study Guide for Chapter Two

A. Questions for Personal Reflection

Record answers in your journal.

1. Read Isaiah 6:1-8. What do you think Isaiah felt when He experienced this scene in heaven? What changed his feeling? Have you ever felt that way or experienced this?

2. Have you recently faced a life issue or a problem that has shaken your world or caused you considerable anxiety? How does Loder's concept of *the Void* (page 42-46) explain what you are feeling? What is the ultimate *Void?*

3. Have you experienced the intervention of *The Holy One* lifting you out of *the Void?* Jot down what happened to you in your journal. Start by describing how you became aware of *the Void.* Describe the transforming moment or dawning that gave you release. How did an awareness of God's action in Christ lift you up? How did you integrate or verify what happened in you with others?

4. Read Colossians 3:1-17. How does the concept of daily dying play itself out in your life? What are the things that you must die to? How does God help you and lift you into things that are above?

B. Exercises (Individual or Large Group)

1. Apply Holy Reading (see page 31-32) to the Emmaus story in Luke 24:12-36. Try to enter into the perplexity of the two disciples who had just witnessed Jesus' crucifixion a few days earlier. How did their world and the world of Israel collapse?
    i. Analyze this story in terms of Loder's transformation logic. (see page 43).

1. Conflict, anxiety or tension – the Void
2. Interlude for scanning – looking for solutions
3. Construction of insight from above – help from God
4. The "ah-ha" turning point – release/ascent
5. Interpretation – public verification

ii. Identify each of the elements of this logic to the disciples, their world (personal, national, spiritual), the Void and the intervention of The Holy One.

iii. What does this tell us about the way God works? How does this help you in the conflicts and tensions of daily life?

2. **Reflecting on your death:** (30 minutes)

In chapter one's Study Guide, we spoke of the discipline of silence and solitude. One aspect of this discipline is that it begins to prepare us for our own death. While this may sound rather somber or morbid, we all know that one day each of us will die. At that moment, we will be alone and face to face with God. Meditating on our own death helps put life into perspective.

i. Take ten minutes to go through the Holy Reading process described in the study guide for chapter one. Reflect on Psalm 23. Use the breath prayer *"Lord, my chief comfort in life and in death is that I belong to you, my faithful Savior"* .

ii. Spend the next ten minutes in silence meditating on your own death. Think of who would organize the funeral. Where would it likely be? Visualize your family and friends gathering and speaking tenderly of you. What would they be saying? What pictures of you would be posted for viewing? At the funeral, what aspects of your life would people be celebrating? Share those with God in prayer. What new perspectives on your life did you gain while doing this?

   iii. Write out your reflections on dying. What are your fears, anxieties and regrets?
   iv. Reflect on Romans 14:7-8. Write down your thoughts.

3. Read Gal 2:20, Col. 3:3-4, Phil 1:21-22, 1 Cor. 15:31. In what way is dying, (entering the Void) a daily occurrence for followers of Jesus Christ? What aspects of your being must die every day?

4. Read Eph. 2:4-6, Col. 3:2, Rom. 8:11. How does living in the light of the resurrection impact you? In what ways is the death and resurrection of Jesus the centre of Christian life?

C. Small Group Breakout (2 or 3)

1. In small groups of 2 or 3 (same gender), share your experience with the meditation on your own death.

2. How did your devotional times go this week? What spiritual challenges are you facing? How is your relationship with God growing deeper?

3. Take some time to pray for one another.

D. Assignment for Next Week

1. As you go through next week, reflect on the paradox of daily dying and being resurrected by Christ. Be aware of how God works transformation around you. Write down your reflections in your journal.

2. Engage in at least five quiet times with God using Holy Reading (see Exercises Chapter 1). Begin with the breath prayer: "*I am yours, save me*" (Ps. 119:94a) Use the following passages and be aware of transformation logic. Gen. 32: 22-32, 1 Sam. 1:1-28, Acts 9:1-21, Gen. 22:1-19, Acts 14:19-23 Note reflections in your journal.

3. Read chapter three. Answer the Questions for Personal Reflection your journal.

* * * * * * *

Solution to puzzle from page 40

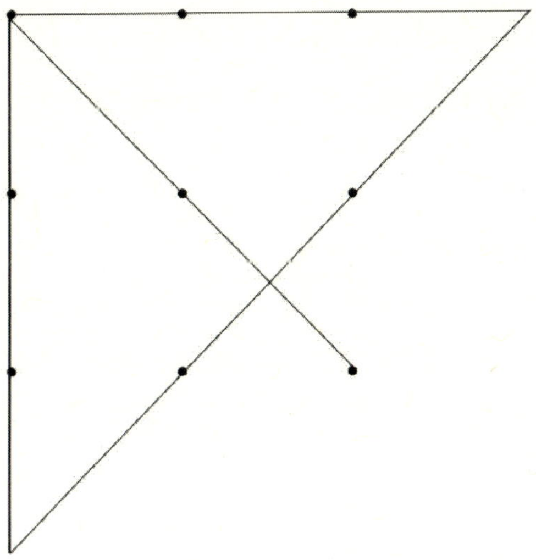

3. The Battle Within – The Victory of Love

"For the desires of the flesh are against the Spirit, and the desires of the Spirit are against the flesh, for these are opposed to each other, to keep you from doing the things you want to do." Galatians 5:17

Transforming faith is a gift of God. Its expression unites the believer with God through Jesus Christ, the object of faith. The substance of that faith is salvation and life in Christ. Salvation is not an event, it is a Person. It is Jesus Christ. As the scripture says: *"He is the source of your life in Christ Jesus, whom God made our wisdom and our righteousness and sanctification and redemption."* (1 Cor. 1:30).

John Calvin identified *justification* and *sanctification* as tandem benefits of union with Jesus Christ.[xxii] For those who are justified, God sees us as clothed with the righteousness of Christ through whom our sins are forgiven and through whom we are declared righteous in His sight. This righteousness is not our own. As Martin Luther stated, it is an alien righteousness[xxiii]. It comes from outside of us[4]. It is not our righteousness but His. In this way God remains both just and justifier of those united with Christ by faith (Rom. 3:26). He remains just, for the righteous requirements of the law have been fulfilled. The punishment for our sins has been laid upon Jesus. God is also Justifier for He initiates this action. As Judge, He is the One who accepts the Son's sacrifice and imputes it to our benefit allowing us to be released from the sentence of death.

For me, such a release requires that God's righteous wrath against me, as sinner is satisfied. This is the meaning of the term *propitiation.* God's wrath at me for my sin is poured out upon His Son at the cross. Jesus absorbs my punishment and with His stripes, I am set right. (Is. 53:5). The curse of sin is removed from me for Jesus is *"the Lamb of God who takes away the sin of the world"* (John 1:29). He is the scapegoat that is led into the wilderness that bears my sin away (Lev. 16:10). The term for this is *expiation.* My justification includes both propitiation and expiation meaning that God's wrath is born away and my sin is forgiven and removed. This gives me a new standing with

---

[4] Latin: *extra nos* (outside of us)

God. When God sees me, He sees me wrapped in the righteousness of His beloved Son. As He is pleased with His son, He is pleased with me.

At the same time, my transformation makes me a new creation (2 Cor. 5:17) and I am sanctified in Christ Jesus. The word sanctification has at its root the Latin word *sanctus* which means holy. Sanctification is being made holy by *the Holy One*. It has both a definitive and a progressive dimension. It is definitive in that it is an accomplished fact by virtue of my union with Christ. The Apostle Paul writes:

> *"you were sanctified, you were justified in the name of the Lord Jesus Christ and by the Spirit of our God." 1 Cor. 6:11*

The tense and mood (aorist, indicative) in the original language indicates that this is a one time act completed in the past. There is a sense in which I have already been sanctified, consecrated to Christ for His purposes. Yet sanctification is also a progressive work of the Holy Spirit within me for while I am in the flesh, I am still influenced by my sinful nature inherited from Adam and Eve. The Apostle Paul writes:

> *"And we all, with unveiled face, beholding the glory of the Lord, are being transformed into the same image from one degree of glory to another. For this comes from the Lord who is the Spirit." 2 Cor 3:18*

This transformation is continuous and progressive, degree-by-degree and is empowered by the Holy Spirit, in a continuing series of transforming moments. It is also a joint work of God and myself for I am commanded to be an active participant in my sanctification. Paul also writes:

> *"Therefore, my beloved, as you have always obeyed, so now, not only as in my presence but much more in my absence, work out your own salvation with fear and trembling, for it is God who works in you, both to will and to work for his good pleasure." Phil. 2:12-13*

I must "work out" what God "works in". In the original language, two different Greek verbs are used for the word *work*. The first "work out" *(katergazomai)* means to "labor to completion" or to "get it done". This is my role. In it, I engage with other Christians who help and mentor me (Prov. 27:17). The second "works in" *(energeo)* has the force of "empowering from within" or "energizing". I am to get it done by dying to myself and obeying the Holy Spirit's promptings to empower God's work in and through me. As Paul writes: *"I have been crucified with Christ, it is no longer I that live, but Christ lives in me"* (Gal. 2:20a) . In this way sanctification is a life long process. It is dying to self and living in Christ continually. It is descent and ascent, living in the death and resurrection of Christ. It is an integral part of salvation.

The biblical concept of salvation has three specific aspects, all of which are ours by virtue of our union with Christ. Theses are justification, sanctification and glorification. Salvation *is both past, present* and *future.* It is very much true that I have been saved (justified), am being saved (sanctified) and will be saved (glorified), provided I remain in Christ. He is the source and the root and the grounding for all of these (1 Cor. 1:30). And it is the Holy Spirit that is the bond that unites me with Him.

The table below summarizes these three aspects of salvation.

Justification	**Sanctification**	**Glorification**
Actual standing	Internal Condition	Glorious hope
Once for all time	Continuous through life	Future fact
Entirely God's work	I work it out as God works in me	Entirely God's work
Perfect in this life	Not perfect in this life	Perfect in future life
The same in all Christians	Greater in some than others	Varying rewards

Glorification[xxiv] is the final step in the application of redemption, which occurs when Christ returns and resurrects the bodies of believers who have died and transforms the bodies of those who are alive, giving them all glorified resurrection bodies like His own. The Apostle Paul sometimes refers to salvation as glorification.

> *"Besides this you know the time, that the hour has come for you to wake from sleep. For salvation is nearer to us now than when we first believed." Romans 13:11*

Our glorification is our ultimate vindication and the victory of the gospel in us. Until that day, while we are in the body, we will struggle with all that is in us to lay hold of that which Christ has laid up for us. That struggle is the struggle of sanctification.

The degree to which any person progresses in sanctification in this life varies widely. Some are just newly born in Christ and have renounced only obvious sins. Others have been walking with Christ for many years and conquered much being progressively transformed more and more into His image. The goal of sanctification is to make me like Christ in every aspect of my life (2 Cor. 3:18). This requires a complete surrender on my part. Jesus said that whoever saves his life in this world will lose it, but he who loses his life for Christ's sake will save it (Luke 9:24). I must continually die to self and live by the faith that He has given me. I must do the things that He commands. I must obey Him, walking in love and in truth as He walked.

As I read the scriptures, as I worship, as I pray, and love others in His name, the Holy Spirit molds me into conformity with Christ. I become a reflection of Him to others. Whereas justification through His sacrifice gives me a new standing with God, sanctification transforms my nature into conformance with His. These dual benefits, justification and sanctification are mine in this life, by virtue of my union with Christ. This union is by faith alone, yet faith is never alone. I must prove my faith as genuine by exercising it in daily life as I walk with God.

Sanctification does not mean that one is without sin. Have you ever wondered why, despite your best intentions and heartfelt desires, you still continue to say and do things that wound people? Despite your best intentions, you continue to disappoint yourself and others. It is a great paradox, for as a new creature in Christ it should not be so. "Am I not in Christ? Does not the Holy Spirit dwell in me? How could I do such a thing?"

The reason for this is that there exists an inner battle in the heart of every believer. This is the battle between the new nature in Christ and the old self that, though crucified, refuses to die. The Apostle Paul testifies to that inner battle when he writes:

> *"I do not understand my own actions. For I do not do what I want, but I do the very thing I hate. 16 Now if I do what I do not want, I agree with the law, that it is good. 17 So now it is no longer I who do it, but sin that dwells within me. 18 For I know that nothing good dwells in me, that is, in my flesh. For I have the desire to do what is right, but not the ability to carry it out. 19 For I do not do the good I want, but the evil I do not want is what I keep on doing." Romans 7:15-19*

Paul later identifies the source of that inner compulsion to sin as "the flesh" (Rom. 8:5). The original Greek word *sarx* means more than just physical flesh. It refers to our earthly descent and encompasses the human mind, heart and will as inherited from Adam and Eve our primordial ancestors. While some might interpret Paul's description of his struggle as a pre-conversion struggle, this interpretation is not convincing. It is clear from this and many other passages that Paul is describing the inner battle of every believer.[xxv] A proper understanding of this struggle requires that we recognize the different ways that the word *sin* is used in scripture.

The Three Meanings of Sin

Sin is a complex topic as that little word "sin" is used in different ways in scripture. In order to appreciate what Christ has done for us and to be able to live in victory, we must understand thoroughly the doctrine of sin. In a broad sense, sin is a violation of God, a violation of His heart, of His will and of His character. It is essentially a defective relationship with God. Yet that little word *sin* is used in different places in scripture with three nuances of meaning. These are:

1. *Sin as actual guilt.*[xxvi] In John's gospel, John the Baptist sees Jesus approaching and declares *"Behold the Lamb of God who takes away the sin of the world"* (John 1:29). We understand that Jesus was the sacrificial Lamb, whose death on the cross atoned for the actual guilt of the world. (The words *legal guilt* are sometimes used as they refer to a courtroom scene where God judges all people. See Rev. 20:11-12.) All of humanity is guilty before God, for "*all have sinned and fall short of the Glory of God*" (Rom. 3:23). In Romans 3:9, we are all described as "*under sin*". Galatians 3:22 states that "scripture imprisoned everything under sin". Everyone who stands before God on judgment day will be actually guilty before God, for everyone has sinned. Jesus' death on the cross changes the outcome for those who cling to Him in faith. They are beneficiaries of His grace and set free from the actual guilt of sin (John 8:36). In this way Jesus makes provision for the "actual guilt" of the entire world to be removed. However, this removal is only apprehended by faith in the finished work of Christ. *"There is therefore now no condemnation for those who are in Christ Jesus"* (Rom. 8:1). Note that actual guilt must be

distinguished from feelings of guilt. A person can be actually guilty before God and have no feelings of guilt or remorse. Likewise, a person can feel guilty about something that is not a violation of God's will. Our consciences have been corrupted by the fall of man and our consequent inner corruption and are not a reliable indicator of actual guilt. Our conscience needs to be reoriented and recalibrated with the word of God.

2. *Sin as inner corruption, defilement*[xxvii]. This use of the word sin refers to our inner corruption inherited from Adam and Eve. Every human being is born with this inner corruption or indwelling sin. Psalm 51:5 says: *"I was brought forth in iniquity and in sin did my mother conceive me."* The Apostle John writes: *"If we say we have no sin, we deceive ourselves and the truth is not in us"* (1 John 1:8). As long as we are in this body we will be influenced by this inner propensity to sin. It is like blood poisoning that runs through our veins that we can never be free of in this earthly life. The difference between a natural person and one in Christ is that indwelling sin rules and enslaves the natural person. There is nothing in the natural person to oppose it. The natural person is a slave to this inner propensity to sin. Jesus said that everyone who commits sin is a slave to sin (John 8:34). When a person comes to Christ, the power of this inner corruption is broken and it no longer rules a believer, however, it continues to influence in varying degrees, creating a constant struggle between indwelling sin and the new creation in Christ (more on this later). When we sin as believers we give way to this indwelling sin. We do this voluntarily for indwelling sin does not rule us. We do have the power to resist through the Holy Spirit. The new creation that we are in Christ has the power and authority to conquer our inner corruption (Rom. 6:12).

3. *Sin as transgression.* The final meaning of the word sin is actual transgression(s), that is thoughts, words or actions that violate the will and heart of God. These can be things done or things left undone (omissions). We transgress when we give way to our inner corruption. Transgressions are the fruit of our unbridled sinnership. When we pray "Forgive us our sins", we are asking that our actual transgressions be forgiven. When we forgive others we forgive their transgressions against us. When Jesus taught His disciples to pray for forgiveness of transgressions, He

assumed that they would occur. As long as we are in the body, we will be praying for such forgiveness.

In reading any passage of scripture in which the word *sin* occurs, we must decide which of these meanings of sin are implied. It may be one or two or perhaps all three. In Romans 7:17 Paul talks about the *"sin that lives in me"*. This is obviously not sin as *actual guilt*, for as a justified believer, he is no longer under condemnation. It cannot mean *transgressions*, for transgressions are external acts and cannot dwell inside someone. It is clear therefore that he is referring to that *inner corruption* that we all have.

In Isaiah 59:2, we read that *"your iniquities have made a separation between you and your God and your sins have hidden his face from you so that he does not hear"*. Here the word *"sins"* and *"iniquities"* cannot mean *actual guilt*, for all humans are born with it and God could not be chastising them for having the imputed guilt of all humanity. For the same reason it cannot mean *inner corruption* as that is universal. So here it refers to actual transgressions.

In 2 Corinthians 5:21 we read: *"For our sake he made him [Jesus] to be sin who knew no sin, so that in him we might become the righteousness of God."* Here sin cannot mean *inner corruption*, for Jesus did not have indwelling sin. He was without sin (Heb. 4:15). Likewise, it could not mean *transgressions* for He never transgressed. So it must mean *actual guilt*. God imputed to Jesus the actual guilt of all humanity. That does not mean that all humanity is saved, for salvation comes through faith, but it does mean that Jesus has provided for the sin of the whole world (John 1:29).

We must also point out that sin is not just immorality. Immorality is transgression of the law. It is possible for someone to keep the entire law and still have a defective relationship with God. In the parable of the Pharisee and the tax collector (Luke 18:10), two men go up to the temple to pray. The one boasts that he keeps all the commandments, and indeed we must assume that this is true or the parable has no force. The other beats his breast and asks for mercy acknowledging himself a sinner. The second is justified before God and not the first. That is because the second acknowledges his own inner corruption and guilt and rightly asks for mercy. The first trusts in his own morality and fails to see himself as he really is. He takes pride in his accomplishments before God and that very pride is evidence of his own inner corruption, to which he is blind. His law keeping is not the fruit of faith in God but an attempt to justify himself, something that law keeping cannot do.

The moral person often uses his morality as a way of fending God off, keeping the relationship at arms length and on his own terms. This was the position of the Pharisees in Jesus' day. God stood before them in the person of Jesus, but they used their Law-keeping to justify themselves and keep Him at a distance. In truth, the moral person is just as far from God as the immoral. Both have a defective relationship with God, the one through pride, the other through a rebellious heart. Sin ultimately is a defective relationship with God. Jesus' death on the cross makes the righting of that relationship possible through repentance and faith. The only appropriate stance before Him is one of grateful humility. *"Have mercy on me, a sinner"* is the prayer of a humble heart who sees himself as he truly is, redeemed by grace yet still inwardly corrupt. Even for the greatest saint, that inner corruption is not finally swept away until death.

One illustration that might help you understand this struggle is to see yourself living in an imaginary "Room of Life". Before you came to faith in Christ, the main influence that affected you was your inner corruption or indwelling sin. Therefore, you sinned by nature for you were by nature a sinner. We will call that inner corruption, *the sinful self. The sinful self* lived in your room as you and was unopposed. So therefore, everything you did was a result of the *the sinful self's* rule. It was restrained only by conscience and consequences. Eventually, your conscience became more and more seared and you descended more and more into your own sinnership. The most merciful thing that God could do for you at that point was to give you up to your *sinful self.* In this way you came face to face with your own depravity (see Romans 1:26-28). When you heard the gospel and saw Christ crucified for you, you were broken and responded in repentance and faith. At that moment, you became a new creation in Christ. We will call this new creation *the new self.* The *sinful self* was co-crucified with Christ, when He died for you and now its power is broken by faith (Gal. 2:20). It is as if the *sinful self* is locked up in a holding cell in a corner of the room of your life. That *sinful self* is now crucified but is not yet completely dead. In fact, it will not be completely dead until that day, when you see Christ face to face as you die physically and cross into eternity. The power of the *sinful self* over you is broken by your union with Christ, but because it is still a part of you, it still has the ability to speak into your life. But, as a believer, the reigning influence in your life is the *new self,* which is empowered by the Holy

Spirit, Christ in you, the hope of glory. This *new self* displaces the rule of the *sinful self*, which is now stripped of its power. In this way, you are "dead to sin" (Rom. 6:11). It is not that the *sinful self* no longer has influence over you, but that its dominating, ruling power is broken.

The Natural Person

Sinful self crucified (imprisoned) yet still alive – seat of indwelling sin

Person in Christ

So too, as a believer, you are released from the power of the *sinful self*. As the apostle John writes in his first letter *"no one born of God makes a practice of sinning, for God's seed abides in him and he cannot keep on sinning"* (1 John 3:9). One born of God is ruled by the *new self,* created in the image of Christ. But at the same time, John also writes in the same letter *"If we say that we have no sin, we deceive ourselves and the truth is not in us"* (1 John 1:8). The word "sin" here refers to our inner corruption. If we deny that we have an inner corruption, we deceive ourselves and the truth is not in us. These statements speak of the reality of the Christian life. We are not ruled by our inner corruption, but Christ reigns in us, so we cannot continually make a practice of sinning. At the same time, we cannot deny that our *sinful self* is still there within us.

So we see that the Christian life is one of a constant inner battle. We are assaulted not only from without as the world and Satan attacks us, but we are also assaulted from within, as we wrestle with our *sinful self.* The good news is that we have within us the power to resist and emerge victorious. The Holy Spirit dwells within us and makes us more than conquerors. The Apostle Paul writes:

> *"Who shall separate us from the love of Christ? Shall tribulation, or distress, or persecution, or famine, or nakedness, or danger, or sword? [36] As it is written, "For your sake we are being killed all the day long; we are regarded as sheep to be slaughtered." [37] No, in all these things we are more than conquerors through him who loved us. [38] For I am sure that neither death nor life, nor angels nor rulers, nor things present nor things to come, nor powers, [39] nor height nor depth, nor anything else in all creation, will be able to separate us from the love of God in Christ Jesus our Lord." Romans 8:35-39*

The Necessity of the Battle Within

The Puritans of the sixteenth and seventeenth centuries understood the nature of this inner battle and have proved to be master diagnosticians of the human condition with regard to indwelling sin. Of these, John Owen stands out as a giant for his volume and breadth of teaching on the subject. Owen was a theologian, professor and pastor who had great influence even to the highest levels of government during the English revolution and the leadership of Oliver Cromwell. During that time, the English parliament declared the last Wednesday of each month a day of prayer and fasting, and Puritan preaching was heard each Wednesday morning in parliament itself. For John Owen, mastering this inner battle was pivotal in the life of the believer. He maintained that those who were not aware of indwelling sin were so fully under it's dominion that they were at peace with it and in mortal danger:

> *"Many there are in the world who find not this law in them..... and have not a spiritual sense and experience of the power of indwelling sin; and that is because they are wholly under the dominion of it. They find that there is not darkness and folly in their minds because they are darkness itself, and darkness will discover nothing.... They are dead wholly in trespasses and sins. They are at peace with their lusts being in bondage to them."*[xxviii]

Owen's point was that the unregenerate person is unaware of the inner battle for that person is under one disposition only, the *sinful self*. In fact, he maintained that if a person does not have a sense of this inner struggle, that person is not truly a believer but is in fact "darkness itself". He goes on to say that experiencing and understanding this inner battle is *the hinge* upon which the whole course of a believer's life turns.

> *"Upon this one hinge, or finding out and experiencing the power and efficacy of this law of sin, turns the whole course of our lives."* [xxix]

To be sure, Jesus taught His disciples to pray: *"Forgive us our debts, as we also have forgiven our debtors"* (Matt. 6:12). He assumed that the disciples would continually ask for forgiveness, for they would struggle with sin. Jesus recognized that transgressions are the fruit of indwelling sin. Yet He also said *"You therefore must be perfect, as your heavenly father is perfect"* (Matt. 5:48). While under the influence of our sinful selves, we are to continually strive for perfection and holiness. This is possible only through what the Puritans called *mortification* and *vivification*. These terms were common among the protestant reformers such as John Calvin.

The word *mortification* means the putting to death of the *sinful self,* that inner corruption that is the result of indwelling sin. *Vivification* is coming to life in the Holy Spirit by which and through which mortification occurs. Vivification must always accompany mortification. It is through the Holy Spirit that we become aware of indwelling sin. Owen writes *"The Spirit is the candle that illuminates indwelling sin."* [xxx]

Vivification is the Holy Spirit's work in us giving us a desire to live a holy and devoted life by virtue of our new birth in Christ. It is through the Holy Spirit that we must continually slay the sinful self. That old self has been crucified with Christ and no longer rules over us, but the body of sin still lingers within us. Therefore, we must daily put it to death. It is only because it has already been crucified with Christ that we are able to put it to death, indeed we must. Hence, our union with Christ, our dying with Him is essential in mortification. Any attempt at putting the sinful self to death apart from entering into Christ's death is doomed to failure. For until the rule of the sinful self is broken, we are powerless against it. It is through the Spirit (vivification), which is the bond of our union with Christ, that the reign of sin is broken. John Calvin writes: *"For the Spirit dispenses a power whereby they may gain the upper hand and become victors in the struggle. But sin ceases only to reign: it does not cease to dwell in them".* [xxxi]

So while the reign of sin is broken, its influence is still present through the sinful self that must continually be put to death. This is the first duty of the believer in sanctification, the continual putting to death of the old nature, the seat of indwelling sin. It is a constant battle.

Our enemy Satan desires above all that we despair of ourselves and become paralyzed in the fight. To do nothing is to allow the sinful self to come to life again. This is how great Godly men fall into sin. Everyone has heard the horror stories of pastors who have consistently preached Spirit-led sermons, have led many to Christ, and yet fall into sin by having an affair with a secretary or a prostitute. How does this happen? It happens because, in their spiritual laziness, they allow the sinful self to have influence over their thinking. It starts with a lustful thought. Then, rather than taking that thought captive to Christ, and putting it to death, they allow it to remain. They ponder over it and enjoy its naughty pleasure. Soon, it becomes a part of their thinking and they are no longer convicted of it. They rationalize it as being "normal". Soon they begin to dwell more and more on their lustful pleasure. Already, at this point desire has given birth to sin. Left unchecked it will soon be acted out. And so they fall openly.

Rather than thinking ourselves impervious to such a fall, let us admit that we are all in the same peril. Perhaps you are already far down that road in some area of your thought life. You must resolve immediately to break the power of this sin by confessing it and putting it off. Through the power of the Holy Spirit, God's heart in you for holiness, you must weep over it, renounce it, confess it, and replace it by it's Godly counterpart. For example, if a person has lustful thoughts for another, the Godly counterpart is to think of that person as a beloved sister or brother whom God has created and for whom Christ died. You can only begin to do this by allowing the Holy Spirit to cleanse and renew your mind. You must also make use of the spiritual resources that God has made available to us. You must also be vigilant in keeping a close watch over yourself. The Apostle Paul writes:

> *"Keep a close watch on yourself and on the teaching. Persist in this, for by so doing you will save both yourself and your hearers." 1 Tim. 4:16*

Spiritual Resources for the Battle

The three main resources that we have been given are the Spirit of God, the Word of God, and the people of God. In order to be victorious, we will need to use all three.

The **Holy Spirit** is the third person of the Trinity. The Holy Spirit is first and foremost a Person. The Holy Spirit is fully God, God in Himself giving us Himself, so that the giver and the gift are one. The Holy Spirit is the breath of God, that breath that carries God's living Word to us. The Holy Spirit is the inspirer of scripture, the illuminating presence of the Word understood. The Holy Spirit is the Paraclete, the one who walks beside us. The Holy Spirit is the divine Counselor and Comforter. The Holy Spirit is a personal reality that convicts of sin, regenerates the believer, converts to faith, sanctifies the believer through union with Christ, quickens new life, gives the gift faith and bestows spiritual gifts on the faithful. The Holy Spirit is the consubstantial communion of the Father and the Son, the bond of love that unites them. Whereas the Father is the divine Lover, the Son the beloved One, the Holy Spirit is that Love itself, God's Person acting in love, moving and quickening new life and holiness in the one receptive. When the Holy Spirit falls on a person, they are broken, converted, renewed, illuminated, filled with God's presence and translated into eternity. Yet the Holy Spirit can also be resisted, grieved, opposed and denied. The Holy Spirit does not force the Spirit's self upon a person, but rather woos and beckons. That is why we are admonished in Scripture to *"be filled with the Spirit"* (Eph 5:18).

The Apostle Paul writes in Romans 7:22-25 of *"the law of sin and death"*. The law of sin is that working of the sinful self that wages war with the desire of my mind to do what is right and holy. Paul writes:

> *"For I delight in the law of God, in my inner being, 23 but I see in my members another law waging war against the law of my mind and making me captive to the law of sin that dwells in my members. 24 Wretched man that I am! Who will deliver me from this body of death? 25 Thanks be to God through Jesus Christ our Lord! So then, I myself serve the law of God with my mind, but with my flesh I serve the law of sin." Romans 7:22-25*

Notice that the law of sin works in the flesh, that is the *sinful self.* It is like the law of gravity. The natural person is subject only to the law of gravity and is kept bound by it. As long as a person is in this world, the law of gravity operates and keeps him on the ground. He is not able to fly, for he is continually subject to the law of gravity. The only way that a person can fly is if another law overcomes the law of gravity. The law of aerodynamics is able to overcome the law of gravity, if a person gets into an airplane and it begins to takes off. As the plane increases its speed, the law of aerodynamics overcomes the law of gravity and a person can fly.

Similarly, the Apostle Paul describes the law of the Spirit:

> *"For the law of the Spirit of life has set you free in Christ Jesus from the law of sin and death." Romans 8:2*

The law of the Spirit is akin to the law of aerodynamics that overcomes gravity. The law of the Spirit overcomes the law of sin and death for the one who is in Christ. Being in Christ is like being in the airplane. It is the airplane that provides the ability for the law of aerodynamics to overcome the law of gravity. So too it is being in Christ that allows the law of the Spirit to overcome the law of sin and death. But there are other requirements as well. The airplane must maintain airspeed, it must have fuel and oxygen to continue to operate. It must not carry excess weight. So too, life in Christ requires that we be diligent to provide fuel and oxygen and minimize weight. The disciplines of worship, prayer, meditating on the Word of God are akin to fuel and oxygen. Putting to death the *sinful self* is to refrain from gaining too much weight. If we are not vigilant, it is possible for one in Christ to descend into sin and cease to fly. It is the Holy Spirit that empowers the flight, by giving us the desire and wherewithal to keep flying. As long as we are in the body, the law of sin and death operates. As long as we are in Christ being filled with the Holy Spirit, we continue to fly above the sin and death of the world. One day, we will be snatched into eternity and will no more have to deal with our *sinful self,* that gravity that propels into sin. On that day our sanctification will be complete. Meanwhile, we see that the Holy Spirit is essential to life in the body.

Another Spiritual resource is the **Word of God**. The Word of God could be compared to the fuel that the plane needs to stay aloft. *"Man does not live by bread alone, but man lives by every word that* *comes from the mouth of the LORD'"* (Deut 8:3b, Matt 4:4). The Word of God is the believer's spiritual food and fuel. Without it, there is no fuel for the plane and strength for the battle. It is essential that we make a daily practice of dwelling in the Word of God. The Spiritual exercises already begun in the study guides are a starting point. However, we all ought to have a personal devotional plan that keep us in the Word of God daily. I am convinced that many people who struggle with sin and depression and relational problems are just not dwelling in the Word of God. Without it, they are starving themselves spiritually. An airplane cannot fly without fuel and a person cannot live long without food. And yet this resource is so readily available to us. It is the one offensive weapon that the Apostle Paul describes as needful in Spiritual warfare. It is the *"sword of the Spirit"* (Eph. 6:17). It is what Jesus used to fend off the tempter in the wilderness (Luke 4). It is so critical in spiritual life that it is the topic of chapter four.

A third spiritual resource is the **People of God**. The Christian life is not designed to be a solo flight. We all need one another to encourage and uplift one another, to pray for one another, to speak the Word into one another's hearts, to hold one another accountable and to love one another. Yet so many Christians try to go it alone. I am convinced that this is due partly to our cultural conditioning. North Americans pride themselves on rugged individualism and independence. Yet the myth of the lone ranger in the "wild west" does not really match historical reality. Lone rangers did not settle the west. Rather, it was the barn raisers, the co-operatives, small communities and extended families working together that were the strength of the "wild west". Similarly, in the Christian life, believers ought to live together in community, having all things in common, devoting themselves to worship, to Apostolic teaching and to prayer.

> *"And they devoted themselves to the apostles' teaching and fellowship, to the breaking of bread and the prayers. And awe came upon every soul, and many wonders and signs were being done through the apostles. And all who believed were together and had all things in common. And they were selling their possessions and belongings and distributing the proceeds to all, as any had need. And day by day, attending the temple together and breaking bread in their homes, they received their food with glad and generous hearts, praising God and having favor with all the people. And the Lord*

> *added to their number day by day those who were being saved." Acts 2:42 -47*

This was not a collection of lone rangers in the Christian life. Whenever Jesus sent out His disciples, He sent them out two by two (Mark 6:7, Luke 10:1). There was a reason for this. Two people make a community and Christian community is essential. Dietrich Bonhoeffer wrote: *"The physical presence of other Christians is a source of incomparable joy and strength to the believer".*[xxxii] One log in a fireplace can scarcely keep burning, yet two or three together create a huge blaze. *"A three fold cord is not quickly broken"* (Eccl. 4:12b). Moreover, we need spiritual friends in order to confess our sins to one another and pray for one another (James 5:16). The disciplines of personal accountability and spiritual direction are not possible without others. We must rekindle an appreciation for community and spiritual friendship in order to stir up one another to love and good works (Heb. 10:24).

How to Win the Battle Within

In recognizing and fighting this battle, we must not allow ourselves to become disheartened nor discouraged. While every believer is under two determinations, indwelling sin and the new nature in Christ, we must understand that these are not weighted evenly. The sinful self has been crucified and stripped of power. It only has power to tempt us as long as we live in denial or indifference to it. We certainly have through the power of the Holy Spirit ample resources to be victorious. While the body of death is in us still, we have in Christ the victory as long as we exercise the resources given us. The Apostle Paul writes:

> *"O death, where is your victory? O death, where is your sting?" [56] The sting of death is sin, and the power of sin is the law. [57] But thanks be to God, who gives us the victory through our Lord Jesus Christ". 1 Corinthians 15:55-57*

So let us learn from our Puritan forefathers who were masters in fighting this battle. Here are some specific steps that I must take daily in order to be victorious. [xxxiii]

1. *I must ask God to search my heart for indwelling sin, bring it out into the open, acknowledge it and put it off, replacing it with Godly attitudes and actions.*

In order to gain victory over the *sinful self,* I first have to appreciate that the seat of this self is the heart. The heart is not just the seat of emotion, but biblically, the heart is the center of the whole person. It includes my mind, understanding, my will, my conscience and my affections. The prophet Jeremiah writes: *"The heart is deceitful above all things, and desperately sick; who can understand it?"* (Jeremiah 17:9). I have to recognize that I am dealing with an inner enemy that is deceit itself. Therefore, I must exercise constant and continual diligence against it. I have to understand that I cannot trust my own heart. The popular admonition "Listen to your heart" sounds great but it is a formula for disaster. If my heart is deceitful, how can I trust it? On the contrary, I can only trust the Holy Spirit of God that dwells within me. Therefore, my first duty in this fight is to humble myself before God in prayer and ask God to search my heart. The Psalmist writes:

> *"Search me, O God, and know my heart! Try me and know my thoughts! [24] And see if there be any grievous way in me, and lead me in the way everlasting!" Psalm 139:23-24*

In asking God to do this, I must be ready to accept His verdict and submit to the promptings of the Holy Spirit. I must hold my own heart up in all humility and allow the Holy Spirit to search it, cleanse it and renew it according to the Holy Spirit's pattern of holiness. I must also examine my motives, especially my motives for doing good. Am I doing this to bolster my ego or reputation? Are my motives completely pure? As I become aware of the nature of indwelling sin, I must confess it, renounce it and repudiate it, asking God to cleanse my heart and humble myself before Him. In addition, I must begin to act in holiness. Having put off what is sinful. I must now put on the Godly counterpart. Paul writes:

> *"put off your old self, which belongs to your former manner of life and is corrupt through deceitful desires, [23] and to be renewed in the spirit of your minds, [24] and to put on the new self, created after the likeness of God in true righteousness*

and holiness." Eph. 4:22-24

For example, if God reveals to me that I have hatred in my heart for an enemy, I must replace that with love, seeing that person as God does. If I struggle with covetousness, I must put on contentment. If I have been stealing, I must confess it, renounce it, make restitution and put on working hard to earn what I need. It is not enough to simply put off sin, I must also replace the attitude of my heart with its godly counterpart. I can only do this through the Holy Spirit working in me.

2. *I must get a clear and abiding sense of the absolute disgust, evil and vileness of indwelling sin and the dangers that it poses to me.*

We tend to have a rather antiseptic view of sin. We see it as a mistake, a moral weakness, or a fault. Yet in reality sin is absolutely vile, disgusting and revolting to God. His absolute holiness is so resplendently beautiful that sin is the most vile stinking disgusting thing imaginable. There is a scene in the movie *Slumdog Millionaire* where a child dives into a smelly outhouse latrine in order to escape being locked in. The child then runs, covered with human excrement through a crowd of people who are mobbing a famous actor. The stench and the disgust of the child covered with excrement is something like what sin is to a Holy God. As John Owen says, we need to "load our minds" with the absolute disgust of sin. In addition, we need to understand the danger that it poses to us. How many lives have been ruined because indwelling sin was not mortified, but allowed to fester and find expression? It is in this way that a man throws away 30 years of marriage for a few moments of passion.

We also need to understand that indwelling sin robs the sinner of peace and communion with God. It isolates the believer, sapping his strength and greatly hinders prayer, worship and any spiritual power. It turns a person into a spiritual dwarf and sets the person up for the onslaughts of Satan. It also puts the person in danger of eternal destruction. We must make no mistake. There is a point of no return in sin. King Saul was chosen by God to be Israel's first king. Yet his persistent and continued acquiescence to his sinful self finally got the better of him and he was rejected by God and given up to his own sinfulness. He finally died from self-inflicted wounds on the battlefield along with his sons (1 Sam. 31:6).

The writer of Hebrews warns that:

> *"... it is impossible to restore again to repentance those who have once been enlightened, who have tasted the heavenly gift, and have shared in the Holy Spirit, [5] and have tasted the goodness of the word of God and the powers of the age to come, [6] if they then fall away, since they are crucifying once again the Son of God to their own harm and holding him up to contempt". Hebrews 6:4-6*

When we give life to our sinful self and allow it unfettered influence, we spurn Christ and cast doubt on our own salvation. When we do so, we are holding the Son of God up to contempt. One can only grieve and quench the Holy Spirit for so long. It is indeed a dangerous road to go down. We are called rather to make our election and salvation sure by fighting this inner battle and allowing the Spirit of Christ in us to conquer and rule. God is with us in this struggle and He is for us. *"In all these things we are more than conquerors through him who loved us"* Rom. 8:37

3. *I must pray for a constant desire to be delivered from the power of indwelling sin.*[xxxiv]

Here the danger is that I might slip into contentment with my own sinful self. I can never allow myself to become comfortable or complacent with my deceitful heart. In the Lord's prayer, we pray "*Deliver us from evil*" (Matt. 6:13). This evil is evil within and evil without. John Owen points out that a city under siege in wartime is in danger from without, but if it also has traitors living within it, it is in greater danger from within. The outer enemy can be readily identified, but the inner enemy disguises himself and pretends to be a friend. I can never let my guard slip so that I become content with my treacherous heart. Therefore, praying to be delivered from evil is also to pray to be delivered from the power of that sin that dwells within me. God loves it when we pray in this way, for it means that we are seeing ourselves rightly. Longing, panting and yearning for deliverance from indwelling sin moves God's heart to grant us that which we long after. Jesus said that if we ask for anything in His name, He will grant it (John 16:24). To pray in Jesus' name is to pray according to His nature and His will.

Surely God wants us to be delivered from indwelling sin. The prayer of faith anticipates victory. As we truly long and pray for such deliverance, we will be bit by bit delivered, especially on that day when we see Him face to face. The one who thus humbles himself, God will surely exalt (James 4:10).

4. *I must be vigilant against putting myself in situations which will give life to my sinful self.*

John Owen called these the occasions of sin.[xxxv] Here the important thing is to know myself. If I have a propensity to lust, then I must stay away and keep clear of any situation that will quicken this sinful desire within me. I may have to stay away from beaches in the summer where women are scantily clad. If I have a propensity to overindulge in alcohol, then I stay away from venues where it will be served. If I struggle with pride, then I must avoid situations that will result in public acclaim.

5. *I must rise mightily against the first actings of indwelling sin.*[xxxvi]

Here the issue is that if I allow sin to take root, even to gain a foothold and think that I can keep it at bay and allow it to spread no further, I am in for a rude awakening. I must not say, "thus far and it shall go no further", for sin is like a dam of water building up pressure trying to fend off a relentless river. The person who allows even the slightest indulgence of small pleasures of sin will soon be overtaken by the flood. Therefore, as soon as there is even an inkling of it, it must be put to death, annihilated and completely destroyed. So, for example, if I begin to feel envy, I must completely annihilate it. To allow it to brew, unfettered will lead to hatred and murder. Vigilance in the arena is critical. There can be no tolerating even traces of it. Rather, I must see it as the horrible loathsome thing that it is and through the Spirit of Christ, completely destroy it.

King Saul was ordered to completely annihilate the Amalekites and leave not even an animal alive (1 Sam. 15:3). Yet, he chose to compromise and leave the king and take the best of the animals for himself. God's judgment on him was swift and complete. His rebellion would cost him the throne and result in his rejection (1 Sam. 15:23). One cannot serve God and allow even the tiniest vestige of sin to remain alive.

6. *I must make a daily practice of confessing sin, not just in thought, word and deed but the deep indwelling sin that resides in my heart.*

There is no substitute in the Christian life for confession. Confession is not an option with regard to forgiveness. The Apostle John writes: *"If we confess our sins, he is faithful and just to forgive us our sins and to cleanse us from all unrighteousness."* (1 John 1:9). Notice that forgiveness is conditional upon confession. If we refuse to acknowledge or confess sin, we cannot claim forgiveness. The blessings and release from confession are lauded in Psalm 32:

> *"Blessed is the one whose transgression is forgiven, whose sin is covered. 2 Blessed is the man against whom the LORD counts no iniquity, and in whose spirit there is no deceit. 3 For when I kept silent, my bones wasted away through my groaning all day long. 4 For day and night your hand was heavy upon me; my strength was dried up as by the heat of summer. Selah 5 I acknowledged my sin to you, and I did not cover my iniquity; I said, "I will confess my transgressions to the LORD," and you forgave the iniquity of my sin." Selah Psalm 32:1-5*

Therefore it is imperative that we include confession in every devotional time that we observe. Confession also presupposes repentance. Repentance requires that we agree with God that our sin is evil and loathsome, that we are broken by it and filled with abhorrence and regret and that we resolve never, by God's grace, to commit it again.

7. *I must fill my mind with the gospel, meditating on the cross and the price paid for the forgiveness of my sin.*

I must dwell on the price paid for my forgiveness. I must meditate on the perfect sinless, Holy God, who abhors sin, immersed in its horrors for me. I must contemplate the pain and the rejection that Jesus suffered on my account. I must meditate the wounds of Christ and listen for his voice to me saying *"Go and sin no more"* (John *8:11).*

Why Fight The Battle Within

Fighting the inner battle with sin is hard work. There is no room for apathy or laziness. Some might ask, if this is not a salvation issue, then why bother? Certainly, we will not lose our salvation if we sin and then repent and confess our sin, however, let us consider the effect of such a cavalier attitude toward sin.

First, when we sin it affects other people. We do not live in isolation. We are all tied together as families, faith communities, larger communities and humanity. When we sin it affects those around us in ways that we cannot fathom. When David committed adultery with Bathsheba (2 Sam. 11), the result was that the child born to them died. Not only that, but the consequences of David's sin resulted in evil being raised up in his own household. One of David's sons raped his sister. Her brother Absalom then murdered that brother and fled for his life. He then led a rebellion that drove King David out of Jerusalem. Eventually he was killed by the leader of David's army. This tragic chain of events stemmed directly from David's sin. Not only did it affect his own family but the entire nation was affected by one man's sin.

Secondly, sin affects our reputation and character. If we think we can recover these, we are mistaken. Once a reputation is soiled, it cannot be cleaned up. Think of the many pastors and Christian leaders who have fallen into sexual sin. It is not the case that they can just repent, confess and pick up where they left off. Their credibility has been severely tarnished. They will never fully rebuild trust after an event like that. The essence of who we are is our character. Every time we sin, we diminish it. Remember, we are defined by what we do. How do we want to be remembered?

Thirdly, sin affects our future rewards in heaven. Those who are faithful in much will be rewarded much. Those who are faithful in little will be still be rewarded (Matt 25:21-23). Those who are lazy and slothful will receive nothing, but will be saved as through fire, barely escaping the wrath to come (1 Cor. 3:15). If we do nothing, we are defining ourselves by our lack of fruit. We may even call into question the authenticity of our faith (James 2:17).

Fourthly, there is a point if one persists in sin, beyond which one cannot recover. Those who continue to practice sin, show that sin is the defining attribute of their life. The Apostle John said that *"no one born of God makes a practice of sinning"* (1 John 3:9). If the habitual pattern of our life is sin, then we do call into question the authenticity of our relationship with God. Saul was a King who started off well, but his repeated infractions led him eventually to the point where he sought comfort in occult practices. He died a tragic death by his own hand.

Ultimately our sin is exposed for what it is by the cross. Seeing the Son of God, the Author of life, crucified on an instrument of torture shows me the true vileness of sin. It also shows me the love of God for even my sinful self and those transgressions that I commit, will not negate the love of God for me. How can I spurn so great a love? How can I treat Him with contempt by returning to the filth from which I have been delivered at such great cost. Let the cross be always before me and the world behind me. Let me cling to my Lord who thus conquered death and sin and rose victorious. Let me see Him now sitting at the right hand of God, still wounded and still weeping over the sins of people for whom He died. Let me meditate on what it will be like to see Him face to face on that Day when He returns to be marveled at by all the saints. Let me see myself in the company of that great host of saints who have conquered through the blood of the Lamb. And let me strive to hear His voice saying to me *"well done, good and faithful servant, enter into the joy of your Master"* (Matt. 25:23).

Study Guide for Chapter Three

A. Questions for Personal Reflection

Record answers in your journal.

1. This chapter opens with the statement that salvation is not an event, but rather it is a Person, Jesus Christ (page 57). How has reading this chapter changed your understanding of salvation? Be specific.

2. In one sense, sanctification is a fact by virtue of union with Christ through faith. Yet, it is also progressive and grows over time. Identify the major events in your life and how they have contributed to your growth in sanctification. Perhaps you can draw a graph with your age along the bottom and your degree of sanctification up the side. Identify key events that cause growth or decline.

3. Read Romans chapter 7. How has the explanation of the three meanings of sin helped you understand this chapter? To what extent have you become aware of the necessity of mortification and vivification in your own life?

Do a Prayer of Examen, described below (B. 1-4) at the end of each day before you retire (10 minutes). Make notes in your journal as led by the Spirit.

B. Exercises (Individual or Large Group)

The **Prayer of Examen** is a method of reflecting on the events of a day in order to give thanks and to bring to light things that went well and things that were tainted with sin. In this prayer, we will go through four steps.[xxxvii]

1. *Reflect on God's continual presence throughout the day. Ask for His help in seeing your day rightly.* Go through your day mentally and see God as being present with you in each activity, conversation, and event. Remember that God loves you and is for you and with you. Ask the Holy Spirit to help you as you reflect on this day (John 16:13).

2. *Look over your day with gratitude.* Give thanks to God for everything that happened (whether good or bad.) Explore your feelings about what happened during the day. Remember that "*all things work together for good for those who love God and are called according to His purpose*". (Rom. 8:28)

3. *Review Your Day.* Ask the Holy Spirit to help you see the events of the day through God's eyes. Ask the Holy Spirit to search your heart and show you if any of the deep inner recesses of your deceitful heart have played out throughout the course of the day. What did you do well? Where did you fail? Let the Holy Spirit bring to light areas of indwelling sin. Let God show you where He is pleased with you and where He is chastising you.

4. *Reconcile and Resolve:* Engage in an open transparent talk with the Lord. Thank Him for His presence. Confess your sins and failings. Express your deep sorrow for sin. Bring to light and confess any indwelling sin that was the root of transgressions. Humble yourself and ask for His help and cleansing. Resolve to move forward in love as a recipient of God's forgiveness and mercy. Resolve to replace ungodly thoughts, words or deeds with their godly counterpart. Thank Him for His forgiveness.

C. Small Group Breakout (2 or 3)

1. Think about a past sin or a temptation that you struggle with. How can you be vigilant to take swift action against the first prompting of this sin?

2. How can you replace this sinful thought or action by its Godly counterpart?

3. What situations do you know of that are likely to give life to your sinful self? Spend some time meditating on this and share with one another as your feel comfortable.

4. Take some time to pray for one another.

D. Assignment for Next Week

1. Continue to observe five devotional times in solitude this week. In each time, follow the pattern that you learned in chapter one. Use the breath prayer: *"Lord Jesus, Son of God, have mercy on me a sinner*." Apply Holy Reading to the following passages throughout the week: Psalm 51, Psalm 32, James 1:12-27, Romans 7, 2 Sam 12:1-24.

2. Take 10-15 minutes at the end of each day to do a Prayer of Examen as outlined above.

3. Read chapter four. Answer the Questions for Personal Reflection your journal.

4. The Presence of God – The Peace of Love

> *"You keep him in perfect peace whose mind is stayed on you, for he trusts in you" Isaiah 26:3*

Those who have a deep and abiding sense of God's presence are truly blessed. Neither circumstance nor affliction can rob them of their inner joy, for they live and move and have their being in God. These people are truly rare. Brother Lawrence, a simple French monk who lived in mid 17th century was one of them. His conversations and letters[xxxviii] exude a peaceful joy that was the fruit of a life lived in the very bosom of God. Every breath that he took, every act and thought was done purely for the love of the God in whose presence he danced through life. His childlike trust in God reflected a simplicity of faith that few achieve. By contrast, many Christians know intellectually that God is with them, but they live as though they were alone, navigating the valleys and forests of life by their own strength. Their prayers are spotty and shallow and they are in frequent anguish over things of this world.

Jesus commanded His disciples to receive Him like little children (Mark 10:15). A child's innocence and trust has yet to be marred by the disappointments of life. A child says what he thinks simply and without pretense. Children by nature take everyone at face value. They converse naturally with imaginary playmates and never attempt to be what they are not. In their innocence, children assume the best about others. While we adults know that not everyone can be trusted, we ought to know that God can be trusted. God assures us that we belong to Him and so childlike trust is what He desires from us. Simple faith moves us to live in Him.

Jesus said:

> *"Abide in me, and I in you. As the branch cannot bear fruit by itself, unless it abides in the vine, neither can you, unless you abide in me. [5] I am the vine; you are the branches. Whoever abides in me and I in him, he it is that bears much fruit, for apart from me you can do nothing."* John 15:4-5

This passage follows Jesus' assertion that He is *the true vine.* The vine throughout the Old Testament represents of the people of

Israel, the lineage of the Messiah. The psalmist writes: *"You brought a vine out of Egypt, you drove out the nations and planted it"* (Psalm 80:8). Whereas Israel was indeed God's vine, it failed as a nation to honor its covenant. Jesus, however, is that one faithful human covenant partner with God with whom the father is well pleased. He is the reason for Israel's existence. He is the source of life for all, who by faith are the branches in that vine. Only through union with Him, do we become the true people of God. It is in Him alone that we must abide. The Greek word for "abide" means to remain, stay united with, dwell, last, endure or continue. We are called to step into union with Jesus and dwell in Him who is the source of that nourishing sap that gives life. Without Christ, we wither. Without Christ, we can do nothing that has eternal significance. As we remain in Him, so He remains in us. (John 15:4) This mutuality of indwelling is such that we derive our life from Him. We live in Him and through Him and He lives in us. We become most truly ourselves, when we give ourselves to Him who empowers us to live and move according to His perfect will for us.

To abide in Christ is to allow His words to abide in us: *"If you abide in me, and my words abide in you, ask whatever you wish, and it will be done for you."* (John 15:7) His words abiding in us move us to act in concert with His own heart and will, in perfect obedience. If we love Him, we will long to do this. As we abide in His love, we abide in the Father's love (John 15:10). When we are in such harmony and unity, we are assured that whatever we ask will be granted. This is so we might bear fruit and that those fruits will also abide in Him (John 15:16). These fruits are those people who will be so impacted by our life in Christ that they too will turn and step into union with Him and bear fruit themselves. God's heart and His great joy is that we live in Him and bear fruit; fruit that also continues to live in Him. If this is our sole purpose in life, God will withhold nothing that we ask for. This is the simplicity of life in Christ that God desires for each of us.

To fail to remain in Him is to wither and be cast off as dry branches, branches that will be burned (John 15:6). No genuine follower could possible want that. Yet through our neglect and our preoccupation with the things of this world, we can choke the life giving sap and begin to wither. As a potted plant sitting on a windowsill withers without water, we too will wither without the living water that only comes through union with Him.

The question is: how do we maintain such union, such intimacy? Christ is our betrothed Bridegroom, yet the consummation of the marriage seems to us a long way off. How do we keep the sap of intimacy flowing? To want it and to possess it are two different things. We must move beyond knowing about God as a concept to knowing Him as Person. Many people know all about God. They might study Him for years. They might go to Bible college or seminary and become theologians. They might even be ordained as pastors. They might rise in influence as leaders in the church. But all this is no guarantee that they will know God as Person. In one of the most chilling passages of scripture Jesus says:

> *"On that day many will say to me, 'Lord, Lord, did we not prophesy in your name, and cast out demons in your name, and do many mighty works in your name?'* [23] *And then will I declare to them, 'I never knew you; depart from me, you workers of lawlessness.'" Matthew 7:22-23*

On that day when we will all stand before Jesus and give account, there will be many who will believe themselves to be disciples, for they will have done many wonderful things in His name. Yet Jesus will say to them that He never *knew* them and He will dismiss them from His presence. Obviously this pronouncement does not mean that Jesus never knew *about* them, for He knows all. It does mean that He had no personal relationship with them. These people did not abide in Christ and Christ in them. They were at best pretenders. They did much in His name, but never connected with Him as Person. Jesus will not take as His bride those who do not know Him, trust Him and love Him.

Two Kinds of Knowing[xxxix]

What does it mean to know someone? There is a clear distinction between *scientific knowing* and *personal knowing*. Scientific or empirical knowing occurs when a subject investigates an object. The subject is someone who is higher in the order of being than the object being investigated. If a researcher investigates the properties of olives, he embarks on a systematic process of gathering information about olives. His objective is to know as much as possible about them, their botanical properties, chemistry, growing patterns, and so on. He then uses this information to make better use of olives. The objective in scientific knowing is mastery, control and manipulation. Such manipulation may be for good or for evil. He may want to find out what fertilizer best enhances the growth of olives. He may want to maximize the amount and quality of oil produced so that people benefit when they use olive oil in food. Or he may seek to determine how olive oil can be used in making chemical or biological weapons to wage war against an enemy. Scientific knowing presupposes objectivity and detachment for the purpose of domination. There is nothing intrinsically wrong with this process when it applies to objects. However, if one applies such empirical methods to gather information for the purpose of controlling or manipulating another *person*, it is totally different. Few things get people angrier that the thought that they are being controlled or manipulated. We have a natural aversion to being treated like objects, because we are not objects. We are people. No one likes to be "*thing-ified*". [xl]

Personal knowing, on the other hand is radically different. To know *about* a person is not the same as knowing *the person*. This is because personal knowing requires intimacy and relationship. The word person comes from the French *per-sonare*[xli]. It means "sounding through". To know a person requires communication, interaction, a "sounding through" of the other. No person can be known personally if they do not want to be. One can shut down any attempt to be known personally by either withdrawing from any interaction, or by pretense. You simply cannot know someone who does not want to be known. This type of knowing is relational, experiential and intimate. The word "know" in scripture when it relates to persons has exactly this context of intimate knowledge. It requires interaction and first hand experience. To know a person this way is to be changed through the experience of such knowing.

If I were to ask you: "Do you know pain?"[xlii] I am not asking you to diagram the neurological pathways that are followed by stimuli from the body to the brain. Rather I am asking you if you have experienced real pain, that excruciating, mind numbing, life altering pain that one never forgets. Anyone who has experienced such pain will be profoundly changed having known it. In the same way, to know a person intimately is to be changed as a result of having known them. In that "sounding through" of another, there is a change that occurs in the one knowing. To have truly known Mother Teresa, for example, is to be personally changed as a result of having known her. Such was the impact of her person on others that almost everyone who met her has had such an experience. Martin Bruber, the Jewish theologian who wrote *I and Thou*[xliii] maintained that we only know another person to the extent that we have been transformed through that knowing. If my knowledge of another has had no impact on me whatsoever, then what I really know is just factual information. I may know all *about them*, but I do not *know* them.

Personal knowing requires openness and vulnerability. I know my wife only to the extent that she has made herself vulnerable and open to me. And she knows me only to the extent that I have opened myself up and made myself vulnerable before her. How many marriages would be transformed if the partners truly understood this? In marriage, both partners must allow themselves to be "sounded through" unreservedly by the other. To do so carries enormous risk, risk of being hurt, ridiculed or cast aside. What if my vulnerability is taken advantage of? What if the other is only pretending to open up, or is only playing a role for the purpose of gaining advantage? This is why commitment and covenant are so important in marriage.

Now if we apply this awareness to God, we can see that we only know God to the extent that we have been transformed through that experience of knowing. If we have not been dramatically changed as a result of our knowing God, then we really do not know Him at all. We may know all about Him, but we do not know *Him*. That is why to truly know God is to be radically changed, transformed in heart, mind and soul.

This happens only as God initiates such knowing through His own self-disclosure. For me to know God intimately means that He must open up and make Himself vulnerable before me. And this is exactly what He has done in Christ. It is precisely what has happened at the cross. As I encounter Jesus Christ crucified, I see Him naked, exposed, humiliated, wounded, bleeding and in agony *for me*. In the cross, we see the total transparency of God. He has withheld nothing, not shame, not ridicule, not rejection, not suffering, not abandonment, not even His own life *for me*. The cross shows me that there is no limit to God's love and no limit to His vulnerability on my account. And His resurrection shows me that there is no limit to the efficacy of His vulnerability. [xliv] In the cross God does His most characteristic work. It takes my breath away. He shows me that He is not out to manipulate me, but to win my love. God can only "know" me to the extent that I choose to make myself vulnerable and open myself up without reservation to Him. His example bids me to open myself up to Him by casting aside all pretense, throwing myself upon His mercy and giving myself completely to Him. As I do so, I respond to God's invitation to enter into a person to Person intimacy in union with Him.

And because He too is Person, He is changed forever as a result of knowing me. We often do not think of this, but God is truly impacted by what we do. We move God by our actions toward Him. This is not to say that we can somehow change God into non-God, for that is impossible, but we do affect Him greatly. In the words of Victor Shepherd, we have *"broken His heart, provoked His anger, mobilized His judgment, had Him delay the day of condemnation and protract the day of grace"*[xlv] all for us. Our sin impacts Him deeply and our continued lack of faith and self-centeredness continues to do so. God continues to suffer and grieve for His people. And He rejoices when they respond in faith, love and obedience.

In the scene in the book of Acts chapter 7, where Steven is martyred, we see Jesus *standing* as Steven is about to be executed. (Acts 7:56). This is significant, for scripture testifies that once Jesus ascended into heaven, He sat down at the right side of the Father, having finished the work He was to do. (Heb. 1:3) To be seated implies rest and control. Kings sit on their thrones. But here Steven, the first martyr, is about to be executed and Jesus *stands up*. Lest, we think that God is unaffected by what we do, let us consider that here all heaven pauses while the Holy One, *stands up* from His throne as Stephen is being executed. We must never forget that everything we think, say and do does impact God. It is precisely in such affecting, that He comes to know us. It is a sobering fact that through our thoughts, words and actions God comes to know us as persons.

> *"For now we see in a mirror dimly, but then face to face. Now I know in part; then I shall know fully, even as I have been fully known." 1 Corinthians 13:12*

Embracing Vulnerability

We have seen that vulnerability is the key to personal knowing by allowing ourselves to be "sounded through" by another. However, most people are cautious in opening themselves up to others, even those close to them. Everyone has been hurt to some extent by another person. The woman who was sexually abused as a child has a deep seated inner defense mechanism against trusting others for, in her innocence, she was brutally violated. And those of us who have never experienced such abuse have experienced being used and manipulated by others. As I write this, CNN is doing a series on the problem of bullying in schools. Bullying is essentially abuse for the sake of gaining social advantage and power. The corrupted human heart is capable of vicious things. Most of us have had the experience of giving our hearts to another only to be rejected and cast off. Life is replete with experiences of vulnerability and betrayal. Yet even human wisdom understands that the appropriate response to such hurt must not be withdrawal. To harden one's heart and to pull back from ever being vulnerable again is to enter a permanent state of loneliness.

Henri Nouwen asserts that we live in a society where "loneliness has become one of the most painful human wounds".[xlvi] The competition and rivalry that many of us face as we grow up has led us into isolation. We are afraid to trust others and so we retreat into ourselves. Yet Nouwen offers up a unique Christian perspective:

> *"The Christian way of life does not take away our loneliness; it protects and cherishes it as a precious gift. Sometimes it seems as if we do everything possible to avoid the painful confrontation with our basic human loneliness, and allow ourselves to be trapped by false gods promising immediate satisfaction and quick relief. But perhaps the painful awareness of loneliness is an invitation to transcend our limitations and look beyond the boundaries of our existence. The awareness of loneliness might be a gift we must protect and guard, because our loneliness reveals to us an inner emptiness that can be destructive when misunderstood, but filled with promise for him who can tolerate its sweet pain."*[xlvii]

Nouwen goes on to say that our expectations are unrealistic. There is nothing in this world that will ever satisfy our loneliness for we were not made for this world. The thirst that we experience is a thirst for something real, but something outside of this life. And there indeed is a quenching of it, but that quenching will never be complete this side of heaven. Jesus said *"If anyone is thirsty, let him come to me and drink. Whoever believes in me as the scripture has said, 'out of his heart will flow streams of living water.'"* (John 7:37-38) The implication here is not that we will no longer thirst, but rather that we will be used as a channel by God to supply "living water" to others who also thirst. Our own thirst keeps us in Christ, so that others who thirst can also drink and become conduits of living water.

Our Deepest Longings

We don't want to negate the thirst, for it is that very thirst that keeps us coming to Christ and keeps us abiding in Him. But, in that thirst there is as Nouwen says a "sweet pain". We cannot deny it. Larry Crabb in his book *Inside Out* states that it is okay to desire, to thirst, but that it is also *"okay to hurt"* ..... *"We do legitimately want what we cannot have in this world. We were designed to live in a perfect world uncorrupted by the weeds of disharmony and distance. Until we take up residence in that world, we will hurt*". [xlviii] We hurt because the world is under sin and under the influence of Satan, whose heart is set on destruction and death. God's people have always understood this.

The psalms are replete with the language of lament. In fact 68 of the 150 psalms (45%) are psalms of crying out to God in anguish or distress. Should it surprise us that almost half of the hymn-book of the Bible are psalms of lament? Not if we truly understand the human condition. Jesus was described as a *"man of sorrows and acquainted with grief"* (Isa. 53:3) because He saw the suffering caused by the effects of sin and the evil one. His response to that suffering was not to withdraw and isolate Himself from it, but rather to enter fully into it and embrace it. Lament is a response to the pain and struggle of living in a world where justice and fairness are constantly frustrated. The psalmists who penned the psalms of lament, making them a vital part of the worship language of Israel, were never concerned with the question of why these things were happening. They understood why. Human depravity as a result of the fall and the influence of Satan make living in the world a painful experience. However, *the question* and plea that keeps coming up in the lament psalms is *"how long?"* (Ps.4:2, 6:3, 13:1-2, 35:17, 62:3, 74:10, 80:4, 82:2, 89:46, 90:13, 94:3, 119:84).

There is implicit in these psalms an understanding that suffering is part of the human condition, but also a continual plea, filled with hope and confidence, that God will make it right. Most of these psalms end with an expression of confidence in God, the only source of ultimate hope and justice.

> *"O LORD, rebuke me not in your anger, nor discipline me in your wrath. [2] Be gracious to me, O LORD, for I am*

languishing; heal me, O LORD, for my bones are troubled. [3] *My soul also is greatly troubled. But you, O LORD- how long?* [4] *Turn, O LORD, deliver my life; save me for the sake of your steadfast love.* [5] *For in death there is no remembrance of you; in Sheol who will give you praise?* [6] *I am weary with my moaning; every night I flood my bed with tears; I drench my couch with my weeping.* [7] *My eye wastes away because of grief; it grows weak because of all my foes.* [8] *Depart from me, all you workers of evil, for the LORD has heard the sound of my weeping.* [9] *The LORD has heard my plea; the LORD accepts my prayer.* [10] *All my enemies shall be ashamed and greatly troubled; they shall turn back and be put to shame in a moment. Psalm 6:1 - 10*

Unfortunately, we live in a culture that has forgotten the language of lament. Many have been taught that the Christian life is one of health, wealth, satisfaction and happiness. This breeds in us false expectations that our lives will be free of trials and deep distress over the things that are not right. As a result, we expect that all of our longings will be satisfied in this life, and when that does not happen, we feel betrayed and sink into depression. We will never achieve complete satisfaction of our longings in this world for we were not made for this world. In Hebrews chapter 11, the writer testifies to all those saints who by faith faced rejection, persecution, trials and torture but continued in faith. They never received in this life that which was promised, for they lived as aliens in this world, but were citizens of an eternal city kept in heaven for them (Heb. 11:13,16). Meanwhile, while we are in this life, it is our very woundedness that God uses to commission us to ministry for Him. It is because we hurt that we can identify with those who hurt. It is because we thirst that we can bring others to drink of Christ. And for that we ought to be grateful. We must also understand that the things of this world and even the relationships of this world will **never** completely satisfy us. If we should ever think so, we would be giving ourselves to pursuit of those earthly things, which will only become idols.

Larry Crabb goes on to identify three kinds of longings that reside within our souls.[xlix] *Crucial longings* are for an intimate relationship with God, who alone can fill the hollow core at the center of our lives. He is the one who empowers us to live life for Him and in so doing fulfills our desire to live a life that has meaning beyond ourselves. David writes: "*O God, you are my God; earnestly I seek you; my soul thirsts for you; my flesh faints for you, as in a dry and weary land where there is no water." Psalm 63:1*

Non-crucial or secondary longings Crabb divides into *critical longings* and *casual longings.* Critical longings are the desire for "*quality relationships that add immeasurably to the joy of living.*" [1] Casual longings are every desire that we experience from the trivial to the significant. They encompass our desire for health, meaningful work, comfortable and beautiful surroundings and so on. Crabb illustrates crucial longings as an inner circle at the core of our being. Critical longings are a middle concentric circle. Casual longings are an outer circle.[li]

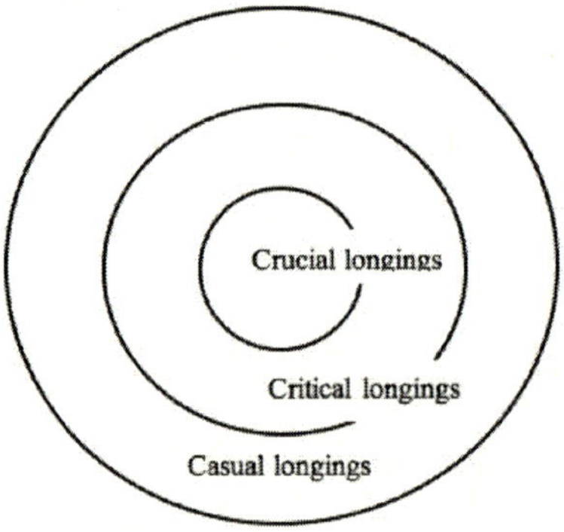

Crucial longings – for an intimate relationship with Christ

Critical longings – for quality relationships with others

Casual longings – for every other human desire (sustenance, things, status, money, power)

The point is that most of us start out in life pursuing casual and then critical longings. We work from the outside in. The desire to supply basic needs and to advance ourselves consumes us so that we ignore the deep crucial longing in our spirit, our inner core. We fill our lives with things and people and put upon them the expectation that they will satisfy the deep inner longings of our hearts. But they will not. In the parable of the sower, we see that the desire for riches and the cares of this world often choke the seed of the Word that is planted in our hearts. (Luke 8:14). As we pursue these things we fall into idolatry. James writes:

> *"What causes quarrels and what causes fights among you? Is it not this, that your passions are at war within you? [2] You desire and do not have, so you murder. You covet and cannot obtain, so you fight and quarrel. You do not have, because you do not ask. [3] You ask and do not receive,*

because you ask wrongly, to spend it on your passions." James 4:1-3

But because God is merciful, He gives us over to our own depravity so that we eventually lose what is most important to us, causing us to fall into despair and ultimately into a personal crisis. Only then do we begin look up and cry out to God. Not only do we need to repent, but we need also to acknowledge that we have often been disappointed in our circumstances and relationships and that these have caused us deep pain. The world around us and we ourselves have created false expectations, expectations that we deserve everything that we desire. When we are disappointed, we often lay the blame on God. After all isn't He in control? Isn't He supposed to give us everything that we want? These false expectations lead us into resentment when they are not fulfilled. A heart full of resentment cannot be at peace. Neither can it give thanks.

Larry Crabb reminds us that we must reorient ourselves to start from the inside out. We must seek first to satisfy crucial longings, that of a relationship with Christ. Then we move to critical longings, involving other relationships and finally to casual longings which are supplemental and easily given up because we are fully satisfied at our inner core.

False Expectations

There is much false teaching afloat today that for the Christian, God guarantees an abundant life full of health, wealth, prosperity and happiness. The reality is that God is not a cosmic Santa Claus to be manipulated by our prayers. We live in a world filled with pain and suffering. The redeemed life is not one of escape from this but is rather one of self-denial and bearing one's cross. In doing so God goes with us, and we have the joy of His presence. We also have the peace that comes from knowing that our names are written in heaven, but in this world, we will have trouble. All but one of the apostles (John) were murdered for their witness, many tortured brutally. Jesus foretold that in this world we would have tribulation, but that we ought to take heart for He has overcome the world (John 16:33).

Not only that, but contrary to popular opinion, God is not in control of everything that happens to us.[lii] In the book of Job, it is God who points Job out to Satan as an example of righteousness. Satan then entices God to turn not only everything Job has, but even his own body over to Satan's sting. It was Satan who was in direct control of Job's situation. God did place limits on what he could do, but allowed Satan free rein, within those limits, to torment Job for a higher purpose.

We might also ask who was in control in the many massacres and genocides that have marred human history? Who was in control in the Nazi death camps, where children, unlike their parents, were thrown alive into the ovens? Who was in control in the Cambodian death camps and in the Rwanda massacre? We need to remember that Satan is alive and active on planet earth and his time is short. God limits his power, and does intervene to protect His saints, but for reasons He alone knows, He often asks us to glorify Him by the way that we endure trial, suffering and even death.

We misunderstand the sovereignty of God if we think of God as a cosmic controller who orchestrates every aspect of life. If we think this, we are likely to blame Him when things go wrong. While it is true that God is the supreme Sovereign of the universe we need to understand how He exercises His sovereignty. He does not wrench people into compliance with His will. He does not treat people as objects to be manipulated. Rather, in love, He gives people up to their own inner corruption because He will not violate their personhood. As He does so, innocent people often get hurt. Job's seven sons and three daughters were casualties of Satan's attack on Job. Because we live in a world filled with sinners, it is given that people will brutalize one another. The question for us is how will we respond when that happens? Jesus' command to us is clear. We are instructed to pray for our enemies, for those who persecute us and for those who despicably use us (Matt. 5:44). Jesus assumes that it will happen. All who live a godly life in Christ can expect it (2 Tim. 3:12).

God does not exercise His sovereignty through a dynamic of control and micro management. Rather, He accomplishes His most powerful act, precisely when He is the most helpless, on the cross. It is through the cross, that Jesus, lifted up, does His greatest work. He draws people to Himself. That is how God operates. The effectiveness of the cross cannot be disputed. Every one of His saints is a product of the cross. It is characteristic of how He accomplishes His purposes. It is also how He asks us to live. We are each to embrace our own cross, whatever it is that He appoints. And we can only do so if we are united with Him, so that His power enables us to live in that sweet dynamic of self-denial and self-surrender that will draw people to Him as they marvel at our faith. This is the sweet discipline of release. It is the discipline of entrusting all of our hurts and wounds into His loving arms.

Some who read this will have been severely hurt by others. Often it is those closest to us that wound us the most. Many others will have been wounded in the church at the hands of brothers and sisters in Christ. One would expect that the church would be the last place to experience such hurt. In reality, the church can be a place where wounds are inflicted most painfully; for it is there that we let our guard down. It is there that we tend to trust people the most. I can only assure you that you have but one safe refuge, and that is in the loving arms of the Savior who died for you. He too has suffered at the hands of those who should have loved Him the most. He is with you. He too feels your pain. He understands it and embraces you in it. One day, He will wipe every tear from your eyes. But today, He asks you to remain in His love by enduring and resting in His presence.

The Discipline of Release - Forgiveness

Forgiving those who have wounded us is critical to a life of peace and is part of the discipline of release. Few things will block peace, joy and love in our lives like unforgiveness. That is why we are commanded to forgive (Mark 11:25). Yet many people find forgiveness difficult because they misunderstand it. They think that forgiveness means that the offender is being let off the hook. How can the woman who was abused by her father for years forgive him, especially if he is in denial and unrepentant? It seems to her that justice is not served by her forgiving him.

The word *forgive* means to release. It is used to describe the release of debts. When someone owes me a sum of money and I forgive that debt it means that I release that person from the obligation of paying it back. I can do so, because I am the one to whom the debt was owed. This works with money, however there is a slight difference when it come to forgiving sin. When someone has wounded me unjustly, there are two debts that are owed. One is to me, the other is to God. When the abuser abuses, he not only sins against the victim but against God. I am commanded to forgive those who wound me because God wants me to release the debt of that wound into His hands and to forgo any retribution or revenge. Jesus said:

> *"You have heard that it was said, 'An eye for an eye and a tooth for a tooth.' 39 But I say to you, Do not resist the one who is evil....*
>
> *You have heard that it was said, 'You shall love your neighbor and hate your enemy.' 44 But I say to you, Love your enemies and pray for those who persecute you," Matthew 5:38-39, 43-44*

I am not to avenge wrongs, for I am not God. I am not in a position to judge another person. Forgiveness means relinquishing judgment into the hands of God. It is necessary because, if I retain resentment or hatred toward that person, then I cannot love them as God commands me. I am called to love my enemies and to pray for those who hurt and abuse me. So I must forgive, releasing that person into the hands of God. A refusal to forgive is an expression of hatred and not love. Because I have been forgiven all of all my sins through Christ, I am called likewise to release every offense against me to Him. Failure to do so is a failure of love and a violation of a direct command of the Lord. It is sin.

But that does not mean that the abuser is forgiven before God. God does not forgive people unless the conditions for forgiveness are met. God requires repentance (see Acts 2:38). Forgiveness without repentance is what Dietrich Bonhoeffer called "cheap grace". [liii] God does not offer blanket forgiveness without repentance. When Jesus prayed on the cross *"Father forgive them, for they know not what they do"* (Luke 23:34), He was not asking the Father to instantly release from punishment all those who crucified Him. Rather He was releasing them from the debt that they owed Him personally as a human being. He was releasing them into the hands of a merciful Father, who would forgive them instantly if they came to Him in brokenness, contrition and repentance together with faith in the atoning work of Christ. Some of those who crucified Jesus became believers on the day of Pentecost and were completely forgiven on the day of their salvation (Acts 2:37-38).

One day every person will stand before God and give an account for everything that they have done. On that day, only those who have repented and whose sins are covered by the blood of Christ will be released by God. Those who have refused to repent will be cast into hell (Rev. 20:15). God is just and will not allow injustice to prevail into eternity. So the abuser who refuses to repent is not let off the hook.

Your forgiveness does not mean that the abuser is released before God. But it does mean that you entrust judgment into the hands of God and bear no resentment or grudge. On the contrary, you are commanded to bless and pray for the person (Rom. 12:14).

In addition, once that person has repented before God, they also have a responsibility to express their sorrow and contrition to those whom they have wounded. This is necessary in order to restore the relationship. The woman who was abused as a child is commanded to release the offense to God and harbor no bitterness. That itself is possible only in the power of the Holy Spirit. But that act does not restore the relationship between herself and the abuser. She is also asked to pray for her abuser and long for that day when he will humble himself and come to her in deep contrition and ask for forgiveness. At that moment her release of the offense to God is accompanied by her expression of forgiveness to the abuser, thus restoring their relationship.

So forgiveness is essentially a two-step process. The first step, the release of the offense to God is required of us immediately. But that does not release the person before God. That release does not ignore the offense or minimize it in any way. It also does not mean that one should pretend that the offense never occurred. Nor does it mean that one should continue to put themselves in danger. Abuse is grounds for separation and no one is expected to stay in an abusive relationship. The second step, the forgiveness of the person eternally is something that only God can do. And God will only release the person when the conditions for that release are met, that is confession, true repentance and faith in Jesus Christ. Repentance and the expression of contrition to the injured party is required in order to restore the relationship between them.

To live having forgiven others who hurt us is to live in peace. There is no peace where unforgiveness, resentment and bitterness dwell. When we release others to God, we allow God to live in our hearts and we are in unity with the God of mercy and compassion. We are then free to enter into other relationships without conditions. Forgiveness brings freedom. Forgiveness brings intimacy with Christ. It also commissions us for ministry.

Wounded Healers[liv]

Jesus calls each of us to pick up our cross and follow Him. He calls us to become wounded healers. Wounded, because He does not ask us to deny our hurts, but embrace them; healers because He wants us to reach out to those who too have been wounded. Not to reassure them that good times will come in this life, but to point them to Himself, the One who was wounded for them, who longs to have them too become wounded healers like Himself.

So, we do not deny pain. We do not blame God for it, but recognize that we live in a sinful world that is under the influence of Satan, who seeks to kill and destroy. Yet we know that God limits His power and uses affliction and suffering to mold us into His likeness. Through it He ordains us to ministry. Those who have been wounded often make the best healers. And in that ministry we embrace others with the love of God. We also hold out to them that peace of God that passes all understanding. We invite them to become a part of the community of faith whereby we together minister to one another by speaking the Word of God into one another's hearts. We no longer become manipulators of others, but we embrace others as divine agents through whom God works. We release them to be what God has called them to be and to do. We love, support, encourage and edify one another.

The discipline of release means also that we renounce prying into another person's life. We have no right, nor are we equipped to judge others, especially their motives. Our task is to release them to God, knowing that God is their judge and He will hold them to account. That does not mean that if we see a brother or sister sinning that we do not admonish them in the name of the Lord to do what is right, but it does mean that we refrain from actively snooping and prying into another person's spiritual affairs.

Each person will have to give an account of himself to God. We ought rather to be concerned with how we ourselves will stand before God. Each one will stand or fall before His own master.

> *"Why do you pass judgment on your brother? Or you, why do you despise your brother? For we will all stand before the judgment seat of God; [11] for it is written, "As I live, says the Lord, every knee shall bow to me, and every tongue shall confess to God." [12] So then each of us will give an account of himself to God." Romans 14:10-12*

Those who consume themselves with worry about the spiritual state of another person, rob themselves of the peace of God and set the stage for strained relationships.

The Discipline of Release – Circumstances & Time

This discipline of release applies not only to people, but also to circumstances that befall us. We live in such a driven culture that, for many, any interruption to our plans and expectations is the cause of great stress and anxiety. If this is our mindset, then our inner peace is always conditional on circumstances. As long as things are going the way that we think they should, then we are content. But if some unforeseen interruption comes along, or if people do not behave the way that we feel that they should, we become sullen, resentful or angry. In doing so, we let circumstances control us. We forfeit the life of peace. Rather, God calls us to release every circumstance to Him. Every event should be seen as an opportunity to allow God's grace to shine through us.

If I see my life as belonging completely to Him, then everything that befalls me, whether an unexpected delight or a sudden tragedy becomes an opportunity to glorify God. To live in such an attitude of continual release is to see every moment and every event as having sacramental significance. Every event, experience and moment will be sacramental when we look through it to see how God is being glorified in it. Even events that are evil glorify God through stark contrast. We would not know what light is, had we not experienced darkness. And so even the darkness brings glory to God through its anticipation of light. To live with this mindset requires a life of continual prayer and surrender. It requires that time itself is seen not as a series of chronological moments but as a series of opportunities given from the hand of God.

There are two Greek words for time used in scripture. *Chronos* is used for chronological time, that is a series of consecutive moments or events like getting up, brushing our teeth, getting dressed, making breakfast, driving to work. The other word *Kairos* has the connotation of opportune time, the right moment, the appointed time. Jesus opens His public ministry with the words *"the time has come"* (Mark 1:15 NIV). His life is governed by God's perfect timing *"my time has not yet come"* (John 7:6) or *"My time is at hand"* (Matt. 26:18). Here *time* is *Kairos,* the right time, the perfect time, the anointed moment. Henri

Nouwen points out that Jesus entire ministry was a series of opportune moments and that "He lived each moment in life as an opportunity to make all things new".[lv] In doing so, time is converted in such a way that what is opaque becomes transparent and we see God at work. [lvi]

The discipline of release means that we release not only circumstances but time to God for His purposes. We see interruptions to our plans not as inconveniences to be endured but divine opportunities, sacramental moments, through which God is to be glorified. Jean Pierre De Caussade writes in the *Sacrament of the Present Moment:*

> *The faithful, knowing God's secret, remain in perfect peace and all that happens, instead of terrifying, reassures them. They accept everything as a blessing and live in forgetfulness of what God is doing in order to devote themselves entirely to their task of unceasing love that inspires them faithfully and exactly to fulfill their obligations"* [lvii]

The "secret" that he refers to is "cherishing God and His divine order without asking for anything more."[lviii] It is to live in an attitude of release and surrender of self to the Word of God in continual self-forgetfulness. If this is our attitude, we will not live in anxiety and stress but in that peace of God that passes all understanding.

We will also become peacemakers for we will teach others by our example how to also see every circumstance and event as a *Kairos* moment, given from the hand of God. To live this way is to be true to Jesus' words to us:

> *"Therefore I tell you, do not be anxious about your life, what you will eat or what you will drink, nor about your body, what you will put on. Is not life more than food, and the body more than clothing? 26 Look at the birds of the air: they neither sow nor reap nor gather into barns, and yet your heavenly Father feeds them. Are you not of more value than they?" Matthew 6:25-26*

Releasing time to God also means that we honor the rhythms of time that He has instituted. The Sabbath cycle is the first of these. God created the heavens and the earth and rested on the seventh day. He also ordered the people of Israel to refrain from unnecessary work on the Sabbath and made this one of the Ten Commandments that were part of the old covenant. While we are not under the old covenant law today (Heb. 8:13), the moral and ethical aspects of it remain normative. The principle behind the commandment stands. Human beings require a weekly cycle of a day of rest. For most believers today, this day is Sunday, a day that we ought to dedicate to rest, worship and reflection. However, the exact day is not important. Many have work schedules that do not permit them to rest on Sunday. It is interesting to note that the *Didache*[lix] an early discipleship document dating back to the second century makes no mention of resting on the Sabbath. The Apostle Paul warned the church about becoming legalistic about the Sabbath and other old covenant festivals (Col 2:16). The early church considered that they had already entered into the Christ's Sabbath rest through faith in His finished work (Heb 4:1).

Yet, we must not ignore the Sabbath principle. Each person or family should develop their own conviction as to how they will devote one twenty four hour period a week to rest, worship and reflection. When this is done as a love offering unto the Lord, it is a devotional act that brings much peace and restoration of soul. To ignore the Sabbath principle and to work relentlessly without taking a day apart each week for rest and reflection will cause a person to stall spiritually. Rather the believer ought to set this one day apart as a day holy to the Lord and allow their soul to be recharged through rest, reflection, prayer and worship.

Similarly, festivals and feast days as well and fast days are an important part of the release of time into the hands of God. Again, we are not under the old covenant and we have been given the freedom to regulate ourselves according to each person's conviction. The Apostle Paul writes:

> *"One person esteems one day as better than another, while another esteems all days alike. Each one should be fully convinced in his own mind. [6] The one who observes the day, observes it in honor of the Lord. The one who eats, eats in honor of the Lord, since he gives thanks to God, while the one who abstains, abstains in honor of the Lord and gives thanks to God." Romans 14:5-6*

Yet to observe no feast or fast days is surely to miss the disciplines of celebration and self-denial. There is a spiritual benefit in observing the seasons of the Christian life. For centuries, the church has observed the Christian calendar beginning with Advent and proceeding through Christmas, Epiphany, Lent, Easter and Pentecost. This has given a rhythm to life that is uniquely Christian. Our lives are governed by how we see and use time. There is something uniquely sacramental in organizing our spiritual lives around the life of Christ. This also provides a basis of unity among believers that come from different denominations and backgrounds. It provides a way that we can give structure to our family life and provides us with opportunities to teach our children through active participation in observances that point us to the Savior and His love for us. Believers ought to acquaint themselves with not only the seasons of the Christian year but also the old covenant festivals that pointed forward to Christ. Some of the most memorable events that my own children remember were the celebration of Passover Seder meals on Maudy Thursday. Christmas celebrations, Easter vigils and fasting during Lent allow us ways of entering tangibly into the life of Christ. The study, reflection on, and celebration of these seasons and festivals provides an opportunity for unique insight into the character of God and a rhythm of life for His people.

The Discipline of Release – Fasting and Self-Denial

There are few things that will move us more completely into the presence of God than the disciplines of fasting and self-denial. Unfortunately few Christians in the western world of prosperity experience it. We live in a society that celebrates the satisfaction of every appetite. Yet Christians impacted the world because believers were seen as those who regularly denied themselves for the love of God and others. John Calvin, the famous protestant reformer maintained that self-denial is a critical element of the Christian life. In his *Institutes of the Christian Religion*, he writes:

> *"We are not our own: let not our reason nor our will, therefore sway our plans and deeds. We are not our own: let us therefore not set it as our goal to seek what is expedient for us according to the flesh. We are not our own: insofar as we can, let us therefore forget ourselves and all that is ours."*[lx]

Our duty, Calvin reminds us, is to present our bodies as a living sacrifice to God (Rom. 12:1). In view of this living sacrifice, Calvin presents three aspects of self-denial. First, we are to deny ourselves and live for God (2 Cor. 5:15). Secondly, we are to deny ourselves with respect to self. Thirdly, we are to deny ourselves with respect to others. Self-denial means that we consider others more significant than ourselves and worthy of our efforts. (Phil. 2:3-4) Self-denial also means that we seek out avenues for withdrawing from self and drawing closer to God. One such avenue is fasting.

Fasting is refraining from eating for an agreed period of time. It is done for a specific spiritual purpose as a spiritual discipline. In fasting, I determine in my own heart before God to refrain from eating either completely or partially (certain foods) for a set time. Mark Nysenwander in his compelling book *The Fasting Key*[lxi] maintains that fasting is the forgotten key that unlocks the door to The Holy Spirit's power. It is the key that unlocks the doors of divine presence, healing, deliverance, anointing, guidance, provision, protection and revival.

Jesus assumed that His disciples would fast. They did not fast when He was physically with them for the Bridegroom was with them. But once He was ascended to heaven, then they would fast:

> *"The days will come when the bridegroom is taken away from them, and then they will fast in that day." Mark 2:20*

Jesus also instructed His disciples to fast in secret (Matt. 6:16-18). It was assumed that they would fast. Jesus fasted in the wilderness as He prepared Himself for ministry. (Matt. 4:1-2). John Wesley, the great evangelist of England stated that *"The man that never fasts is no more on the way to heaven than the man who never prays."*[lxii] Wesley was not making fasting a requirement of salvation but was pointing out that one of the *fruits* of salvation is a life of self denial and earnest wholehearted prayer which ought to include regular fasting.

Why is fasting such a powerful spiritual discipline? When I fast, I release the hold of the physical over me. I deny my body that which is good (food) for a higher purpose. I also humble myself before God and declare by my actions that I am in desperate need. I acknowledge that I am too much tied to my senses and my appetites and I practice self-denial in order to draw near to God. The scriptures are full of examples of people of God fasting in times of distress, in times of seeking guidance, in times of great need. Moses fasted for forty days before receiving the Ten Commandments (Ex. 34:28). Queen Esther fasted with all the Jews when they were faced with certain destruction, just before she was to put her life on the line by going into the king (Esther 4:16). Daniel fasted for three weeks in order to understand the vision that he was given about the end times (Dan. 9:3).

When I fast for a specific purpose, be it guidance, healing, as a sign of repentance or sorrow for sin, or to plead for healing or for the salvation of someone, I come before God and show Him my earnestness by my self-denial. God takes notice when I do this. My physical hunger in fasting parallels my desperate hunger for God and His help. In the process, all my spiritual senses are honed and made more acute. I become more in tune with God and I allow the Holy Spirit to move me in profound ways.

In addition, fasting breaks the power of the flesh in me. The old man, that *sinful-self* that we described in chapter three is mortified with Spiritual power as I fast. In fasting I declare myself master over my body. I declare that I will not allow my bodily appetites to rule over me. Fasting ought not be legalistic, wherein someone else mandates it. Rather it ought to be as a purely voluntary act, with a specific purpose in mind that I lay before God in prayer. In this way, fasting and prayer go together. The time that I would have spent eating, I spend in prayer.

If you have not made a habit of fasting, I encourage you to begin. Identify something that is on your heart for which you wish to seek God. This might be as simple as wanting to draw closer to Him in prayer. It might be on behalf of a friend or family member who is struggling with a health or spiritual issue. It might be for the salvation of certain people whom God has placed on your mind. Then decide that you will go without food for a certain period for this purpose. You may skip a meal or two or fast for an entire day. Offer this up to God in prayer. If possible, keep your fast secret; but do not lie about why you are not eating. Simply tell people that you are fasting, but not in a boastful way. Keep your purpose private. As you fast, ensure that you drink lots of water or clear liquids to keep yourself hydrated. A fast that includes liquids should be done only for a maximum of three days under special circumstances where you will not get dehydrated. As you fast, be aware of how your body is hungering for food. Let this motivate you in your hunger for Christ, your Bridegroom. Spend much time in prayer. If you get a headache or cramps, offer these to God as a sacrifice. Once you have mastered a fast for one day, try one for three days. After three days, your body will cease to hunger and you will have an acute sense of well-being. This will also give you the benefit of cleansing your body of toxins. The health benefits of fasting are well known. After three days, once you start to feel hungry again, you should break your fast. Always do so gradually, starting with soups and light fare.

In fasting and self-denial, we release ourselves to God in physical ways that acknowledge that we are indeed His. Our Bridegroom stands ready to sweep us into His arms for He knows of our hunger and will reward us with His incredible presence in ways that will astound us.

The Discipline of Release - Simplicity

Jesus lived a life of simplicity in total dependence on His Father. Simplicity is more than just being free from the hold of material possessions. It is an attitude of the heart toward what is important. Matter is not evil. Wealth is not evil. But a constant quest for more of the world's goods while people in parts of the world are starving ought to raise a red flag. Jesus condemned covetousness. (Luke 12:15) Covetousness is a lack of contentment with one's lot in life. Comparing ourselves with others and feeding the passions of our inner corruption fuels covetousness. We also fuel it by allowing our desires, appetites and wants to dictate our actions. When we make ourselves the center of our universe, we impose our will on those around us. Conversely self-denial and seeking God's heart for others will lead us into a life of simplicity and love.

When Jesus was invited into a certain home, two sisters, Mary and Martha, sought to honor Him in different ways (Luke 10:38-41). Martha busied herself with much serving in order to provide for her honored guest. Her sister Mary simply sat at Jesus' feet and hung on His words. Martha became upset that she was left to serve alone. She had in her mind a set of expectations as to what needed to be done. Her world revolved around her perception of what was needed and she allowed this to distract her from what was more important. She even asked Jesus to rebuke her sister for not supporting her in her expectations. Jesus refused to do so and affirmed that Mary had chosen the "better portion". There was nothing intrinsically wrong with what Martha was doing, but she failed to appreciate the spiritual significance of Jesus' presence. Mary on the other hand entered into the opportunity of the moment by recognizing that Jesus' words were life giving and much more needful to her than food. She released her agenda into God's hands.

Like Mary, we can break the grip of anxiety by committing ourselves to a life of simplicity. Simplicity brings great freedom for it allows us to focus on what is really important in life.

> *"Better is a dry morsel with quiet than a house full of feasting with strife." Proverbs 17:1*

Those who choose simplicity and quiet above anxiety and strife choose wisely. Peace is often forfeited in search for more and more. The more that we have, the more we must maintain, the more anxious our lives become. Materialism is the great idol of our day. Marriages are ruined, children are neglected and lives are destroyed by a constant pursuit of power, pleasure and things. Corporations, which exist solely to make a profit, entice us with slick advertising to fuel our discontent and a constant craving for newer, better and more. We spend resources on what could be used for Godly purposes to satisfy our constant craving for more and more stuff.

A life of simplicity clears the way for the peace of God, for it frees us to concentrate on loving God and our neighbor. It frees us to live in a simple rhythm of solitude, ministry and community. It allows us to devote our time to one another. Life becomes about the simple enjoyment of one another's company and not continuous entertainment and endless distraction.

Simplicity is learning to say no to things that take us away from what ought to be our first love. As we walk hand in hand with God in the simplicity of a life devoted to Him, God fills us with His peace. This peace is not a peace that is conditional on circumstances or our situation in life. Rather it is the deep inner assurance of His presence in good times and bad. Our peace is that we belong to Him and He is forever with us. We belong to Him. And He is ours. It is simplicity.

> *"Fear not, for I have redeemed you; I have called you by name, you are mine. [2] When you pass through the waters, I will be with you; and through the rivers, they shall not overwhelm you; when you walk through fire you shall not be burned, and the flame shall not consume you. [3] For I am the LORD your God, the Holy One of Israel, your Savior." Isaiah 43:1-3*

Study Guide for Chapter Four

A. Questions for Personal Reflection

Record answers in your journal.

1. To what extent do you feel that you know God personally rather than just knowing about God? How has the discussion on vulnerability in relationships helped you understand how to draw near to God?

2. Reflect on Larry Crabb's discussion of Crucial, Critical and Casual longings. (pages 91-93) To what extent have you pursued secondary longings and neglected Crucial longings? How do you respond to the notion that these longings will never be entirely satisfied in this life?

3. Reflect on situations and people in your life who have hurt you deeply. At the time, did you have an awareness of God's presence? To what extent did you feel that there must be something wrong with you? How has it helped you to realize that it is OK to hurt and that there is nothing wrong with you? How has God used your pain for a higher purpose?

4. What has struck you the most about the discipline of release? How has the discussion on forgiveness helped you lay down some of the burdens that you have been carrying? What changes in your life is God calling you to?

B. **Exercises** (Individual or Large Group)

1. Read John 15:1-17 three times using the Holy Reading process (pages 31-32). What is God saying to you and how are you responding?

2. Read Psalm 13, an individual psalm of lament. Answer the questions below:

    i. What are the four questions the person asks?
    ii. What do these questions reveal about the psalmist's life?

iii. What is the person asking God to do?
iv. How do you account for the change in verse 5?
v. Express the pattern of lament in this psalm in your own words.

C. Small Group Breakout (2 or 3)

1. Share with one another a situation in which you were deeply hurt. How did this affect your relationship with God? Reflecting on this now, what have you learned? Have you been able to release those who hurt you?

2. What have you learned personally about the discipline of release, regarding yourself, time, circumstances, other people? What have you learned about the discipline of fasting and simplicity?

3. Take some time to pray for one another.

D. Assignment for This Week

1. Continue to observe five devotional times in solitude this week. In each time, follow the pattern that you learned in chapter one. This week use the breath prayer *"Lord, I am continually with you. You hold my right hand, you guide me with your counsel."* (Ps. 73:23-24) Apply Holy Reading to the following passages throughout the week: Psalm 79, Mathew 18: 23-35, Eccles. 3:1-8, Matt. 6:19-34, Rom. 8:31-39.

2. Continue to take 10-15 minutes at the end of each day to do a *Prayer of Examen* (pages 80-81).

3. Decide this week to fast for a meal or two for a specific purpose. Write down the reason for your fast in your journal and commit this to God in prayer. Write down your reflections on your fast in your journal.

4. Read chapter five. Answer the Questions for Personal Reflection in your journal.

5. Prayer and Worship – the Breath of Love

"Pray without ceasing." 1 Thess. 5:17

A person can survive an extended period of time without food, but no one can live more that a few minutes without breathing. Breathing supplies oxygen to the blood, which is essential in allowing living cells to live. Deprived of oxygen, cells die. Similarly, our spirit dies if cut off from God. We don't often think of it, but it is only by the grace of God that we continue to live at all. God's providence is such that it is in Him that we live and move and have our being. *"He himself gives to all mankind, life and breath and everything*" (Acts 17:25b). Not only did Jesus Christ create the world and everything in it, but it is only in Him that it all continues to hold together (Col. 1:17). Should God for one second withhold His sustaining power, the earth and everything in it would be destroyed. He is the invisible force that holds all atoms and molecules together and He gives life by His providence and grace to everything as He wills.

God is Love and He loves us with an incredibly deep and profound love. While God loves all of His creatures, He has a special love for those that He created in His image. For, while we share our physicality with the animals, we are also different from the animals. God created both humans and the animals on the same day, the sixth day, but we are the only creatures on earth to whom God speaks. He speaks to us, He does not speak to the animals. God not only dignifies us by His address but He has made us able to respond to Him. In that sense we are *response-able.* And in speaking to us, He expects us to respond and so holds us *response-ible.*[lxiii] It is the height of rudeness not to respond to someone when spoken to. God expects us to respond to Him, and He expects us to do so in reverence. The only appropriate response is worship and prayer. It is a response to God that acknowledges that He exits and that He is worthy of both adoration and address. Hence prayer is one of the definitive characteristics that makes us human.[lxiv] The animals cannot pray. They relate to God through instinct. But humans can pray. To refuse to pray is to refuse to acknowledge God and His claim upon us. A refusal to pray is a sign of unbelief and results in condemnation and an eternity spent in torment apart from God, the source of all life and love. The Apostle Paul writes in Romans chapter one:

> *"For the wrath of God is revealed from heaven against all ungodliness and unrighteousness of men, who by their unrighteousness suppress the truth. [19] For what can be known about God is plain to them, because God has shown it to them. [20] For his invisible attributes, namely, his eternal power and divine nature, have been clearly perceived, ever since the creation of the world, in the things that have been made. So they are without excuse. [21] For although they knew God, they did not honor him as God or give thanks to him, but they became futile in their thinking, and their foolish hearts were darkened." Romans 1:18-21*

To refuse to acknowledge God or to address Him as God is to denigrate one's own humanity and consider it no better than the animals.

PRAYER – A HUMAN EXPRESSION

The idea of praying to a deity is not a uniquely Christian concept. Since the beginning, people have had a sense that forces outside of themselves control their destiny. Various creation myths such as the Babylonian Epic *Enuma Elish*[lxv] depict the origin of the world as a result of a battle between primal gods. The forces that govern existence are seen as many and varied. The Greek and Roman notions of many gods with differing spheres of influence meant that anyone who had a human venture was wise to entreat the favor of these gods. They would do so by offering up prayers together with sacrifices to entreat the favor of the particular deity whose favor they sought. These imaginary gods were not particularly moral, but had power over human affairs. They were seen to vary in strength and influence and had to be appeased. Even today, in many parts of the world, various gods are worshipped with earnestness. In India, shrines and temples to such deities characterize Hinduism. Millions of people pray to these gods. Religion is humanity's vain attempt to appease and seek the favor of unknown, arbitrary gods. Prayer in this context is not simply a matter of petition, but of finding the right god to petition.

Instinctively, people do cry out for help when in distress. Dietrich Bonhoeffer, the famous German theologian, experienced a fellow inmate in a Nazi prison crying out to God in desperation during a bombing raid. He was unable to bring himself to give the man any Christian comfort, for he describes the man as a "flippant" type and he didn't feel that he was really praying at all.[lxvi] Praying to an imaginary and unknown god is useless and destructive because any deity imagined or inferred is an idol. It is useless because the god is not real. It is destructive for it opens people up to demonic influence. Indeed, the nations all around Israel would make pleas to their own idols, who were really not gods but demons. In the showdown between Elijah and the prophets of Baal in 1 Kings 18, the 450 prophets called out in prayer to Baal for hours without answer. Such prayer is not heard by YHWH, the true God, for the one praying does not acknowledge Him as God, but rather offers it up to the work of human hands. The word idol in Hebrew actually means "nothing". The idols of the nations were nothings. (see Isaiah 44:14-19). However, in praying to such nothings, the people were opening themselves up to demonic influence. Sacrifices to idols are actually offered up to demons (1 Cor. 10:20). Satan is the great pretender and prince of demons who desires that people worship him (Luke 4:5-7).

PRAYER IN ISRAEL

Israel, by contrast, had an experience of the one true God YHWH, initiated by Him through the deliverance from Egypt and the covenant at Mount Sinai. By virtue of His abiding presence with them symbolized by the tabernacle, and His promises, they were able to worship the One who saved them. Their prayers, were a reflection of the fact that they were as a people commissioned to be a *"kingdom of priests and a holy nation"* (Ex. 19:6). As such, YWHW was interested in their preservation and continued holiness. Individuals could pour out their hearts to Him and make petitions. The tabernacle and later the temple were places towards which they could pray. Even in captivity, once the temple had been destroyed, Daniel prayed three times a day with his face toward Jerusalem. It was not *prayer* per se that got him into trouble with the king, but prayer directed to YHWH and toward Jerusalem (Dan. 6:10).

Prayer was not just the prerogative of prophet, priest and king. The common person in ancient Israel could also cry out to God and petition Him, for He was not only God of the nation, but a personal God. The story of Hannah is an example (1 Samuel, chapter1).

HANNAH'S PRAYER

Hannah and her husband Elkanah lived during the time when Israel had settled in the Promised Land and was governed by a secession of judges. The times were characterized by cycles of idolatry, oppression and deliverance. Elkanah and Hannah were ordinary Hebrews who would go up yearly to Shiloh to sacrifice at the Tabernacle. Hannah was in great distress due to her childlessness. Childlessness was often seen as a punishment from God for some besetting sin. To make matters worse, her rival wife would often provoke her about this during the annual pilgrimage. Despite her husband's love for her and generosity, she was in great distress. In a poignant moment, she approached the Tabernacle, pouring out her soul to YHWH, weeping bitterly and asking Him to take way her reproach and give her a son (1 Sam. 1:11).

In her prayer, she made a vow that if YHWH gave her a son, she would give him to the LORD, all the days of his life as a Nazarite[5], one whose life would be devoted to God and His service. The presiding priest, Eli saw her distress and assumed that she was drunk. When she corrected him and explained her distress and anxiety, he blessed her and added his own prayer that YHWH grant her petition. Encouraged by this, she rose and went her way and was no longer sad. In due course the LORD remembered her and she conceived and bore a son, Samuel. When Samuel was weaned, she took him back to Shiloh and gave him to Eli as a helper. Samuel eventually became one of Israel's great prophets, an anointer of kings, the judge and priest of Israel. Hannah eventually was blessed with five additional children (1 Sam. 2:21).

The story is compelling for it depicts the anguish of a woman who cries out to YHWH and asks for a very personal favor. Childlessness in those days was seen as a curse. Her personal relationship with God was in question. Was God not pleased with her? Her anguish was not simply childlessness, but that of feeling rejected by God. Others around her, who likely had a questionable relationship with God, were blessed with children. Why not her? And so, on this occasion, she was driven to make a desperate plea. Her petition was not accompanied by a sacrifice, but by bitter tears and vexation in spirit. Her prayer was in no way selfish, for she promised to give this son back to God. She would get little personal benefit from her son. He

[5] See Numbers chapter 6

would not be there to help her husband in the fields nor help with the chores around the home. Her willingness to give him up to God's service showed her heart. She wanted assurance above all that God did remember her. God heard her prayer and responded, giving her what she asked for. She reciprocated by faithfully fulfilling her vow. Her husband supported her in all of this. The son that she bore became the most famous judge in Israel, a man of God and anointer of kings.

Imagine the lift that this episode would have given to her spiritual life and her devotion to YHWH. Her amazing prayer of thanksgiving is recorded in scripture for future generations (1 Sam. 2:1-10). All the people would have know her testimony. Her story illustrates that God does care for the individual. He hears their prayers and he responds to selfless devotion to those that seek Him.

It is noteworthy that Hannah's prayer occurred in the context of the community of worship. The festival and the tabernacle were the occasion of her prayer. The role of Eli, the priest in her obtaining inner assurance indicated that the context of the worshipping community and the established priesthood, were important aspects of her petition. Self-denial and personal sacrifice accompanied her prayer, but were not the heart of it. It was her deep distress and her passion for the assurance of His favor that moved her to pray.

In the same way, the prophets reminded the people constantly that it was their inner heart attitude and their holiness that God noted and not the quality nor quantity of their sacrifices. (Hos. 6:6) God was not to be bribed like a pagan deity. If they were faithful in their spirit, YHWH would be faithful. When God no longer answered their prayers it was because of their continued hardness of heart and their sin.

> *"Behold, the LORD's hand is not shortened, that it cannot save, or his ear dull, that it cannot hear; [2] but your iniquities have made a separation between you and your God, and your sins have hidden his face from you so that he does not hear. [3] For your hands are defiled with blood and your fingers with iniquity; your lips have spoken lies; your tongue mutters wickedness." Isaiah 59:1-3*

The message is clear. God does not respond to the prayers of sinners who continue in their sin. In contrast, the one who is repentant, humble and contrite before God gets an immediate hearing (Is. 66:2b).

JESUS – MAN OF PRAYER

Israel, at the time of Jesus was led by a religious elite whose life centered around the Temple and its sacrificial system and a zealousness for the law. Three times a year, people made pilgrimages to the temple to celebrate the three primary feasts, bringing sacrifices and offerings. For most people, daily spiritual life revolved around the local synagogue, which was a place of prayer as well as a place to hear the reading of scripture every Sabbath. Various teachers of the law, Rabbi's, would gather disciples around them and teach them their particular interpretation and amplification of the law. It was at the synagogue and at the temple that Jesus ran afoul of the religious establishment. Hence, most of His teaching was done in the open air. His compassion for people, His authoritative teaching and the healings that He performed drew great crowds. Jesus would often rise early and withdraw for times of personal prayer. As dawn broke, people would come looking for Him and His ministry would begin once again.

Prayer characterized Jesus' entire ministry. Immediately after His baptism, the Spirit led Him into the wilderness where He fasted and prayed for 40 days. It was in this context that the tempter, Satan came to Him with his enticements to sin (Luke 4:1-13). Jesus also prayed before He chose His disciples, spending all night in prayer (Luke 6:12). On the mountain of transfiguration He took three of His disciples with Him to pray (Luke 9:28). Often, He would arise early in the morning, while it was still dark and retreat to solitary places to pray (Luke 5:16). Many of His miracles and healings were preceded by prayer. When His disciples asked Him why they could not cast out a demon, He replied that *"this kind cannot be driven out by anything but prayer"* (Mark 9:29). In Gethsemane, Jesus struggled over His pending crucifixion and prayed so intensely that He staggered to His knees with drops of blood falling from His brow (Luke 22:44). Even on the cross, Jesus prayed for His tormentors and asked the Father to receive His Spirit (Luke 23:46). Jesus' disciples were so impacted by His prayer life that the only recorded request that they ever made to Him was to teach them to pray. Jesus not only taught them by giving them a template, the Lord's Prayer, but also encouraged them to be persistent and diligent in their prayers (Luke 18:1).

JESUS' ATTITUDE IN PRAYER

In contrast the rabbi's prayers, which could be pretentious and formal, beginning with phrases like *"Blessed art Thou Lord, God, King of the Universe.... ",* Jesus' preferred way of addressing God His Father was: *Abba*. This is a term of familial endearment that suggests complete intimacy. Much like our term *daddy* or *dad,* it expresses a close fondness that was a sharp contrast to the aloofness expressed by the rabbis. Jesus often attracted their condemnation for He was addressing God as if He were His own Father (John 5:18). In addressing Jesus as *Abba* Father, Jesus was emphasizing God's affectionate love and fondness for His children. He was testifying that God seeks to relate to His children, not as a distant, transcendently stern Monarch, but as a loving, gentle, kind and merciful Father, who is also King. As heavenly Father-King, He desires the best for His children and desires above all that they flourish and be released from the slavery of sin and the evil one. In Mark's gospel, whenever Jesus comes across disease, demonic possession or death, He reverses it. He sets people free, heals the sick and raises the dead. His work was not independent of God, but in accordance with God's own heart. *"My Father is working and until now I am working."* (John 5:17) By word, deed and in His prayers, Jesus revealed the true nature of God and His compassion for His children.

Jesus' own unique relationship with His Father was grounded in an assurance that God acknowledged Him and was working through Him to accomplish the specific work that He had sent Him to do. Prayer and thanksgiving preceded His miracles, in confidence that God was working in Him and through Him.

We have much to learn from Jesus' prayer life and attitude in prayer. The first thing is that Jesus, though He was fully God, felt the need to withdraw and spend significant periods of time in prayer. Such was His understanding of the human need for intimacy and communion with God that, though He was God, He humbled Himself and took the form of a child communicating with his Father. As God, He claimed no exemption from an intimate life of prayer. If Jesus then, who was God, was compelled to spend much time with God in prayer, how much more should we who are mere mortals do the same and more?

Secondly, Jesus' day-to-day life was bathed in prayer. He had no grand master plan for reaching the people of Israel. Each morning, He would pray and ask God to direct Him. He was so immersed into the Father's heart that His decisions and His daily life throbbed with that same heart. Everything that He did was preceded by and immersed in prayer. He was simultaneously in the Father and in the world. And He invited His disciples to also live in Him and in the world. This invitation is also extended to us, His adopted sons and daughters. We too are not to be "of the world", for everything that is of the world moves against the Kingdom of God (1 John 2:15). To be in the world but not of the world requires constant prayer. The Apostle Paul exhorts us to *"pray without ceasing"* (1 Thess 5:17). To pray without ceasing is to never stop praying. Prayer is to be a continual activity, like breathing. In breathing, we inhale and exhale. To inhale is to be filled with the Spirit. To exhale is to let the impurities of our hearts depart from us, giving them up to God. Prayer is renewing and cleansing. It allows the pure oxygen of God's Spirit to infuse us, giving life to our spirit. It allows our deepest burdens, anxieties, contradictions and heartaches to be released to God. It opens us up to be filled with His Spirit.

Thirdly, Jesus prayer life was thoroughly evangelistic. His passion was to reach people with the good news of the Kingdom of God. His message was: *"The time is fulfilled and the Kingdom of God is at hand, repent and believe in the gospel"* (Mark. 1:15). The phrase *"Kingdom of God"* occurs 52 times in the gospels. The sister phrase *"Kingdom of heaven"* is preferred by Matthew who uses it 32 times in his gospel. Jesus Himself is the embodiment of the Kingdom, for He is the King. With His physical presence, He proclaimed that the Kingdom was there among them. The Kingdom of God is the rule of Christ, the rightful King over His subjects, the citizens of the Kingdom. His parables told this story over and over again. The King comes, commissions His citizens, gives them gifts and resources and then departs for a season (Luke 19:12-27). He will return and call to account those whom He commissioned, giving them rewards commensurate with their results. The Kingdom is here now, but is seen only through eyes of faith. One day it will be fully manifest, and those who rejected the King will be brought to account. It will not be pleasant for those who reject the King. They will be destroyed (Luke 19:27, Rev. 20:15).

Hence, Jesus' ministry is a call to embrace the Kingdom and Himself as King. This requires a radical realigning of priorities. We are to seek first the Kingdom (Matt. 6:33) and not overly concern ourselves with the things of this world. Those things that we need will be provided as we seek the Kingdom. This is not only thoroughly evangelistic but also eschatological for the Kingdom is both now and not yet. Wherever Jesus Christ is worshipped and acknowledged as

King, the Kingdom is manifest. In acknowledging Him as King now, we proclaim His coming again to rule publicly and openly as King. At that time *"every knee [will] bow .....and every tongue confess that Jesus Christ is Lord" (Phil 2:10-11).*

Jesus' priority in prayer and in ministry was that people would embrace the Kingdom and Himself as the King whom God had sent. To refuse to believe in Him was to die in sin.*"Unless you believe that I am he, you will die in your sins."(John 8:24)* Jesus rejoiced in the Spirit when people accepted Him and declared that salvation had come to that household (Luke 19:9). He sent His disciples out two by two to declare peace, heal and proclaim the Kingdom (Luke 10:1-12). He rejoiced, for in the proclamation of the Kingdom, He saw the defeat of Satan (Luke 10:18). Hence the Kingdom represented the restoration of all things and the end of the rule of the Evil One, both personally and corporately. "Thy Kingdom Come" was to characterize the disciples' prayer. It was both a declaration in confidence, and a petition that it be so, not only in the life of the individual but also in the world. This Kingdom comes continually as people turn from sin and embrace Christ as King, and will come in all its consummated fullness when Jesus returns and is openly and expressly King over the entire earth. He is the *"King of Kings and Lord of Lords"* both now and into eternity *(Rev. 19:16).*

CHRISTIAN PRAYER

Following Jesus' resurrection, Jesus spent forty days with His disciples, impressing upon them the meaning of the Kingdom. During this time, He explained to them the full significance of everything that had happened and explained the scriptures that bore witness to it all (Luke 24:27). Upon His ascension into Heaven, he told them to remain in Jerusalem and wait to be clothed with power by the Holy Spirit. They actually waited ten days and during that time, they were together and devoted themselves to prayer (Acts 1:14). At that point, they understood much of what Jesus had said, but they had not been empowered to proclaim it. Jesus had told them that the Holy Spirit would bring to their remembrance everything that they needed. During those ten days of waiting, the disciples were in deep prayer.

It was on the day of Pentecost, while they were all together, that the Holy Spirit came upon them with extraordinary power. They were filled with the Holy Spirit and began speaking in tongues (other languages) and proclaiming the mighty works of God. On that day, the

New Covenant church was born. Because of the festival of Pentecost (one of the three required feasts where all Jews were to gather in Jerusalem) the city was full of people from all the surrounding areas. The Apostle Peter stood up and spoke clearly and boldly to the people. Even though the city was full of foreigners, each person heard the message in his own language. Peter explained the meaning of what was happening and proclaimed the good news of salvation through repentance and faith in Christ. On that day, three thousand souls repented before God and came to the Lord (Acts 2:41). This passage from the book of Acts gives us a very concise description of what the early church looked like:

> *"And they devoted themselves to the apostles' teaching and fellowship, to the breaking of bread and the prayers. [43] And awe came upon every soul, and many wonders and signs were being done through the apostles. [44] And all who believed were together and had all things in common. [45] And they were selling their possessions and belongings and distributing the proceeds to all, as any had need. [46] And day by day, attending the temple together and breaking bread in their homes, they received their food with glad and generous hearts, [47] praising God and having favor with all the people. And the Lord added to their number day by day those who were being saved." Acts 2:42 - 47*

We see that they devoted themselves to these four things: the apostles' teaching, fellowship, breaking of bread and prayer. A life of prayer defined and characterized the early community of faith. J.C. Ryle in *"Practical Religion"*[lxvii] says that *"the habit of prayer is the secret mark of the true Christian"*. Without prayer no one can be saved. No one can repent for another. No one can invite Jesus Christ into someone else's heart. No one is saved apart from prayer. Prayer is the only way to start the Christian life and prayer is the way to continue in the Christian life.

The first thing that a newborn baby does is cry. Crying requires exhaling and then inhaling. It kick-starts the breathing cycle. It is also a declaration of dependency. A newborn is totally dependent on others for everything. Similarly, "*If anyone is in Christ, he is a new creation."* (2 Cor. 5:17), a newborn of the Spirit. As new creations, we have a Spiritual life that is just as dependent on Him as is our physical life. The breath that sustains such life is our communion with Him. He is the vine, we are the branches. If we fail to remain in Him, we wither and die. To remain in Him is to remain in His love (John 15:10). The essence of a relationship between two lovers is communion. Communion is that deep sharing of one another that is "the between" of the relationship. And what sustains that communion is communication. Two lovers who never communicated with one another would not long remain lovers. On the contrary, true lovers can never get enough of spending time with each other in deep conversation. As we awaken in rebirth to our Bridegroom, so too we should earnestly desire to remain in communion and conversation with Him.

Prayer is essential in this relationship. The disciples in the early church engaged in prayer at every opportunity. It was at the hour of prayer that Peter and John went up to the temple where the lame beggar was healed (Acts 3:1-10). After their arrest and release, the disciples gathered together and prayed earnestly for the ability to continue to speak the word of God with *"all boldness"* (Acts 4:29). As they were praying, the place was shaken and they were all filled with the Holy Spirit and *"they continued to speak the word of God with boldness"* (Acts 4:31).

When Herod imprisoned Peter in Jerusalem, the church gathered together and offered up earnest prayer for him. That night an angel delivered him from four squads of soldiers and Peter appeared at the prayer meeting to their utter amazement (Acts 12:16). Every time a major decision was to be made, or someone was commissioned and sent out for ministry, the believers would pray. Prayer prefaced healings and miracles. Prayer was the one constant for people in the early church. The letters of the apostles were filled with prayers and exhortations to pray continuously (Rom. 8:26, 12:12, 1 Cor. 7:5, 14:15, 2 Cor. 1:11, Eph. 6:18, Phil. 4:6, Col. 4:2, 1 Thess. 5:17, 2 Thess. 3:1, 1 Tim. 2:8, 5:5, Jas. 5:13, 16; Jude 1:20).

The way in which the disciples prayed in the early church was characterized by plain language and petition. There were no lofty phrases being strung together in the rabbinic tradition. Rather, their prayers were much like Jesus' prayers, intimate communication with the heavenly Father. Secondly, they were not reticent to ask for things. Even before the Holy Spirit fell upon the Apostles at Pentecost, they were gathered in the upper room and came to the conviction that someone should be appointed an apostle to replace Judas Iscariot who betrayed Jesus. They prayed that God would show them which of the two proposed candidates should be chosen and they had confidence that God would show them His will.

Stanley Grentz points out that many Christian leaders over the past two hundred years have suggested that petitionary prayer is a lowlier form of prayer that should be avoided.[lxviii] They suggest that mature believers should move away from "beggarly" prayers asking God to intervene in human situations, and focus rather on simply being in the presence of God. We certainly do not see that in the scriptures. Peter was not reticent to ask for difficult things, even praying for people to be raised from the dead (Acts 9:40). The Apostle James writes *"you do not have because you do not ask"* (James 4:2). Jesus said: *"Until now you have asked nothing in my name. Ask, and you will receive, that your joy may be full."* (John 16:24) The Apostle Paul writes in Philippians:

> *"Rejoice in the Lord always; again I will say, Rejoice. [5] Let your reasonableness be known to everyone. The Lord is at hand; [6] do not be anxious about anything, but in everything by prayer and supplication with thanksgiving let your requests be made known to God." Philippians 4:4-6*

Petitionary prayer is the heart of prayer and the heart of any child's relationship with their father. It would be a strange child indeed that never asked his or her father for anything. Yet respect, honor and obedience are prerequisites to having a father consider anything that a child might ask for. A good father would only grant requests that would actually be beneficial and safe for his child.

Grentz continues to point out that the emphasis on petition in the early church testifies to the eschatological outlook of the early church. They embraced the prayer that Jesus taught them as a cry for the Kingdom ("*Thy Kingdom come*"). The believers yearned with all their heart, soul and strength for Jesus to intervene in their own situations and embrace them as Bridegroom and King. But their primary concern was not so much for themselves but for the glory of God and the advancement of His Kingdom. They would pray for God's Kingdom to come and wait on God to answer.

And so, they rejoiced in the miraculous healings and wonders that accompanied the proclamation of the gospel. These were the authenticating signs that God was indeed working and that the Kingdom was indeed coming. At the same time, personal petitions were answered with a call for endurance and reliance on God's strength to bear up under the trial (2 Cor 12:9). In all cases, petition was a vital part of the prayer life of the early church. It was not viewed as beggarly but seen as a way of participating in what God was doing. Grentz summarizes:

> *"According to the New Testament, petition can be voiced boldly because of the presence of the two great eschatological signposts: the resurrection of Jesus and the presence of the Holy Spirit. These events encourage the faithful community to petition God and bring about the completion of God's work in the world, in the church and in the life of every believer."* [lxix]

THE LORD'S PRAYER

The gospels record many events in the life of the disciples who were with Jesus, but the only recorded specific request for instruction was that Jesus teach them to pray. Jesus taught them to avoid the formalism, repetition and public spectacle that characterized the prayers of "hypocrites" (Matt. 6:5). Rather, they were to go into their prayer closet and pray in secret (Matt. 6:6). The Father who hears all would hear them for they would not be praying for pretense or to impress others but their motivation would be to draw near in personal intimacy and engage only Him. Their prayer was not to be characterized by vain repetition and empty phrases, but by simply letting their requests be made known to their heavenly Father who already knows what they need. As an example, Jesus gave them what we now know as the Lord's Prayer. Unfortunately, many traditions have turned this wonderful example of how to pray into many occasions of "vain repetition".

> *"Our Father in heaven,*
> *Hallowed be your name.*
> *Your kingdom come, your will be done,*
> *On earth as it is in heaven.*
> *Give us this day our daily bread,*
> *and forgive us our debts, as we also have forgiven our debtors.*
> *And lead us not into temptation,*
> *but deliver us from evil." Matt. 6:9-13*

Our Father in heaven. The first part of this prayer acknowledges God as heavenly Father of all who know Him. The first phrase reminds us that we are all brothers and sisters for He is Father of all of us. We share collectively in His Fatherhood. The prayer starts with a call to community. It is not "my Father" but "our Father". Whenever, we pray, we must note that we are not alone. Others are also praying and this serves to humble us insofar as our requests go. How will the quality of our petition stack up against those in desperate situations and severe affliction? This is not to say that we should not ask for what we need, but we must be aware that God's heart is to supply our needs but not our fleshly desires.

Heaven is not just the physical location of our Father, but His field of concern. Heaven is His throne and earth His footstool. His priorities are heavenly. Reminded of this, we pray knowing that we too should be concerned with heavenly issues. This is not to say that God is not concerned about "our daily bread", for that phrase follows, however, it does remind us that God's priorities are not the same as our own.

"Hallowed be your name" reminds us that God is Holy. It is a call to reverence. We adopt a posture of worship before the One who rules all creation. We bow down before Him. We acknowledge Him as He really is. We acknowledge Him as King.

"Thy Kingdom come" is the first petitionary phrase and summarizes our hearts cry for His righteous rule. In saying this, we acknowledge that all of the problems in this world will be dealt with justly and righteously, when His kingdom fully comes. It is our heart's cry for His Kingdom to come now, in greater measure than we currently see. It is both eschatological and current, for we know that it is both now and not yet. We long to see more of it and we cry with the psalmists "how long" will it be before God makes it all right. In praying it, we agree that the Kingdom is our first priority. We long for it, we yearn for it, we acknowledge it.

"Your will be done" is an admission that we do not understand what is best for ourselves or our world. It is a humble submission to God's desire for us and an acknowledgement that our Father really does have our best interests at heart. To pray this sincerely demands that I give up my pride in thinking that I know what needs to happen in any situation. It is reminiscent of Jesus' prayer in Gethsemane, when He asks that the cup of suffering pass from Him. Jesus does not hesitate to express His desire for another way and His horror for what is ahead for Him. Yet His words echo into eternity as He submits *"Nevertheless, not as I will, but as you will"* (Matt. 26:39). In praying this, we enter into the spirit of Christ, who drank the cup that the Father had prepared for Him. (Further amplification on what it means to pray according to God's will follows in the next section.)

"On earth as it is in heaven" acknowledges that our desire for God's will extends to all of the created order. There is no room here for a dualistic view of God reigning in heaven and humanity on earth. In reality, we know that the earth is Satan's realm, but that he has already been defeated and his kingdom is being displaced by the rule of God. In praying this, we acknowledge that we are on God's side and stand opposed to Satan, his demons and all evil here on earth.

Give us this day our daily bread. Up until this phrase the prayer is focused vertically on God. It is fitting that the first half of the prayer is entirely affirming, hallowing and deferring to God. Adoration and acknowledgement of who God is and unity with His purposes is essential in prayer. We ought to yearn for His purposes to be accomplished in us and in the world. Only then do we ask for our needs. "Daily bread" is the most basic human need. This simple phrase summarizes all those things that we need to exist as people on the face of a crowded planet. The Father knows what we need before we ask Him, yet He encourages us to ask. He also encourages us to be persistent in asking (Luke 18:1). "Daily bread" also reminds us that God supplies our needs one day at a time. Jesus does not model asking for a year's supply. We are to trust that He will indeed supply what we need.

Forgive us our debts as we forgive our debtors. *"Debts"* is the Greek word *hophehlema.* It refers to something justly owed, that which is legally due. When we sin, we offend God and we owe Him an apology. Confession of sin is an integral part of prayer. Jesus reminds us here that we do have an inner corruption (the sinful-self) that will manifest itself in transgression. We are to confess these transgressions to God daily in prayer. To fail to confess sin to God is to refuse to acknowledge that we do sin. We sin in thought, word and deed as well as words left unspoken and deeds left undone. While Jesus paid the penalty for our sins, past, present and future, sin does affect our relationship with God. It is presumption to ask Him favors if there is something between us. We ought always to search our hearts and ask Him to search our hearts to see if there is anything offensive to God in us (Psalm 139:23-24). Jesus reminds us in the same breath that we too must forgive those who are indebted to us. As discussed at length in chapter four, forgiveness is a release of the offender to God. It is therapeutic for us to do so for it relieves us of bitterness and any desire to get even. Insofar as a restoration of the relationship is concerned, that requires repentance and confession by the offender to us. God does not expect us to excuse or condone sin against us by simply pretending that it never happened. However, in releasing the offender and offense to God, we maintain an attitude of having released them already and we pray for those who abuse us, yearning for their restoration, just as the Father yearns for ours.

Lead us not into temptation. Temptation *is pierasmos* in Greek. This word means to test, to subject something to a trial to ensure that it is genuine. In a negative sense it can also mean to entice to evil. However, in this case it does not mean this of God, for God will not entice us to evil. The Apostle James makes that clear when he says *"Let no man say when he is tempted, I am being tempted of God; for God cannot be tempted with evil, and he himself tempts no man."* (Jas. 1:13) Rather, what we mean when we pray this is that we are asking God not to lead us into situations of weakness where Satan would be able to entice us. We know that God does test His people, yet He always provides a way of escape (1 Cor. 10:13). He will not test us beyond our ability to endure it. This phrase is an appeal to God to go easy on us in terms of trials and ordeals. We will have trials for they do build character in us but it is legitimate for us to ask God to not overly test us nor to allow us to be enticed too easily by Satan and his hordes.

Deliver us from evil. Here we are asking God to guard us from the snares of the devil. Satan does indeed "*prowl around like a roaring lion looking for someone to devour"* (1 Peter 5:8). He is our adversary and he will come after us. It is legitimate to ask for protection. We ought also to have confidence that God will provide it. We should not be overly anxious and fearful, for *"greater is he who is in you than he who is in the world."* (1 John 4:4) Neither should we be cavalier about Satan for he is treacherous and loves to appear as an "*angel of light"* (2 Cor. 11:14). We must maintain a keen sense of our own vulnerability and so ought to be sober and watchful. We are to pray for deliverance and to rest in the assurance that God will provide it.

The Lord's Prayer is a divine template for prayer for it includes all the elements that Jesus Himself commended to His disciples. Because it has been extensively memorized, it should always be prayed slowly, allowing the implications of each phrase to sink in. A good practice is to pray each phrase and then elaborate upon it in one's own words. This pattern of "praying scripture" can be extended to other scripture as well, particularly the Psalms. As each phrase is read, I allow God to speak into my spirit and I answer back, by putting my response into my own words as if I were speaking to someone present. I must always remind myself that God is ever present with me. I do not pray into a vacuum, but He hears my prayer and, like a loving Father, earnestly desires to converse with me.

PRAYING ACCORDING TO GOD'S WILL

Jesus frequently identified faith as a critical component of healing and restoration (Matt. 9:2, 22, 29, 15:28). He also said *"whatever you ask in prayer, you will receive if you have faith"* (Matt 21:22). Some have interpreted these statements of Jesus as proving that faith is the only determinant factor for prayers to be granted. They maintain, that if we only had enough faith, then everything we prayed for would be granted and every sickness healed. Unfortunately, this is not consistent with the totality of scripture. Faith is not a magic wand that forces God's hand to give us whatever we ask for. In fact the Apostle James chastises his readers for asking for the wrong things, in order to satisfy their passions (James 4:3). The key thing about faith is the object of that faith. We are to have faith *in God* and not faith in the quality of our faith. To place our faith in God is to unite our hearts with His purposes and His will. The Apostle John writes in his first epistle:

> *"And this is the confidence that we have toward him, that if we ask anything according to his will he hears us. 15 And if we know that he hears us in whatever we ask, we know that we have the requests that we have asked of him" 1 John 5:14-15*

We are to ask *"according to His will"*. And if we do so, we know that we have the reality of we have asked for. To pray according to God's will is to embrace God's willingness to act on behalf of His people, who desire and ask for things in harmony with His eternal purposes. These purposes have to do not only with the thing asked for, but also with the spiritual development of the one asking and also, those in the surrounding community and in future generations and events. Hence there are many factors that go into determining God's will. From God's perspective, we might ask: Is the thing asked for the right thing for the petitioner at this point in time? Is the petition itself the right thing for the development of the Kingdom of God at this point in time? Is it the right thing for the development of others who are affected at this point in time and in the future? Because God sees the entirety of eternity past to eternity future, His perspective greatly overarches ours. We see only this tiny slice of time in which we now live. Our entire lives are but a sliver in the grand scheme of events and circumstances that interrelate millions of people, situations and events.

The point is that when we pray for something, we certainly do not know for certain if the thing we ask is consistent with God's eternal purposes, given the complexities of life on earth. However, we do know that God is entirely consistent within Himself. The things that He has done or promised to do are also consistent with who He is. Hence, prayer according to God's will aligns itself with God's character and His purposes. Both of these are revealed in scripture. Therefore, prayer according to God's will will be thoroughly Biblical. We also know that God does not hear the prayers of those who are separated from Him through their sin (Isa. 59:2). The spiritual condition of the petitioner is a huge factor in God's willingness to act. Both the motivation of the petitioner and the extent to which the petitioner is in synchronization with God's heart are extremely important. One reason that fasting is such a catalyst for prayer is that it puts the petitioner in the right spiritual mindset, that is one of self-denial and humility.

For example, the Apostle James instructs the church to deal with sickness by calling together the Elders of the Church and having them pray and anoint with oil the sick person. He then states *"The prayer of a righteous person has great power as it is working."* (James 5:16). He goes on to give the example of Elijah who prayed that it might not rain for three years, in order to bring the king and nation to repentance. Hence, in praying for the sick, we note that sometimes people are healed, instantly, miraculously and sometimes they are not. Faith is one determining factor, but the other factors are the spiritual condition of the petitioner, his or her motivation, and the current situation in the community among which the petition is made and God's particular purpose in this situation. For example, we know that interpersonal problems in the church hinder prayer. Those who bring their gift to God, yet are in a situation where a brother has something against them, are to leave their gift and first be reconciled to their brother (Matt 5:23-24). Husbands who do not live well with their wives are likely to have their prayers hindered (1 Peter 3:7, Mal. 2:16).

To maximize the probability that what we ask will be in accordance with God's will, we must know God's character thoroughly and have His pulse on the situation at hand. A critical discipline is reading, reflecting and meditating on the scriptures in humility and gratitude. A friend of mine has read the Bible cover to cover every year for the past 30 years, spending at least an hour each day in personal devotions. Someone so steeped in scripture will understand the character of God much better than someone who has never even read the Bible through once.

Secondly, the spiritual gift of discernment is crucial. We must have the wisdom to see the situation at hand according to the spiritual context. Things are not always as they appear to be.

Thirdly, the personal holiness of the one praying is critical. God simply will not listen to those who persist in sin. For many, hidden sins such as pride, selfishness and arrogance block prayers for the simple reason that God does not want the pride situation to worsen.

Finally, an understanding of God's purposes is important. For example, we know that God desires all people to be saved and to come to knowledge of the truth (1 Tim 2:4). So praying for the salvation of people is always in accordance with God's will. However, we also know that God's character is such that God will not violate the free will of another person. To do so would be to treat that person as an object and so to negate their humanity. We also know that no one comes to a saving knowledge of Christ unless the Holy Spirit moves in them, convicting and converting them. Knowing these three biblical truths, helps us then to formulate a prayer that will invite God to move in a way that is consistent with who He is and His eternal purposes. In praying, we can preface our prayers with a statement of these three truths. We can then ask God to move in such a way that will be consistent with these things but focused on a particular individual or group. We must then be patient to allow God to move in a way that is consistent with His nature and will not violate another person.

THE "ACTS" ACROSTIC

ACTS stands for Adoration, Confession, Thanksgiving, Supplication. This simple tool has helped many to remember the elements of effective prayer. Adoration requires that I see God rightly for who He is and myself for who I am. I meditate on God's eternal attributes and praise Him, offering up my worship. It is especially helpful to bring to mind those attributes of God that bear upon my needs. If I am hungry and need food, I bring to mind how God fed the Israelites in the wilderness with manna. He allowed them to hunger for a season to test them (Deut. 8:3). He also provided all their needs and preserved their health (Ex. 15:26). I then praise God for His great providence, His mercy and wisdom. I might also recall, that the Spirit led Jesus into the wilderness to fast for 40 days and nights. Again I praise Him for His faithfulness and providence.

In confession, I humble myself and acknowledge my inner corruption. I also confess and repent of any transgressions. I commit to making restitution if necessary and commit to doing any things that I should have done but have not. Confession means clearing the slate between God and myself. Confession also brings to mind God's promise that if I confess my sin, He is faithful and just to forgive my sin and to cleanse me from all unrighteousness (1 John 1:9). Confession leads naturally into thanksgiving.

In thanksgiving, I express my gratitude to God for what He has done for me. He has forgiven my sin, saved me from a life of sin and death and recreated me after the likeness of His Son. He has adopted me as son or daughter, bestowed upon me an eternal inheritance, filled me with His Holy Spirit and betrothed me as part of His eternal bride for His Son. In addition, He has blessed me with all sorts of temporal blessings in this life. He has answered my prayers and given me much of what I have asked for. He continues to provide for all my needs and has given me a community of faith to encourage and support. Thanksgiving is essential in prayer for it reminds me of God's faithfulness and His promises. Gratitude displaces sins of anxiety, worry, complaining and criticizing. As I express my thanks, I align myself with the way things really are and enter into a frame of mind that is consistent with His Kingdom.

Supplication is the final aspect of prayer, for it follows worship, confession and thanksgiving. I am now in a frame of mind that is more in tune with God's heart and am more likely to ask for things that truly matter to Him. I can ask for wisdom, endurance, faithfulness and knowledge because I know, according to scripture, that these things please God. In faith, I rest in the assurance that I am receiving what I have asked for. In asking for things that I need or for prayers for others, I must always defer to God's will. This does not mean that I refrain from asking because of uncertainty, but that I ask wisely from a knowledge of God's character and His eternal purposes.

THE COLLECT

The Collect is a pattern of prayer that is used in worship after a time of prayer to summarize or "collect" the prayers of the people. The pattern is useful in composing prayers for it applies the principle that we have discussed. The Collect has a general form as follows:

1. Address (the person of the Trinity who is being addressed).
2. An attribute or quality of God based upon what He has done or promised to do that is related to the petition.
3. The petition, consisting of a request linked to the above attribute.
4. The reason for, or result expected from, the petition.
5. Conclusion or doxology (blessing).

For example, the following well-known prayer takes the form of a collect.

> *"Almighty God, to you all hearts are open, all desires known and from you no secrets are hidden: cleanse the thoughts of our hearts by the inspiration of your Holy Spirit, that we may perfectly love you and worthily magnify your holy name, through Jesus Christ our Lord, Amen"*[lxx]

The Address = Almighty God

The Attribute = omniscience – to you all hearts are open, all desires known, no secrets hid
The Petition = cleanse the thoughts of our hearts by the inspiration of your Holy Spirit
The Reason = that we might perfectly love you and worthily magnify your Holy name
Conclusion – through Jesus Christ our Lord, Amen

Remembering the general form of a Collect is useful in fashioning our prayers for it helps us to think through that attribute of God, which has a direct correlation to our petition. It also helps us think through the reason for the petition and frame it in a way that is likely to be in accordance with God's will.

For example, if I am praying for the salvation of a friend, Jake, I recall that it is the Holy Spirit who convicts and converts people. I also recall that God's heart is for all people to be saved, so that Jesus Christ might be glorified and His Kingdom enlarged. So in praying, I might fashion the prayer as follows:

> Holy Spirit of Truth, who convicts sinners and gives new life to those locked in sin, have mercy on my friend Jake and bring him to a place where he sees himself clearly and understands what you have done for him in Jesus Christ. For you desire that all people be saved and come to a knowledge of the truth. Fall upon Jake in power and help him respond to your grace, so that He may glorify you with his life and bring honor to your name. In the precious and Holy name of Jesus I ask these things, Amen.

If you prayed this prayer in a public gathering, no one would likely know that what you were praying was in the form of a Collect, yet they would be deeply touched by your prayer because it addressed God in a way that is consistent with who He is and His eternal purposes. It also expresses your own heartfelt compassion for Jake to God, but frames it in a way that consistent with God's will.

THE PSALMS – PRAYER BOOK OF THE BIBLE

Perhaps the greatest resource that the community of faith has for both prayer and worship is the book of Psalms, also known as the Psalter. The early church laid much emphasis on using Psalms in worship and community life.

> *"Let the word of Christ dwell in you richly, teaching and admonishing one another in all wisdom, singing psalms and hymns and spiritual songs, with thankfulness in your hearts to God." Colossians 3:16*

The Psalms depict the raw emotion of a soul seeking God. They are filled with lament, anguish, thanksgiving, praise, petition, confidence and worship. Many psalms are the heart cries of people in deep anguish and frustration over evil, treachery, oppression and sin. They are not so much to be analyzed but to be experienced. They are poetry. They throb with concrete imagery and pulsate with God's own heart.

The devotional life of any disciple must include the psalms. They are to be read aloud, memorized, and prayed through. Many faith communities over the centuries have used the Psalms as a centerpiece of worship and prayer. We express a solidarity of faith and experience with them when we pray the psalms. The psalms become a link to the universal community of saints who pray with us as we pray.

Dietrich Bonhoeffer, in *Life Together* made an interesting observation about using the psalms in prayer. [lxxi] He called it the "*Secret of the Psalter"*. As he began to use the psalms as his own personal prayers, he found that there were certain psalms or portions of psalms that he could not pray. In these Psalms, it was clear that there was another voice praying. That voice was Jesus Himself. The clue was that only God would have the right to pray that prayer. For example in Psalm 101, the first four verses are worship and consecration, which we would have no trouble praying, but in verse five, the tone changes and includes the verse *"Whoever slanders his neighbor secretly, I will destroy."* (Ps. 101:5) As mere humans, we have no right to make such a statement. However, God has every right to make such a statement and in fact, we find the rest of the psalm makes sense when we understand that it is Jesus praying on our behalf. This is true also of the psalms where the psalmist calls himself innocent devout and righteous (Ps. 18:20, 24, 35:27) and of the imprecatory psalms that call down judgment on the wicked (Ps. 5:10, 69:24, 109:7, 137:9). It is also true of psalms such as Psalm 22, where it is Jesus Himself praying through the entire psalm.

Once we realize this "secret" we can be tuned into those portions of the psalm where Jesus is praying with us. We remind ourselves that Jesus is now at the right hand of the Father ever interceding for us (Rom. 8:34). We do not pray alone. We also pray together with David, who wrote many of the psalms and that countless community of saints who have prayed these psalms in ages past. We allow ourselves to enter with them into the unspeakable misery and suffering that God's people have endured over the ages and still endure today. We become one voice with the Son crying out to the Father in communion with the Spirit. In Psalm 73, Asaph, a musician and worship leader in David's court[lxxii], is profoundly comforted in God's presence and, in the language of worship, expresses his thirst for God and his eternal confidence the Holy One of Israel.

> *"Nevertheless, I am continually with you; you hold my right hand. [24] You guide me with your counsel, and afterward you will receive me to glory. [25] Whom have I in heaven but you? And there is nothing on earth that I desire besides you. [26] My flesh and my heart may fail, but God is the strength of my heart and my portion forever."* Psalm 73:23-26

Another characteristic of the psalms is their frequent chiastic structure. An understanding of this helps us to identify the centerpiece of each psalm and to appreciate the parallelism that is evident in Hebrew poetry. Chiastic structure means that the phrases in the psalm follow the pattern ABCBA or ABCDCBA. This can also be diagramed as:

A A
B B
C C
D

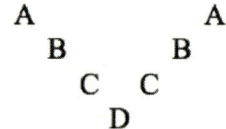

For example, take Psalm 54:

[1] *O God, save me, by your name, and vindicate me by your might.*

[2] *O God, hear my prayer; give ear to the words of my mouth.*

[3] *For strangers have risen against me; ruthless men seek my life; they do not set God before themselves. Selah*

[4] *Behold, God is my helper; the Lord is the upholder of my life.*

[5] *He will return the evil to my enemies; in your faithfulness put an end to them.*

[6] *With a freewill offering I will sacrifice to you; I will give thanks to your name, O LORD, for it is good.*

[7] *For he has delivered me from every trouble, and my eye has looked in triumph on my enemies.*

Note that the pattern ABC D CBA corresponds to verses 1 through 7. Verses 1 and 7 go together, as do 2 and 6, 3 and 5. This makes verse 4 the centerpiece or turning point of the psalm. It is the main idea and the main confidence expressed by the psalmist. This main idea is that "*God is my helper; the Lord is the upholder of my life.*" The remaining verses are centered around this idea. Notice that the two A's correspond together as verse one is a cry for salvation and verse seven, the receipt of the salvation prayed for in verse one. Likewise verse two is a petition to be heard, whereas verse six is thanksgiving for the prayer having being heard. Likewise verse three is the detailed description of the problem and verse five, the confidence that God will deal with it. This structure is both an aid to memory, and a lesson in how to pray. We begin by crying out to God to save us (vs 1). We ask that He hear our prayer. (vs 2) We then describe the problem that we are facing (vs 3). We express our faith in God as our helper (vs 4). We express our confidence that He will act on our behalf (vs 5). We give thanks for deliverance received, praising His name (vs 6). We testify to His salvation (vs 7). As you study and reflect on the psalms, you will find this same pattern in many of them, especially the shorter ones.

The Psalms have been given to us as a great treasure. In them, we have prayer modeled for us by the psalmists who wrote them but also by Jesus who prays along with us. As we pray the psalms, we join our voice to His voice and we glorify God together. In praying the psalms, we, as the betrothed bride, join our voices harmoniously together with our Bridegroom. We also suffer together, rejoice together and together yearn for the consummation of the Kingdom where our eternal wedding will take place. Our hearts cry out *"come Lord Jesus come!"* (Rev. 22:20b)

WORSHIP AND PRAYER

Like prayer, worship is the soul's response to God. Prayer and worship are intertwined for prayer rightly offered must begin with adoration (i.e. "*hallowed be thy name*") Adoration is the only appropriate response to the Bridegroom who has given Himself up to suffering and death for His bride. In worship we ascribe worth to the One who alone is worthy of adoration.

The word commonly used for worship in the New Testament is *proskuneo*. It literally means to fall down and kiss. Bernard's of Clairvaux in his *Song of Songs,* states *"the believer does not leap immediately to the intimate union of the kiss of the mouth, but rather must begin by prostrating himself before the Bridegroom and kiss his feet".* [lxxiii] Worship is the bride's sweet surrender and giving of herself with total abandon to the One who has swept her off her feet. There is a holy reverence and a complete giving of oneself in worship that makes worship first an attitude of the heart. There is a reverence and submission in true worship that comes from deep within. Worship that does not begin with the heart is just going through the empty motions of externalism. The ability to worship is a gift, for it is born entirely of faith.

A marvelous picture of faith and worship comes from an episode in Jesus life. In Luke chapter 7, He is at the home of a Pharisee, Simon for dinner. As He is reclining, a woman with a seedy reputation comes up behind Him and weeps, kissing His feet, soaking them with her tears, wiping them with her hair and anointing Him with ointment. Simon is deeply troubled in his spirit that Jesus, a rabbi would let such a woman touch Him, in what might be perceived as an erotic act. Jesus, on the other hand, uses this as an occasion to illustrate that much love is generated by much forgiveness (Luke 7:41-42). He commends the woman for her faith, which has saved her. This woman rightly understood who Jesus was, and she worshipped Him. Her worship was personal, intimate, costly and passionately steeped in gratitude for her forgiveness. Simon, on the other hand did not even offer Jesus the common courtesy of a basin to wash His feet, nor a simple kiss of fellowship. He did not see Jesus for who He was. He was not a worshipper.

Only one who has accepted Jesus Christ for who He is, worships in Spirit and in Truth, for only the Holy Spirit gives Spiritual life by empowering new birth from above. It is only through the Holy Spirit that a person can see the truth of the Kingdom (John 3:3, 5). Hence true worship is very much a *"gifted response"*. [lxxiv] As faith itself is a gift (Eph. 2:8), so also is the heart song of faith, worship. It is a movement of the Holy Spirit who descends and quickens worship directed upwards at Jesus Christ and the triune God.

Robert Webber observed that worship is also rooted in an event. In scripture, Hebrew worship most often looks back to and rehearses the divine deliverance from Egypt. Psalms 113 to 118 *(The Hallel from which we get our word Hallelulia)* are a high point of praise and thanksgiving, rehearsing and celebrating God's saving act of deliverance and pleading for continued salvation amid life's trials. Likewise Christian worship looks back to and rehearses the cross of Christ. Webber says: "*Worship tells and acts out the living, dying and rising of Christ... it celebrates God's saving deed in Jesus Christ.*"[lxxv] Hence, a component of worship is meditation on the cross of Christ and a rehearsal, celebration and retelling of the gospel. The believer's worship is rooted in the cross of Christ and is an intimate pouring out of affection and love on Christ. Hence both worship and prayer must be offered in the light of the cross, empowered by the Holy Spirit and directed toward the Triune God who alone is worthy of worship.

We often think of worship as something that is only done in church at a worship service. Yet this is not the Biblical picture that we get of worship. Jesus worshipped the Father together with His disciples without any of the trappings of a modern western worship experience. Certainly, worship often involved singing and dancing. But, it was highly participative, personal and heartfelt. It also took place in a community setting in both small groups and large gatherings during the feasts and festivals of Israel. Worship was both personal and communal, but always highly participative.

True worship comes from the heart and requires no external trappings. It is deeply personal and resonates with praise, thanksgiving and love expressed to God. Because worship is also seen and heard, it is subject to the temptation to glory in the act of worship rather than in the One who is worshipped. We must give ourselves to God alone in worship, and fight against the tendency to be so enthralled in worship that we worship the very act of worship.

Worship also extends to action. Like a faith that is without deeds is dead, so worship must include acts of worship. Acts of worship include prayer, fasting, stillness before God, solitude, meditation, scripture reading, reflection, singing, raising hands, dancing before the Lord, praising God and serving others in His name.

Worship is offering up our bodies as instruments of righteousness in His service. Old Testament priests served YHWH in that tabernacle which was for them an act of worship. Under the New Covenant, we are all called to be a royal priesthood (1 Pet. 2:9). The Apostle Paul writes:

> *"I appeal to you therefore, brothers, by the mercies of God, to present your bodies as a living sacrifice, holy and acceptable to God, which is your spiritual worship."*
> *Romans 12:1*

We are to present our bodies as a *living sacrifice*. To present a sacrifice means that the thing presented is no longer available to the one presenting it. When I present my body as a living sacrifice, it means that I surrender control over it to the One to whom I present it. Worship means surrendering myself to God and acting on His behalf. In the words of the Apostle Paul, I worship because *"it is no longer I that live but Christ who lives in me." (Gal. 2:20)*

Worship, then is the heart's response to the God of love who lavishes love on me. I worship because I am His. I worship because He is worthy. I worship because, to do otherwise, would be to live life as one ungrateful for the gifts and blessings of God. I spend my life in service of the God who died for me. I spend my life in anticipation of the promise of His return for me. I worship as an expression of my longing for the consummation of the heavenly wedding when I will be united, together with all the saints, in marriage to the Bridegroom, the King of Kings and Lord or Lords, Jesus Christ, my One and only.

Study Guide for Chapter Five

A. Questions for Personal Reflection

Record answers in your journal.

1. How would you characterize your own prayer life? Is it a natural activity like breathing or do you find that you have to force yourself to pray? What might this be symptomatic of?

2. What do you think of the notion that we are most authentically human when we pray? If Jesus was God, why was it necessary for Him to pray? (see Heb. 4:15, Heb. 5:7-8)

3. What attitudes should characterize us when we pray? (See Matt. 6:5-6, Matt. 6:7, Luke 18:10-14, Micah 6:8, Jude 1:20, Mark 11,24-25, Phil. 4:4-6)

4. Select one of the scriptures below that have to do with your own situation. Read the passage and reflect on this scripture in light of your own situation. Pray this text back to God.

   a. Protection (Gen 32:9-12)
   b. Wisdom (2 Chron 1:7-13)
   c. Healing (Mark 9:17-24)
   d. Blessing (1 Chron 4:9-10)
   e. Peace (John 14:26-27)
   f. Unity (John 17:20-23)

5. Read Psalm 69. As you read, identify those verses where Jesus is the one praying. Which sections of this psalm are natural for you to pray? Take some time to read this psalm slowly and pray sections of it back to God. Be aware of Jesus' presence with you as you pray.

B. Exercises (Individual or Large Group)

1. Read Luke 17:11-19, the story of the ten lepers. Then do the three part exercise below. The purpose of this exercise is to experience the passage and not to analyze it. Allow yourself to enter into the experience as one who was there.

    i. Imagine yourself to be one of the ten lepers who did not return to give thanks to Jesus. Why didn't you return? (5 min.)

    ii. Now imagine yourself as the one leper who did return to thank Jesus. What was it like? What did He say to you? How did you feel afterward? (5 min.)

    iii. Think of the times when God has healed you or the ways that He has blessed you. List some ways that you can give thanks to Jesus. (5 minutes)

2. In your journal, write down a particular prayer request that has been on your heart lately. Then using the pattern of the Collect on pages 127-128, write out a prayer to God. Then pray this prayer each day this week.

C. Small Group Breakout (2 or 3)

1. Read Psalm 27. Identify the Chiastic structure of this psalm. Which verse(s) are the centerpiece?

2. What does this psalm teach us about worship? What does it teach us regarding what our life should be about?

3. What is the "one thing" that your would ask God, if you had a special audience with Him?

4. Share prayer requests and take some time to pray for one another.

D. Assignment for This Week

Continue to observe five devotional times in solitude this week. Use the breath prayer *Lord God of hosts, I worship you, hear my prayer (Ps. 84:8)* . Begin with the ACTS formula. As you pray, think of the attributes of God that have a bearing on what you are asking for and incorporate these into your prayers.

1. Each day select one the Psalms below.

    a. Read the Psalm out loud.
    b. Go through the psalm 2-3 verses at a time and pray these back to God.
    c. Identify the centerpiece, turning point or main idea of the Psalm. Write this out on a card or in your journal
    d. Reflect on this as you go through your day. Commit a key verse to memory.

    (Psalm, 5, 11, 23, 46, 52, 54, 63, 84, 121, 127)

2. Continue to take 10-15 minutes at the end of each day to do a Prayer of Examen (see pages 80-82).

3. Continue the regimen of fasting, once this week (one or more meals) for a specific purpose.

4. Read chapter six. Answer the Questions for Personal Reflection your journal.

6. God's Word – The Nourishment of Love

"Man shall not live by bread alone, but by every word that comes from the mouth of God" – Matt. 4:4

Food is essential for life. Without food, the body shrivels and dies. As new creations in Christ, we require spiritual food to continue to thrive. Both Moses and Jesus likened bread to the word[6] of God (Deut. 8:3, Matt 4:4). As bread sustains and nourishes the human body, so the word of God sustains and nourishes us. It is essential to our spiritual life. As we hear the words of God, the Holy Spirit vivifies us by bestowing Himself on us. We are enlightened, convicted, restored and encouraged and our spirits are refreshed. Through the living Word, God reveals Himself, speaks to us, convicts us, blesses and bestows Himself on us.

Yet human beings by nature do not desire such heavenly food. Rather they seek to satisfy spiritual hunger and thirst by venturing into the spiritual marketplace of religion. In Isaiah chapter 55, the question is asked: *"Why do you spend your money for that which is not bread, and your labor for that which does not satisfy?"* (Isa. 55:2a) He is not referring to physical bread here, but spiritual food. The "marketplace" is full of spiritual stalls. In the midst of these, God cries out above the tumult *"Come to me everyone who thirsts, come to the waters, come buy and eat! Come buy wine and milk without money and without price.... Listen diligently to me, and eat what is good, and delight yourselves in rich food."* (Isa. 55:1,2b) God's plea to humankind is to come to Him and buy real food. We are to buy it, but it is without money or price. The metaphor of buying requires intentionality. To buy something is not just to receive it, but it is to approach the vendor and indicate a desire to make a transaction. We are to be intentional about purchasing that which God supplies without cost. What He supplies without cost is Himself, His own self-bestowal, His Son, the living Word, through whom we hear God speak and through whom the Holy Spirit grants us understanding as we listen to His voice.

---

[6] I have chosen to capitalize *Word* of God, only when referring to the incarnate Word of God, Jesus Christ. Where it refers to scripture or the uttered word, I leave it lower case, i.e word of God.

Jesus, at the high point of feast of Tabernacles, utters a similar invitation, which would have rung true with those who were familiar with Isaiah's words. He stands up on the last day of the feast, the great day, and cries out: *"If anyone thirsts, let him come to me and drink.* [38] *Whoever believes in me, as the Scripture has said, 'Out of his heart will flow rivers of living water.*'" (John 7:37-38) In doing so, Jesus restates the divine invitation to come and drink, to be intentional about seeking nourishment and refreshment from Him alone. His invitation echoes the invitation of the Holy One of Israel to buy and eat of the true bread. He also states: *"I am the bread of life; whoever comes to me shall not hunger, and whoever believes in me shall never thirst.*" (John 6:35) He is the true bread that gives life to the world (John 6:32). Jesus also admonishes His hearers to not labor for that which does not satisfy, but to seek that which truly satisfies and gives eternal life. This bread that He gives is Himself the living Word that comes down from heaven. So too the words that He speaks, give life to those who internalize them.

Meaning of the "Word of God"

The word of God is both the self-utterance of God and the Person of Jesus Christ, the incarnate Word of God. They cannot be *the word* of God in exactly the same sense for one refers to words spoken and written while the other is Person. The word of God as speech is that which God utters through the prophets and that which He endorses as speaking for Him. Hence the word of God is an aspect of revelation. What God reveals is not a book, but Himself. He is both the Author of such revelation and the content of it. The incarnate Word *(logos)* of God is the self-revelation of God in Jesus Christ, the Son who takes on human flesh. God has never been without His Word, for Christ was there in the beginning with God and it was through Him that God created everything that has been created (John 1:1-3). *Logos* (translated *word*) in Greek means word or reason. The concept was rich in Greek philosophy for it embodied the complete rationale for all that exists. *Logos* was understood to be the ultimate *reason* for all that is. The gospel writer, John, takes this Greek concept and boldly declares that the reason *(logos)* for all that exists is a Person, God incarnate, Jesus Christ. He is the self-begotten of God because He is the only begotten Son of the Father while yet fully God. In this way both word and Word of God are the self-utterance of God and the incarnate One, Jesus Christ.

It is common to refer to scripture as the word of God. Yet scripture is only one aspect (yet a crucial aspect) of God's self-utterance and is not *in itself* that self-utterance. God does not reveal words on a page, but reveals Himself. The action of the Holy Spirit is essential in such revelation for without the Spirit's illumination and action, scripture would only be words on a page.

In revealing Himself to us, God acts.[lxxvi] He then illuminates those who are the beneficiaries of such action by explaining to them exactly what He has done, is doing or will do and its significance for them. Without such illumination, we would be unaware of the significance of any of God's acts. For example, when Jesus died on the cross, two other men also died along side Him. The significance of the death of Jesus is not self-evident. We have to be told. The disciples themselves were quite confused about what it all meant. After His resurrection, Jesus spent forty days with His disciples explaining to them in detail the significance of what had just happened. That explanation then became the apostolic witness to Jesus Christ that we call *the gospel*. In that gospel, the self-revelation of God, through the proclamation of it, was illuminated by the Holy Spirit in those who would by faith be transformed into new creations as a result of hearing it. Their own testimony also became a part of the continuing apostolic witness. Subsequently, that apostolic witness was written down as gospels, history, revelations or letters to churches. These writings were then compiled by the church under the superintention of the Holy Spirit and declared to be authoritative because they were the occasion of God's self revelation through the Holy Spirit through human authors. The *Canon*[7] of scripture is that faithful prophetic and apostolic witness to Jesus Christ. The *Canonical Collection* is that list of books that the church has recognized as being faithful to that witness and now make up our Bible.

Scripture is therefore both a human witness to divine revelation and God's witness to such revelation. The human witness of such revelation endorses it and owns it as a testimony to what God has revealed to him. God also endorses it as His own words because it speaks completely and thoroughly for Him. Hence there are two authors of scripture. Both the human author and God are equally and fully co-authors.

---

[7] *Canon* means rod or standard.

Authors are intentional. They know what they wish to say and they say it. What is written can only mean what the author intended it to say. Subsequent derived or implied meanings, not intended by the author, must be rejected. This is an important principle in interpretation. A scripture can never mean what the author did not intend. But, because there are two authors, the Holy Spirit may have inspired human writers to write things whose significance they did not fully appreciate at the time. The Old Testament prophets wrote many prophecies that had an initial fulfillment close to the time of writing and also a future significance, the implications of which they themselves might not have been aware. Did the human authors fully and completely understand all the intentions of God as they wrote? Not completely, but the way scripture functions is that the Holy Spirit illuminates the readers as to God's intended meaning as that meaning is appropriated by faith and confirmed by the body of believers (see 1 John 4:1).

The Word of God is Active

While God reveals His glory to all peoples through the majesty of creation, His Personhood is revealed only through what He says and does. The laws, precepts and testimonies of God bear witness to what He is like. In Psalm 19, the psalmist begins by bearing witness to creation declaring the glory of God. He then moves into a magnificent account of the blessings that God's revelation generates.

> *"The law of the LORD is perfect, reviving the soul; The testimony of the LORD is sure, making wise the simple; The precepts of the LORD are right, rejoicing the heart; The commandment of the LORD is pure, enlightening the eyes; The fear of the LORD is clean, enduring forever; The rules of the LORD are true, and righteous altogether. More to be desired are they than gold, even much fine gold; Sweeter also than honey and drippings of the honeycomb. Moreover, by them is your servant warned; in keeping them there is great reward." Psalm 19:7-11*

Note the verbs in the passage above. God's words *revive*, *make wise*, *rejoice*, *enlighten* and *endure*. They are also *perfect, sure, true, right, desirable*, incredibly valuable and *sweeter than honey*. The words of God revive and refresh us because they are what God has given us as spiritual food. We are contingent spiritual creations who owe our very existence to God. It is through the word of God and the Holy Spirit that we come to understand that Jesus is the Christ and that He died to redeem us to Himself. The hearing of the word of God and the action of the Holy Spirit are the occasion that introduces us to the living Word Jesus Christ who is the Source of that life. The words of God give spiritual life for it is in them that God acts through the Holy Spirit to impart life to that which is dead. These words also sustain, refresh and renew us for it is through them that the Holy Spirit operates.

Moreover the word of God operates on us in ways that perform divine surgery on our calcified hearts. "*For the word of God is living and active, sharper than any two-edged sword, piercing to the division of soul and of spirit, of joints and of marrow, and discerning the thoughts and intentions of the heart.*" (Hebrews 4:12) The human heart is sick and deceitful above all else (Jer. 17:9). Our inner corruption inherited from Adam and Eve defiles our heart so that it cannot be trusted. In our natural state, we are unable to do the good required of us, for our sinful selves taint even our most loving acts. It is the Holy Spirit who vivifies us as we hear the word of God, making it that alive and active surgical scalpel that pierces into the depths of our spirit, laying bear the thoughts and motives of our inmost being. As this happens, we are cut to the heart and convicted of sin. Such conviction leads us into repentance and bids us to put to death that which is the source of sin in us, our sinful-self, through the power of the Holy Spirit, who then moulds us bit by bit into the image of Christ. Sanctification is the fruit of the activity of Holy Spirit through the word of God.

So we have in the Holy Scriptures an immense treasure. Yet how are we to approach this treasure? For centuries the church entrusted this treasure solely into the hands of a clergy class, who alone were allowed to interpret it. It is astonishing that as late as 1965, it was against church law in one major denomination for ordinary people to read the scriptures. Moreover, many reformation saints, such as William Tyndale, and John Huss, were burned at the stake for daring to make the scriptures available in the language of their people. These men believed that the scriptures ought to be available to the common person because the reading and hearing of scripture was the occasion of God's self-revelation through the Holy Spirit. The scriptures were the words of life that sustained God's people and fed them. Hence scripture was not to be bound nor controlled, but was to be made freely available to all.

The Origins of the Bible

In a pocket Bible, given to my parents on the occasion of our family becoming Canadian citizens, is this inscription from the coronation service of Queen Elizabeth II:

> *"OUR GRACIOUS QUEEN, WE PRESENT YOU WITH THIS BOOK, THE MOST VALUABLE THING THAT THE WORLD AFFORDS. HERE IS WISDOM; THIS IS THE ROYAL LAW; THESE ARE THE LIVELY ORACLES OF GOD"*

Our modern Bible is indeed a product of God's amazing grace in faithfully creating and preserving this treasure for us. The Old and New Testaments which make up our Bible were written by the Prophets and Apostles, men who had a first hand experience of God. They experienced God in action. Moses met God at Horeb and watched as God performed amazing signs before him. He heard God's voice, coming out of the fire. God subsequently commissioned him to be the agent of the redemption of God's people out of slavery in Egypt. As Moses wrote down God's words, he learned of how God created the world and of God's acts throughout the generations from Adam to the time in which Moses lived. Through this process, God revealed Himself to the nation Israel as Creator, only *after* He had revealed Himself as Redeemer. So too, we only come to understand the origin of human life as we come to faith in Jesus Christ, our Redeemer who then illumines us to understand and place our faith in the divine account. What Moses and the other prophets wrote, God superintended and claimed as His own words. He also superintended the collection and duplication of the scriptures by providing scribes who faithfully and meticulously copied the ancient texts for each generation.

The Old Testament was written in Hebrew, with portions in Aramaic, while the New Testament was written in Greek, the global language of the first century. We have a great many ancient manuscripts written in these languages, which show an amazing degree of consistency. In the few places where there are textual variants, these are noted in most modern translations and impact very little on the overall meaning.

The discipline of textual criticism is the study of these manuscripts to determine dating and to establish probabilities of which ones were likely original copies. Bible translators diligently practice this discipline. In the middle ages, these original language texts were translated into Latin for the Western (Roman) church. This translation became the Vulgate, the Latin version of the Bible. During this era, common people were not permitted to have or read the Bible, as it was feared that it would be misinterpreted. Most could not read Latin in any case, so it was up to the priests and clergy to interpret the content. The Old Testament translation into Greek by a group of seventy scholars became known as the Septuagint and was used extensively in the Eastern church.

During the Protestant Reformation, the idea gained prominence that the scriptures alone were to inform faith rather than the traditions and decrees of the church. It was through a careful reading of the scriptures that the reformers, men like Martin Luther, Jean Calvin, John Wycliff and William Tyndale became convinced that the traditions of the Roman church obscured the gospel and distorted the revelation of God. Their passion was to provide translations of the scriptures into the language of the people. As these translations were published and multiplied through the advent of the printing press, modern versions of the Bible began to emerge in German, French, English and many other languages. The translators, who created these translations, were Godly men, many of whom were martyred for going against the religious establishment.

Today, there are many English translations of the Bible available. The early versions, ones such as the Wycliffe Bible were translated from the Latin Vulgate. Later translations such as the King James were translated from the original Hebrew and Greek, but were translated by committees that sought conformity with the ecclesiastical structure of the current church and so preserved certain terms that were already in use. More modern versions each have their own philosophies of translation. Some, like the English Standard Version (ESV), seek to preserve as closely as possible the original word structures without sounding wooden. Others like the New International Version (NIV) and the New English Bible (NEB), tend to be sentence for sentence translations. Paraphrase versions like "*The Message*" [lxxvii] try to interpret and restate the meaning into colloquial language. The English-speaking believer today is faced with a vast range of options in selecting a Bible. The choice is a personal one. However, for those who wish to be detailed exegetes, it is important to select a translation where the translators have not already done the interpretive task. My own personal preference is to use a version that is close to the original language and make my own interpretive decisions, so I use the English Standard Version (ESV) or the New Revised Standard Version (NRSV). When studying, I look to the original language or consult good Bible commentaries, where credible scholars examine the original language usage and nuances.

Approaching the Scriptures

In reading scripture, we must begin with faith and a humble, prayerful stance. God discloses Himself through eyes of faith. If we come to the scriptures as skeptics, we encounter only words on a page, for the Holy Spirit will not normally illuminate skepticism. When I first began to study the Bible, I realized that I needed to adopt some sort of stance. Intuitively, God gave me insight to know that if I approached it from a position of doubt, then I would not likely gain much. So I consciously decided to assume that it was all true and the word of God. As I read, the Holy Spirit began to testify to my spirit and I found it not only true, but life giving. I had discovered living water. Yet I soon came up against many questions. I discovered among the Old Testament patriarchs a lifestyle that was foreign to what I felt God desired. They had several wives, many concubines and frequently fell short of righteousness. I found that I needed someone to guide me in interpreting what I was reading. And how was I to assume that any one school of interpretation was correct? I needed to learn some principles that would keep me from error. I needed to learn how to extract the meaning of the text properly. This is the discipline of exegesis.

Exegesis

To determine the meaning of a particular text or portion of scripture, we must begin by asking the right questions of the text.[lxxviii] What message is a Biblical author communicating to the people to whom he writes? There are of two kinds of questions we can ask of a text, context questions and content. *Contextua*l questions force us to examine the time, the culture, the political situation, the historical context, covenantal obligations and the language of that people. These questions force us to examine what the situation was with the people to whom the original words were written. *Content* questions relate to identifying what the Biblical author was actually saying about the subject that he was writing about. In considering content issues it is important to look at the meaning of the words chosen, literary constructs, metaphors and the implications of grammar and idiom.

A key principle is that "meaning" is located primarily in the author's divinely inspired intended message. Authors are intentional. A text can never mean what the author did not intend. Authors do not take kindly to being misquoted, misinterpreted or misconstrued. What makes scripture unique is that there are two authors. The human author is writing, but his writing is being superintended by the Holy Spirit, the divine Author. God as Author is intentional in His word. He means one thing and not another. The goal of exegesis is to discover that divine intent. Because the Holy Spirit is the ultimate Author, we must not allow the *reader's response* to be the measure of what the text means. The reader's response is important and impacts *the significance* of the text in the life of the reader, but it can never determine the meaning of the text. There is a difference between significance and meaning.

Significance is the application of that meaning in the life situation of the reader. Meaning is grounded in the intentionality of the author. The Apostle Paul was intentional when he wrote correcting the misunderstanding that the Corinthians had about not associating with immoral people (1 Cor. 5:9-10). He wrote intentionally to correct the misunderstanding that they had concerning the intent of his previous letter. They understood it to mean people outside the church. Paul meant those inside the church. It was his intent that was the issue. Similarly, God has intended certain meanings to be taken from scripture. Jesus often had to correct the experts in the law for their interpretation was wrong (Matt. 22:29).

There is a danger in subjective reading of scripture that meanings not intended by God be taken from the text. One woman, that I knew, felt that God was telling her to leave her church because she had read in the Bible that morning *"But seek not Bethel ....and Bethel shall come to nought"* (Amos 5:5 KJV). The name of her church was Bethel.

We understand that the role of the Holy Spirit is to guide us into all truth (John 16:13). However, we also recognize that there are other spirits in the world, which are not the Spirit of Christ (1 John 4:1). In addition, our own hearts are deceitful and can lead us astray (Jer. 17:9). Well-intentioned people who claim divine illumination can misinterpret certain texts and lead others astray. Therefore, it is important that every disciple of Christ have a basic understanding of principles of interpretation that are theologically sound.

While the first task of the exegete is a historical one, that is to determine the author's intended meaning, this first task is not the ultimate one.[lxxix] The ultimate task is a spiritual one, to hear the text in such a way as to allow the Holy Spirit to lead the reader/hearer into the worship of God and into conformity with His will and His ways.

For example, what value is it for us to exegete Galatians 2:*20 "I have been crucified with Christ. It is no longer I who live, but Christ who lives in me."* in purely descriptive terms, if we do not engage in Paul's own intent that the Galatians themselves take this view of their present life? As a reader, I must enter into their experience and be confronted by the reality of what *living* means to me. What statement would I use to describe my life? (i.e. "for me to live is to be free to do what I want") By contrast, as the Holy Spirit convicts me, I am cut to the heart and repent crying out with Paul "I too have been crucified, and Christ lives in me." In this way, I enter into Paul's own experience and my spiritual life becomes like his in unity with God.

Because we are self-centered beings, when we approach scripture, we tend to see ourselves as the subject trying to make sense out of the text, which is the object. This is a classic "scientific knowing" approach. However, we must understand that, when we read a text of scripture, we are encountering a Person, God Himself who seeks to speak to us. The appropriate stance is to consider ourselves the object being addressed by God who is the Subject. Because the scripture is God's word, it is the means through which God (the divine Subject) operates on us, the object. During the process of exegesis, we *momentarily* reverse the roles as we act as subject examining the text, which becomes the object. In doing so, we apply the principles and the process of interpretation. But the process is not complete until we return to the proper posture of humbling ourselves as human objects being molded by the Subject, the Holy Spirit. God desires to transform us through an encounter with Him.

In Biblical exegesis, we are studying God's word. God speaks to us and we listen, but we must hear the text on God's terms and not on ours. We must be careful not to place too much emphasis on the reader/hearer and not enough on the intentionality of the author. Thus the practice of Holy Reading, which we have been practicing in our devotional times, must be balanced by a proper exegetical approach to the text. We must desire to hear what God is saying to us and be ready to obey, to order our lives around it. Our obedience is acted out in the community of faith in which we live and move, a community committed to listening to God and walking in His ways. Together we move into a unity of Spirit with the divine Author, who says to us "Follow Me".

Interpretive Issues

CONTEXT

In approaching any text of scripture, we must first become aware of a number of contexts. A context is the setting in which the text was written or the setting in which the reader sits. There is the human author's context and reader's context. Most of the interpretive questions involve the human author's context, however, in identifying both meaning and significance, it is essential that we also consider the context of the reader. As we approach the scriptures we must be aware that our own cultural situation can lead us away from the true meaning of the text through any pre-understanding and bias that we bring to the text. Our own cultural situation is a result of our familial upbringing as well as the country, region and city in which we grew up. These influences color our thought processes in ways that are both conscious and unconscious.

For example, Americans generally grow up with positive feelings about the origin of the United Sates. The Boston tea party, which was essentially a tax revolt, is seen in a positive light as is the American Revolution itself. However, for someone who grew up in Canada just a north of the 49th parallel, the American revolution is seen in less favorable light. From a Christian ethical perspective, we might ask: "Was it right for the rebels to dump someone else's property into the Boston harbor because they disagreed with the government's taxation policy?" In light of Romans 13:1, is it right to rebel against the ruling authorities for economic reasons? You would have received two different opinions in 1776 depending on which side of the border you were on. Many Americans fled the American States and moved north to Canada and were called United Empire Loyalists by those north of the border and traitors by those south of the border. The origins of the United States are seen differently by school curriculums in the U.S. and Canada. These result in many different points of view on issues such as the "right to bear arms", gun legislation, the role of government, defense, health care, civil liberties and so on. This is just one example contrasting two cultures, which in many ways are very similar. Now if you take that same principle and imagine yourself growing up in South Africa or India or China, you can begin to appreciate the role of cultural context in interpretation.

Because of this, we all tend to come to the scriptures with a certain amount of pre-understanding. The conviction that our particular pre-understanding is correct breeds pride, through which we prejudge that our pre-understanding is right even before we study the text. Similarly, we can approach a text with certain theological presuppositions based upon our church background and spiritual history. So we must always be aware of our own context.

LANGUAGE

Moreover, we use language and approach literature in certain ways, which are culturally specific. People in different parts of the world who speak different languages approach language differently than we do. For example, the entire Old Testament was written in Hebrew (small portions in Aramaic), which is an Eastern language. That part of the world thinks differently than we do and uses language differently. Our own heritage is decidedly Western, Roman and Greek in origin and so when we come to the Old Testament we come to it with a Greek Roman mind-set. The New Testament, however, was written in Greek. Therefore as we go back and forth between the testaments, we need to shift gears in our understanding of language. The two tables that follow, list some of the differences between the Greek and Hebrew approach to literature and thinking.

Generally Hebrew language uses concrete word pictures to get and idea across. Phrases such as *"stiff necked people"* (Ex. 32:9) and *"brood of vipers"* (Matt. 3:7) are used to convey the ideas of stubbornness and wickedness. In Greek thinking, we tend to use abstract language with philosophical and sociological terms rather that such concrete word pictures. In addition, Greek thinking is preoccupied with details and "how" questions. Hebrew thinking is primarily concerned with "why" and "what does it mean" questions. So when we as Westerners come to the creation accounts in Genesis 1 and 2, we come with all sorts of how questions and tend to focus on the details or the narrative rather that the overall message that the narrative conveys.

Hebrew Thinking	**Greek Thinking**
Reality = God	Reality = Matter
Main Concern = Theology	Main Concern =Technology
Approach = Holistic	Approach = Analytical
Asks "Why"	Asks "How"
Asks "Meaning"	Asks "Cause"
Supernatural / Mystery	Natural
Concrete – Picture Language	Abstract
Corporate	Individual
Figurative/Symbolic	Literal
Involved	Detached
Feelings/Intuition	Thought

For example a Western author might write a description of a family situation as:

> If the mother cannot control her emotional feelings in the context of the marriage relationship and the father is unable to express the nuances of tenderness, then it is likely that the child will develop feelings which are difficult to reconcile, extremely complex and a frustration to his own emotional development.

A Hebrew author might write the same description as:

> If the father chews garlic and the mother eats onions, you can't expect the child to smell like a rose.

Note the dramatically different approaches in expressing a simple truth. Therefore it is essential in approaching scripture that we become aware of the differences in our own cultural and linguistic predispositions. We also approach the Old and New Testaments differently.

COVENANT

We must appreciate that the Old Testament was written to a people who were under the Old Covenant. Moses wrote the Pentateuch (first five books) after the people of Israel were redeemed from Egypt. Then they were brought to Mount Sinai, where God held a very specific covenant ceremony with them described in Exodus 24. In that covenant, God identified Himself as the God who brought them out of slavery in Egypt and redeemed them with an outstretched arm (Ex. 20:2). Consequently, they were to be a Kingdom of priests and a holy nation, and were to obey the laws, rules and statutes that God gave them through Moses. Such obedience was to be the fruit of faith, trust, love and gratitude. Essentially God was saying to them something like: "You were slaves in Egypt facing genocide and annihilation. I brought you out of Egypt and have taken you as a people for my own possession in order to proclaim my Holiness, Glory and Wisdom to the nations. So then, you are to be Holy and you shall live according to this law." The law was God's creative will and work in a society that was called to live in love, justice, compassion and gratitude. It was never meant to be a means of righteousness, but was to be a faith and love response to the God with whom they already had a relationship, initiated by God.

Everything about Old Covenant Israel, it's laws, festivals, priesthood, tabernacle and temple worship, and sacrificial system pointed forward to Jesus Christ, that one true human covenant partner with God, with whom the Father is well pleased. Jesus is the fulfillment and the culmination of the Law and the Prophets (Matt. 5:17). Consequently, upon His death and resurrection, the Old Covenant was fulfilled and is now obsolete. The Greek word translated "fulfilled" in Mathew 5:17 is *playrao.* It means to bring something to fullness, to completion. In the eighth chapter of Hebrews, the writer discusses the relationship between the Old and New Covenant and concludes:

> *"In speaking of a new covenant, he makes the first one obsolete. And what is becoming obsolete and growing old is ready to vanish away." Hebrews 8:13*

So we as believers now live in the era of the New Covenant in Jesus' own blood (Luke 22:20, 1 Cor. 11:25, Heb. 12:24). We are no longer under the Old Testament law, for it has been fulfilled and completed in Christ (Rom. 6:14, 7:6, Gal. 5:18). So then how are we to interpret much of the Old Testament? We cannot interpret Old Testament laws as divine commands that are still in force today in the same way that they were in force in ancient Israel. If we were to do that, we would have to enumerate all 613 individual commandments (the Hebrew *Mishnah)* and live by them. These commandments include stoning adulterers and rebellious children (Deut 22:24, 21:21), the laws related to animal sacrifices, the priesthood, temple service, the feasts and festivals of Israel, the dietary laws and the laws relating to the Sabbath.

Moreover, Gentile (non Jewish) believers have never been required to obey the Old Covenant laws. The Jerusalem Council in Acts chapter 15 was convened for the express purpose of considering the question of Gentile converts to Christ. Were they to be required to keep the Old Testament law (Acts 15:5)? The Council, presided over by James, concluded no. They need only abstain from sexual immorality, from drinking blood and eating meat from animals strangled or sacrificed to idols (Acts 15:20).

Nevertheless, despite the clear teaching of the New Testament regarding the Old Covenant law, there are faith communities, who maintain that keeping of the Old Testament law (The Torah) is required for Christians today. Clearly, we have a major interpretive issue here that illustrates the importance of developing a proper hermeneutic for the Old Testament. What these communities miss is the clear teaching of the New Testament that we are released from the Old Testament law and now live under the law of love articulated by Jesus in the Sermon on the Mount (Matt. 5-7). Yet the moral and ethical aspects of the Old Covenant law are still applicable, for God's heart and will have not changed. We must not disregard the Old Testament. Everything written in scripture is for our instruction and is profitable (Rom 15:4, 2 Tim 3:16). So we need to establish an interpretive process that will faithfully show us how to extract and apply both the meaning and the significance of the Old Testament today.

The Interpretive Journey

Scott Duvall and Daniel Hays in their book *Grasping God's Word*[lxxx], outline an interpretive journey that can be used to determine the meaning on any text. They point out that we do not create meaning from a text but rather discover the meaning that God intended. We also determine the significance and the applicability of that meaning to our context today. Because the text was written to an ancient audience, we must consider the context in which that audience lived. We must also consider the context in which we live today. This interpretive journey will allow us to discover the theological principles, which come from God's communication to His people throughout different periods in history. While the specifics of a certain passage may only apply to their situation, the principles behind the message are universal and applicable for any time and any people. God is the same yesterday, today and forever (Heb. 13:8) and His character, His heart and His purposes are eternal. Discovering the theological principle between any passage allows us to construct a *principalizing bridge*[lxxxi] that will allow us to span the river of differences between the two contexts. In some cases, the bridge will be very small and perhaps even non-existent because differences are minimal. In other cases, the differences in context will be large and we will have to build a large principalizing bridge.

The journey starts with a careful reading of the text. The journey ends with an understanding of the meaning of the text so that we can respond to the Holy Spirit's call to change our lives as a result of hearing God's voice through it. Duvall and Hays outline four steps in this interpretive journey.[lxxxii]

STEP 1: UNDERSTAND THE TEXT IN THE ORIGINAL CONTEXT

Question: What did the text mean to the Biblical Audience?

In this step we must read the text carefully and observe all that we can. We have to identify the broad context of this passage. How does it fit into the entire biblical narrative? What is God doing among His people at this point in their history? What is the cultural, geographic, political, religious situation? Who is the author? What is the author's situation, role and context? Secondly, we have to identify the immediate context. What specifically is happening? What sort of literature (genre) is this passage? There are differences in how one communicates a message in poetry, historical narrative and prophecy. Apocalyptic passages cannot always be taken literally, but paint vivid, concrete pictures of events and scenes in a way where the author seeks to communicate a certain message. What is the content of the passage? We must also observe the specifics of the passage, identifying key words, parallel structures, metaphors, comparisons, sentence structure, nouns, verbs and adjectives that are used.

STEP 2: DETERMINE THE DIFFERENCES BETWEEN THE ORIGINAL CONTEXT AND OURS

Question: What are the differences between the Biblical audience and us?

As believers today, we are separated from the Biblical audience to whom the text was written by differences in culture, language, time, situation and, in many cases, the covenant that we live under. As Duvall and Hayes put it, "these differences form a river that hinders us from moving straight from meaning in their context to meaning in ours".[lxxxiii] Sometimes the width of this river is enormous and we cannot simply take the text at face value. Other times, the width of the river is minute and we can just step across without any difficulty. For example, through Moses, God gave the Israelites the Ten Commandments. Most of these commandments are moral laws such as "Thou shall not murder" (Exodus 20:13). This particular commandment is a moral one and means exactly the same then as it does now. It doesn't matter that they lived in the wilderness, under the Old Covenant (Ex. 24:7-8) and we live under the new covenant in Jesus blood (Luke 22:20). The principle is the same. It is morally reprehensible to take another person's life and God prohibits it. However, in the very next chapter of Exodus, we have this commandment: "Whoever curses his father or mother shall be put to death" (Ex. 21:17). While the prohibition of murder is a moral law that is just as applicable today, we must recognize that this particular commandment was part of the civil law of the people of Israel who were nomads wandering in the dessert. This law identifies not only an offense (cursing parents), but also prescribes the penalty (death). Together with other civil and ceremonial laws, these laws and penalties were part of the Covenant that God had made with the people at Mt Sinai, which they had agreed to obey (Ex. 19:8). Today, we are not under the Old Covenant. It has been fulfilled and completed in Jesus Christ and we are now a part of His people who are under the New Covenant in His blood (Heb. 8:13). In the case of this text, the width of the river of differences is large. So we must construct a principalizing bridge in order to deduce the principle behind this commandment and then translate that principle into our context today.

STEP 3: IDENTIFY THE PRINCIPLE THAT SUPERCEDES CONTEXT

Question: What is the theological principle in this text?

This is the most difficult step of the interpretive journey for in it we are seeking the theological principle represented by the text. We are really seeking God's heart and God's will about the subject at hand. This theological principle is part of the meaning of the text. It is what God wanted to communicate to the people of that day. The principle should apply equally to them and to us. It should also be consistent with the teaching of the rest of scripture. It should reflect God's heart and will for both them and us. In the example above regarding cursing parents, we can conclude that God has instituted the relationship between children and parents. Children are placed under the authority of their parents. They are to honor their parents (Ex. 20:12). Therefore to curse parents is not only to fail to honor them, but to do the opposite. It is an act of outright rebellion against the authority that God has instituted and should be punished most severely. Under the Old Covenant, rebellion was not to be tolerated and threatened the entire faith community. Such evil needed to be purged. The offender was to be put to death. So the principle behind this text is that deliberately cursing parents is an evil act of rebellion and will not be tolerated in the community of faith. In the next step, we will construct how to apply this today.

Duvall and Hayes identify five criteria for formulating theological principles.

> *"The principle should be reflected in the text.*
> *The principle should be timeless and not tied to a specific situation.*
> *The principle should not be culturally bound.*
> *The principle should correspond to the rest of the teaching of scripture.*
> *The principle should be relevant to both the Biblical and the contemporary audience."*[lxxxiv]

STEP 4: APPLY THAT PRINCIPLE TO OUR CONTEXT

Question: How should individual Christians today apply the theological principle in their lives?

In this step, we take the principle, which reflects God's heart and the message of the passage and apply it to our own situation today. In the example above, if a child curses a parent, we first must conclude that this is a very serious issue. It is an issue of rebellion against God ordained authority and hence a rebellion against God. If this were to happen in our context, we would certainly not execute the child (that would violate our current criminal law). But we ought to sit down with the child and explain this principle. We should sit down and show them the Old Testament passage and explain the situation then and now. We should point out that rebellion against Godly authority breaks God's heart and provokes His anger. Rebellion is dealt with very harshly in scripture. It is like the sin of witchcraft (1 Sam. 15:23) and will not be tolerated. If the sin were to persist, the child ought to be severely censured by the community of faith. The leadership of that community would determine the details of that censure.

In approaching the text in this way, we do not minimize the text, nor do we blindly follow it to the letter, but we seek the true meaning and it's significance to us today. We seek to order our lives around it, for these words reflect the heart of God.

Identifying the "Main Idea"

In identifying the message of any text to the original audience, it is useful to ask "What is the *Main Idea*?". Haddon Robinson, a professor of preaching, discovered that effective communication always articulates a main idea. This idea consists of two parts: *Subject* and *Complement.*[lxxxv] The Subject will be one concept. The Complement could consist of several.

Subject = What is the author is talking about?

Complement = What is the author is saying about it?
(the Subject)

This terminology is taken from grammar where a simple sentence like "God is Love" has a subject, *God* and a complement, *Love.* To understand the *Main Idea*, it is essential to know both the subject and the complement. Often communicators cause great confusion because they go on and on without ever telling people what exactly they are talking about and then what exactly they are saying about it. It is helpful to state the subject in the form of a question that is then answered by the complement. For example, if we take as a sample text, Psalm 117:

> *Praise the LORD, all nations!*
> *Extol him, all peoples!*
> *For great is his steadfast love toward us, and*
> *The faithfulness of the LORD endures forever.*
> *Praise the LORD!*

To undercover the main idea, we must ask ourselves "What is the author talking about?" One might say: "Praising the Lord" but that is much too general. To make it more specific, it helps to put the subject in the form of a question. We could say that the author is focusing on the question "Why should people praise the Lord?" This then would the subject. It is what the author is talking about. The complement would then be the answer to this question according to the author. Here we would have:

Subject: Why should people praise the Lord?

Complement: because His steadfast love towards them is great
because His faithfulness endures forever.

Note that here Complement has two parts because there are two reasons given in the text. Having understood the main idea, we are now in a better position to understand the meaning of the text to the original audience.

Main Idea thinking can help us to discover not only what the text meant to the original audience and can also help us to determine the overall principle and how to express that meaning today. It is very helpful for us to examine passages of scripture in this light. We should always be asking ourselves what the author of a particular passage is talking about, and what message he is communicating. While this sounds like a highly intellectual exercise, it can happen very intuitively. The role of the Holy Spirit in reading scripture is to lead us into all truth (John 16:13).

For example, let's take a Biblical passage that most of us will be familiar with, David and Goliath. This passage occurs in the book of 1st Samuel chapter 17. This story is about a time when the Hebrew army was being intimidated by the Philistine army, especially by the giant Goliath. The Hebrews were hiding in caves and among rocks and cowering in fear. David comes along as a young boy who is just visiting and is astounded that the armies of God are paralyzed in such fear. His experience with God was that God is a faithful deliverer of His people. David steps up and volunteers to face Goliath and prevails with a sling and a stone. He kills Goliath and the armies of God are energized to rout the Philistines.

So, in asking the question what is the author talking about, we see that it is not just a story about some battle. Rather the message behind the story is that God's people ought not to cower in fear of their enemies. So we might say that the Subject is: "How should God's people respond when they face enemies and situations that seem insurmountable? That is what the author is talking about. Then the Complement is the answer to that question given through the story. "They should remember who they are and who God is and step out in faith with confidence, for God has promised to be with them and deliver them. Others will be inspired by their courageous action."

That is the primary message of the story. David is presented as a faithful Hebrew for he has a keen sense of who he is, who God's people are and God's faithfulness. His courage inspired an army and a nation. We can then apply this principle to our own situation today. We are not the Hebrew people fighting the Philistines. But we are God's people and we are engaged in spiritual conflict with the powers and principalities of the world (Eph. 6:12). So when we are faced with insurmountable odds in the spiritual realm, we must step forward in confidence that in Christ the evil one has already been defeated and God will deliver us and enable us to be victorious in our struggle against evil. We too should step out in faith and courage like David did.

The Discipline of Feeding on the Word of God

In giving us the scriptures, God has given us Himself. The word of God in scripture is an aspect of the incarnate Word of God, Jesus Christ. He is the *"living bread that came down from heaven"* (John 6:51). The scriptures are also a love letter that our betrothed Bridegroom has given us to sustain us until He returns. If we truly love Him, we will earnestly desire to read and re read His letter to us. A love struck teenager, who receives his first love letter from his girlfriend, will pour over it again and again, mulling over every word and relishing its content. How much more should we pour over the scriptures, which have been given to nourish, encourage and strengthen us.

MEDITATION

Meditation (reflecting or pondering) on scripture is an essential aspect of devotional life. Imagine the love struck teenager described above. As he goes through his girlfriend's letter, he will ponder over passages and phrases, rolling them over in his mind. Why did she use that word, why not another? What was in her heart when she penned that? He will relish each sentence and word, reflecting on them over and over in his mind.

In the same way, we should we also approach our Bride-groom's letter to us. Meditating on scripture ought to be done in very small chunks. We might take one verse or a portion of a verse and mull it over in our minds for an entire week. We might memorize it and pray it back to God, we bask in the glow of a promise and think about the implications. As we do so, we press into Christ and increase our yearning for Him. Meditation invites us to bask in the glow of a verse that has jumped out of the scriptures and seems to have a special significance to our situation. We might easily hang onto a phrase, an admonition or a promise that the Holy Spirit wants us to internalize. As we do so, we begin to act in concert with God's heart. We become more and more in tune with Him. We become more completely His.

MEMORIZATION

Memorizing scripture is a powerful way of making God's word a part of us. When we commit a verse to memory, it is instantly available to us at any time, to reflect on, to share with others or to pray. We also make it available to our subconscious so that even in our sleep, it can form us. A friend of mine works daily at memorizing scripture. He writes scripture passages out on small cards and takes them into work with him. As he works, he goes over each scripture and reflects on it. This allows him to have a vast array of passages instantly available when he is speaking or praying with others. As he car pools to work, fellow commuters will often notice his scripture cards and ask him about them. He has had the privilege of leading several people to Christ as a result of this practice.

Another variant of chapter/verse memorization, is committing to memory what scriptures say from the familiarity of having read them over and over again. Due to my own personal discipline of scripture reading, I have read the entire Bible ten times over the past ten years. This practice makes me so familiar with scripture that I can quote the essence of a passage from memory, and I know generally where it is found if I need to look it up. The author of the book of Hebrews is continually quoting Old Testament passages that he knows exist, even though he does not give chapter and verse. In this way, he makes it part of his argument for the superiority of the New Covenant in Christ over the old.

PRAYER

Scripture reading, meditation and memorization should always be accompanied with prayer. As we read, meditate and memorize, God speaks to us through His word. It will become a one sided relationship if we only receive but never respond to our Lord. Hence, pausing to pray often is vital. We pray for clarity of understanding, for open hearts, for the putting to death of our sinful self, for the cleansing of our hearts and minds and for the anxieties that beset us as we read. We pray worshipping and adoring the One who addresses us through His word. We pray that the Holy Spirit will work deep in our hearts to form us through our reading, reflecting and memorizing. We can also pray scripture back to God. As we read, we express to Him whatever a scripture brings into our hearts. Such prayer will be a spontaneous response to that which we hear God saying to us through His word.

Prayer facilitates our taking a humble posture with regard to God's word. We do not approach Him as experts but as little children sitting at His feet. We submit to Him and learn from the One who took on the form of a servant, lowly and humble. We imitate Him in His love and we pray for others as His Spirit directs us. Abiding in Him means to abide in His word and to abide in prayer and in worship.

* * * * *

The scriptures give us so much inspiration and life on so many levels. They do this because hearing or reading scripture is the occasion of revelation through the Holy Spirit and a continual abiding in Christ. But, if we rarely read or hear scripture read, we do not benefit. Just living next to a grocery store, does us no good if we never go in and buy food to eat. So many Christians go to church once a week and fill up with spiritual food but then never eat again until the next Sunday. In doing so they gradually starve themselves spiritually, impoverish their souls and allow their love to grow cold. The discipline of being daily in God's word is critical to spiritual life.

As a pastor, when couples come to me for counseling with all sorts of problems, a common problem is that they are not daily reading scripture. They are neglecting one of the great Spiritual resources that God has given to us. Not being in the Word, they give no occasion for the Holy Spirit to feed them. They are not feeding on the Bread of life that came down from heaven. They are not relishing their relationship with their divine Bridegroom, Jesus Christ. In this sorry state of spiritual starvation, their own relationships wither. As they are both drifting away from Christ, so too they are drifting away from each other.

To avoid this, every follower of Christ must have a plan for being daily in the word of God. There are many such plans, which have been published, but the simplest is the *three bookmark plan*. In this plan you simply take three bookmarks. Place one in your Bible in Genesis 1, the second in Psalm 1 and the third in Matthew 1. Each day, you read one chapter in the Psalms and Proverbs, one chapter in the Old Testament and one chapter in the New Testament. Once you complete a section, you start over again. In this way, you will read through the Old Testament every two years, the New Testament every eight months and the Psalms and Proverbs every six months. As you read, it is important to read formationally, allowing the Holy Spirit to form you. As you study a passage, you should also apply the interpretive principles we have examined to help you meditate on God's Word.

Reading, meditation, memorization and immersion into scripture ought to become a cornerstone of your devotional life. As you read and respond in worship and prayer, God will begin to move your heart and mold it into conformance with His. He will sustain you and renew you daily in your relationship with Him. He is the living Word. He commands you to abide in Him. So pick up and read, listen, memorize and reflect. Then do what the Holy Spirit asks of you.

Study Guide for Chapter Six

A. Questions for Personal Reflection

Record answers in your journal.

1. Have you ever experienced acute physical hunger? What do you recall about that experience? In what ways is spiritual hunger similar? How would you classify your degree of spiritual hunger (on a scale of 1-10)? How is spiritual hunger good for us?

2. What are the similarities in feeding on the words of God in scripture and feeding on the Word of God, Jesus Christ? What are the differences?

3. It has been said that we ought to read God's word in the same way that a love struck teenager would read his first love letter.[lxxxvi] How do you imagine that a love struck teenager would read such a letter? Be specific.

4. Apply the interpretive journey (pages 155-159) to the following scriptures (Joshua 1:1-9, Malachi 1:6-8). Write down your observations in your journal. What research could help you as you answer?

5. Articulate the *Main Idea* of the two passages above according to Haddon Robison's pattern. (pages 159-161) Record the Subject and Complement in your journal. How has this way of looking at a passage helped you?

B. Exercises (Individual or Large Group)

1. To help identify the meaning of a text, we must analyze the use of language looking for things such as repetition, contrasts, comparisons, lists, cause and effect, figures of speech, conjunctions (and, but, however, therefore), verbs and pronouns. One technique that helps analyze sentences and paragraphs is to reproduce the text by printing it out and then using

a pen or pencil to circle words, patterns, lists, verbs and so on. This technique allows us to make as many detailed observations as possible. It is called "Content Analysis".

Use the space below to circle and make notes of the features listed above in the following passage.

Romans 12:1-2 *I appeal to you therefore, brothers, by the mercies of God, to present your bodies as a living sacrifice, holy and acceptable to God, which is your spiritual worship.* [2] *Do not be conformed to this world, but be transformed by the renewal of your mind, that by testing you may discern what is the will of God, what is good and acceptable and perfect.*

i. What is the Apostle Paul talking about in this passage? (The Subject). Make sure you put this in the form of a question. What is he saying about it? (The Complement). Articulate this in your own words.

ii. The final step in studying a passage is to determine its application to your own life. This means applying the main idea to your current situation and the Biblical principles to yourself. What things in your own life would represent "being conformed to this world"? What would "presenting your body as a living sacrifice" look like in your situation?

iii. Application always means taking a good hard look at yourself and then taking the matter at hand to God in prayer. You must allow the Holy Spirit to do His work in your life through the living word. Take some time in prayer to reflect on this passage in prayer. Record your reflections in your journal.

iv. Apply the steps above to another passage of your choice.

C. Small Group Breakout (2 or 3)

1. Share with one another the struggles and successes that you have experienced in feeding on the word of God regularly.

2. What aspects of this chapter have been particularly helpful to you?

3. Take some time to pray for one another.

D. Assignment for This Week

Continue to observe five devotional times in solitude this week. In each time, follow the pattern that you learned in chapter one. This week use the breath prayer "Lord, speak for your servant is listening" (1 Sam 3:10).

1. Study the following passages, using Content Analysis, the Interpretive Journey or Main Idea thinking. Make notes in your journal. Judges 6:11-16, Proverbs 23:1-5, Amos 5:21-24, Luke 7:41-50, 1 John 2:15-17

2. If you do not already follow a Bible reading plan, take three bookmarks and place one in your Bible at Genesis 1, Psalm 1 and Matthew 1. Begin the practice of reading one chapter a day from each section. Find one verse from your reading this week and memorize it. Reflect on it throughout the week.

3. Continue to take 10-15 minutes at the end of each day to do a Prayer of Examen (pages 80-81).

4. Read chapter seven. Answer the Questions for Personal Reflection your journal.

7. Love's Rule – The Disciplines of Love

"For whatever does not proceed from faith is sin" Rom 14:23b

Saving faith is a gift of God. It is entirely free, given to those whom God has called and quickened through His Spirit. Faith ushers us into an unexpected relationship with God. We suddenly become aware of an entirely new dimension of being. Our world is transformed and we become new creations through Him who loved us and gave Himself for us. We joyfully respond in worship, thanksgiving and prayer, entering into a new reality of life in the Holy Spirit. For the first time in our lives we become truly free, free to be what we were created to be. Jesus Christ has ushered us into a new humanity, a redeemed and transformed humanity that is now able to rest in a covenant partnership with God. This covenant is ratified in His own blood. As Moses sprinkled the Israelites with the blood of the Old Covenant at Mount Sinai (Ex. 24:8), Jesus sprinkled us with the blood of the New Covenant that He inaugurates Himself (Luke 22:20). All of this is by faith in the completed work of Christ, who died, rose again and ascended to sit at the right hand of the Father, having finished the work that He was given to do. We, who were once slaves to sin have now been set free by the Son of righteousness.

This freedom that we now have is often misunderstood. It is not the freedom to be or do anything that we want, but is rather the freedom to be what we were designed to be. There is now no longer any impediment to our being authentically human as God designed us to be. As long as we are fallen in sin and enslaved to sin, we are inhibited from being what we were designed to be. Consider the example of a train. It is free to run along its track as long as there is no impediment to its doing so. But if a tree falls across the track, it is no longer free to run. There is a blockage; an impediment to it being able to do what it was designed to do. Once the tree is removed, it is once again free to run. But the train is not free to fly, for trains are not designed to fly.[lxxxvii] It is only free to be what it was designed to be. Similarly, human beings, in their fallen state are not free. There is an impediment to their freedom. They are enslaved to sin. It is all that they can do for it is their nature. But if the Son sets them free, that impediment is removed and they are made free, recreated to be what they were once designed to be (John 8:36). But they are not to go beyond the limits of what they were designed to be. Their inner corruption, once an impediment, no longer rules, but it does tempt. It tempts them to forget who they are and seeks to derail them once again.

When the people of Israel were freed from bondage in Egypt and brought across the Red Sea to Mount Sinai, it was not long before they forgot God and constructed their own gods (Exodus 32). They forgot the very God who saved them and created idols to meet their spiritual need. Having been set free, they reverted back to that which would enslave them again. Unfortunately this is a universal human tendency.

Religion is our attempt to satisfy God by the performance of religious duties. We have a tendency to take something that is good and mandate it as a requirement to please God. For example consider worship. Worship is good and ought to be a heart felt response of adoration to the God with whom we have an intimate relationship. But as soon as we take worship and make it a requirement, we have subconsciously set up a system in which acceptability before God means that we *must* worship. We have legalistically made worship the measure of our favor with God and we measure others by it. We have just created a religion centered around worship. And the net effect is to say that, to be acceptable to God, we need both Jesus Christ and worship.

But, as soon as we add something to Christ, we are implying that Christ is not sufficient. We are saying that we need Christ plus.... something. But to add anything to Christ is to denigrate Christ. In truth, all we need to be acceptable to God is Jesus Christ, nothing more, nothing less. He is the all-sufficient One in whom we have our being. As we abide in Him and His love, we will spontaneously worship. But we must never make worship a means of righteousness or a measure of spirituality. We must continually fight against religion. Religion always seeks to say that *"this is what we must do"* to please God. In reality God is not at all impressed by what we do. The things that we do only become sources of pride which God hates.

The Law

Our tendency to move away from faith in Christ into religion is no more acute than when it comes to the law. The law was given to Moses at Mount Sinai as a part of the Covenant made with Israel at Horeb. This covenant was in the unique relationship that YHWH forged with Israel. They were called to be a *"kingdom of priests and a holy nation",* God's own people, bearing witness to His Glory and faithfulness (Ex. 19:6). The law was to be an expression of life in the covenant community of Israel, a community that was grounded in a saving relationship that YHWH had initiated. The most important aspect of the law was that relationship. God's Word in the preface to the Ten Commandments grounds that relationship:

> *"And God spoke all these words, saying, "I am the LORD your God, who brought you out of the land of Egypt, out of the house of slavery." Exodus 20:1-2*

The preface declared the basis of the relationship between YHWH and Israel. The rest of the law was to be a living out of that relationship. Because God saved them from extinction and brought them to Himself, they were to respond in gratitude and humility by obeying the decrees and rules that God established for them. These rules were an expression of His righteousness and a reflection of His character. But, these rules were never meant to be a means of righteousness, nor were they to become a religion, a way of earning God's favor. *They already had God's favor.* Rather, they were to be a love response to the God who had saved them and made them His own.

There is a great difference between doing something as a love response in faith and as an imposed requirement. We can best understand this by relating it to our own children. Every parent desires that his or her children obey. But our hope as parents is that children will obey us because they love us deeply and have a strong relationship with us. We hope they would never want to disappoint us. Such filial reverence is the desire of a son or daughter to always please a loving parent. Jesus has such filial reverence for His Father. His heart was entirely united with His Father and He always did what was pleasing to His Father (John 5:19). When our children obey us because they love us, their obedience is not a requirement but rather a joy. They are united in heart and mind and purpose with us. A child who is thus disposed brings great joy to a parent. However, if the relationship between the child and parent is distant and stressed, the child may obey only out of duty or fear of punishment. Such fear is a servile fear, the fear of a servant who is regularly punished for not living up to expectations. The absence of a relationship causes the child to obey, only out of fear and impending punishment. The child may obey, but their heart is not united with their parent. Actually, they are in a state of resentment and tacit rebellion, for whenever they feel that they can escape detection, they will cease to obey.

Similarly, we can see the difference between obedience grounded in faith, love and reverence for our Heavenly Father who loves us deeply and obedience out of duty and fear of punishment by a God whom we perceive to be a harsh spoilsport. It is the difference between a life of freedom to be who God designed us to be and a life of religious duty to an arbitrary and capricious deity whom we do not really understand. It is the difference between life giving faith and life destroying religiosity.

In His teaching, Jesus always transcended the written law, going beyond it to the heart principle that was behind the law. He chastised the Pharisees and the Scribes for they had made the law an end in itself. They had also added to and multiplied the requirements of the law through their rabbinic interpretations. The law had become a legal code that was to be obeyed. Such obedience had become a measure of righteousness. While the scribes and Pharisees were focused on the law, they had lost touch with the Giver of the law and no longer knew Him. They had made keeping of the law into a religion that made people slaves to the written code. Jesus, on the other hand, told them that if they really had a relationship with the Father, they would go beyond the written code toward the Godly perfection that stemmed from a unity of heart and spirit with the righteous Father. The Sermon on the Mount is replete with Jesus' admonitions to transcend the written code out of love for God (Matthew 5:43-46).

FUNCTIONS OF THE LAW

The law given on Mount Sinai consists of moral, ceremonial and civil laws that were given to Israel at a specific point in time for a specific purpose. These laws are beautiful reflections of the love of God for His people and the way in which He desired them to live. One cannot read these laws without being overwhelmed at the right-eousness, wisdom and holiness of God. YHWH called a people out of slavery in a pagan culture and gave them a code of conduct that pointed in every way to the superlative nature of God's love. What other nation had such righteous rules (Deut 4:8)? These rules were designed to establish Israel as a holy nation, God's own people. They reflected the heart of God for people, their need for weekly rest, and their need for redemption from debt, their need to receive cleansing from sin and restoration, their need for worship and a mediated approach to God through the Levitical priesthood.

For Israel, in the wilderness, the presence of the Tabernacle and the priesthood were daily reminders of God's special relationship with them and their status as a holy nation. Once they had settled in the promised land, the temple, the city of Jerusalem and their feasts and festivals established a rhythm of life that was the envy of nations all around them. In contrast to the idolatry and despicable paganism of the nations, Israel stood as a beacon pointing to the love of YHWH, the God of the universe.

Hence, we see that the first function of the law is to reflect the character of God, His love, righteousness, justice and holiness. Every time that I read the last half of Exodus, as well as Leviticus and Deuteronomy I am struck with awe by the love of God, the holiness of God and the righteous wisdom of God. In God's prescription for living for ancient Israel, we have a testament to His glory, justice and righteousness.

The Israelites were to obey the law in faith, out of a heartfelt gratitude and reverence for what God had already done for them. The law was to be their guardian to teach them what God was really like and to exhort them to live according to His heart (Gal. 3:24).

When Jesus came into Israel in the first century, He was appalled at their lack of understanding and their hardness of heart, for they had turned the law into legal code severing it from the love and mercy of God. They focused on the minute details of the law and forgot the God of love behind the law. They had turned faith in YHWH into a legalistic religion that was satanically corrupted. For Satan always seeks to move people away from a relationship with God into religious pride (John 8:54-55). This religion allowed the religious establishment to profit and actually kept people from entering into a vibrant relationship with God (Luke 11:48, Matt. 23:15). The law was designed to show people what God was like, but they had turned it into a complex code of obedience, with themselves as the only interpreters. The law was designed to point toward the Messiah, Jesus, who was one fully righteous fulfiller of the law. He was the embodiment of the law and He brought it to completion. Jesus' radical simplification of the law made the religious leaders assume that He was intent on abolishing it. To this Jesus replied:

> *"Do not think that I have come to abolish the Law or the Prophets; I have not come to abolish them but to fulfill them". **Matthew 5:17***

Jesus did not abolish the law, for its righteous testimony to God's heart stands forever, however He did come to fulfill it. The word "fulfill" in Greek is *playrao*. It literally means to bring to fullness, to complete, to finish. One no longer needed the law to see God's character, one only had to see Jesus. He exemplified the love of God and the heart of God for He was God. In Christ, all the righteous requirements of the law are instantly fulfilled through faith in Him. Jesus is the end of the law for all who believe (Rom.10:4). He was the one faithful covenant partner with God who kept all the requirements of the law and fully pleased the Father in every way. As we rest in Him through faith, we are clothed with His righteousness and deemed to have fulfilled all those requirements through faith in Him. In giving Himself as a once for all sacrifice for sin, He inaugurated the New Covenant in His blood, which made the Old Covenant at Sinai obsolete (Luke 22:20).

> *"In speaking of a new covenant, he makes the first one obsolete. And what is becoming obsolete and growing old is ready to vanish away." Hebrews 8:13*

As believers who are redeemed by the New Covenant in His blood, we are not bound by the Old Covenant code given at Sinai. That matter was settled once and for all at the Jerusalem council in Acts 15. The issue raised by certain Pharisees, who had become believers, was that Gentiles who had come to faith in Christ ought to be circumcised and taught to obey the law of Moses (Acts 15:5). That position was soundly defeated and the council did not impose the Old Covenant law on Gentile believers (Acts 15:10, 19-20). Moreover, the Apostle Paul vehemently warned throughout the New Testament of the futility of reverting back to the Old Testament law as a means of gaining favor with God (Gal. 3:10-13). For those in Christ have died to the law:

> *"But now we are released from the law, having died to that which held us captive, so that we serve not under the old written code but in the new life of the Spirit." Romans 7:6*

Rather, as believers, we are under a new law, the law of the Spirit. God's righteous requirements are written on our hearts by faith. We are actually held to a higher standard than the law, for it impossible to legislate against every offense. Rather, we are to observe the law of love. The one who truly loves has already fulfilled the law. (Rom. 13:8) We are to love God with all our heart, mind and strength and we are to love our neighbor as our self (Matt. 22:37-39). As we live in the power of the Holy Spirit, we bear the fruits of the Spirit (Gal. 5:22-23) and live a life pleasing to God. So the first function of the law is to reveal the character of God and motivate us to love, fear and obey Him.

The second function of the law is that, for believer and unbeliever alike, it reveals sin. We would not know explicitly what sin is without the law. The law declares sin to be sin (1 John 3:4). For Israel, failing to observe the law was an act of rebellion. The moral law, the ethical component, still functions as that which defines and convicts of sin. For where the moral law says *"do not covet",* I am convicted of sin if I find within me any covetousness. Thus the law has done its work in convicting me of sin.

And so the moral law is the mirror that shows us what we are like. When we allow our sinful self to influence us, when we get puffed up with pride or self-righteousness, the law is there to convict us and to drive us to our knees. In such moments, the grace of God through the gospel is there to lift us up and restore us through Christ our Lord.

A third function of the law is that it restrains evil in the world. It is not by accident that most civil laws in jurisdictions around the world are based on the moral law of God given at Sinai. These laws are universally recognized as basic requirements to preserve the sanctity of human life and to allow society to function. International law is based upon these rules and they are used to prosecute criminals who feel that they can get away with murder, genocide and other violations.

However, the law was never designed to be a means of righteousness nor was it designed to be a way of earning favor with God. Righteousness before God has always been through faith in the God of salvation. In such faith, loving reverent obedience is the only appropriate response. Obedience that proceeds from any other motive, always descends into legalism and religiosity. The one who obeys the law apart from faith is obeying a moral code divorced from the One who gave it. Because such obedience is not grounded in relationship and does not proceed from faith, it does not meet the requirement of the law, but actually violates the first commandment (and preamble), which requires faith and trust in the God of redemption.

A moralist who obeys the law apart from faith has elevated the keeping of the law above the call to love God and neighbor and has turned the law into an idolatrous means of righteousness, thus violating the second commandment (no idols).

A fourth function of the law is that it allows us to derive principles that lead us to convictions about righteous behavior. As described in chapter six, every Old Testament law can be analyzed to determine God's heart in the matter at hand. Hence we must never reject the Old Testament as being irrelevant, but rather we must recognize that, in the Old Testament, we have a deep treasure that reveals the heart and character of God and His desires for His people.

Just as we must guard against Legalism, that is making the law an end in itself and divorcing it from faith in the law Giver, so too we must guard against licentiousness. Licentiousness is disregarding the law entirely and living according to the desires of our passions and sinful self. It is for freedom that Christ has set us free, but we must never use our freedom as an indulgence to sin (Rom. 6:1). Rather, we ought to have a reverent fear of offending a holy God The admonition to "fear God" reverberates through scripture (Ecc. 12:13, Luke 23:40, 1 Pet 2:17, Rev. 14:7). This means that we need to develop deep convictions about how to live and disciplines that will enable us to do so consistently.

Putting Off and Putting On – Replacing Sin with Godliness

Many people are convicted of sin by the Holy Spirit and earnestly try to reform their sinful behavior. That approach to holiness does not work. Reformation is not the way to freedom. The alcoholic who simply tries to stop drinking is never successful. If he refrains for a season, he is simply a "dry drunk". Similarly, one who tries to stop sinning by human effort is never successful. He is just a sinner who is not acting out his sin at the moment. The solution, as we have seen in chapter three, is to put the old sinful self to death through the Holy

Spirit who then gives life to the New Creation that a person is in Christ. It is not enough to just put the old self to death. The old self must be put off and the new self in Christ must replace it. Similarly, when it comes to sinful behavior, it is not enough to simply "stop it". The sinful behavior must be replaced by its godly counterpart through the power of the Holy Spirit. That is why the Apostle Paul writes:

> *"And do not get drunk with wine, for that is debauchery, but be filled with the Spirit, [19] addressing one another in psalms and hymns and spiritual songs, singing and making melody to the Lord with all your heart...". Ephesians 5:18-19*

It is insufficient for an alcoholic to simply stop being drunk with wine. For when alcoholics drink, they are controlled by that drink. Rather, they must replace drinking by some superintending motivation that displaces the desire to drink. Likewise the sinner cannot simply stop sinning. Rather he must surrender to the Holy Spirit's control. He must be filled with the Spirit, responding in worship and thanksgiving. This is the pattern of putting off and putting on. The Apostle continues:

> *"....put off your old self, which belongs to your former manner of life and is corrupt through deceitful desires, [23] and ...be renewed in the spirit of your minds, [24] and... put on the new self, created after the likeness of God in true righteousness and holiness." Ephesians 4:22-24*

Hence to displace any sinful behavior or attitude, I cannot try in my own strength to "stop it", but must first identify what the godly counterpart is. Then, I must *put that on* through the power of the Holy Spirit. For example, to stop lying, I must put on the godly virtue of truth telling. This is only possible by submitting myself to God in the power of the Holy Spirit. It requires conviction, discipline and an act of the will empowered by the Holy Spirit. It is only possible if I have surrendered my life to Christ and seek to live entirely for Him.

The Ten Commandments as Disciplines of Love

In the remainder of this chapter we will examine the Ten Commandments and identify the sinful attitude and behavior that each reflects. Then we will identify the principle that is behind the law. We will also identify the discipline and Godly attitude and behavior that must replace it. To live a Holy life, we must be proactive in replacing our predisposition to sin by Godly behavior empowered by the Holy Spirit.

REMEMBRANCE

As we have seen, the preamble to the Ten Commandments is the most important part, for it establishes the relationship between God and His people.

> *"I am the LORD your God, who brought you out of the land of Egypt, out of the house of slavery." Ex. 20:1*

This is the discipline of **remembrance**. The reason that the preamble is such an important part of the commandments is that we must never forget what God has done. The sinful attitude and behavior highlighted in the preamble is our tendency to forget God and to live our lives independently of Him. When Israel made the golden calf, they forgot God. They were slaves in Egypt and subjects of genocide. They owed their lives and their continued existence to YHWH. They were continually admonished by scripture and prophet to never forget that they were a people doomed to destruction whom YHYW had rescued by His own hand. They were to replace the sinful attitude of forgetfulness with the godly attitude of remembrance.

> *"You shall remember that you were a slave in the land of Egypt, and the LORD your God brought you out from there with a mighty hand and an outstretched arm." Deuteronomy 5:15*

The Hebrew concept of remembering does not simply mean to call something to mind, that is to think about it now and again. *Remember* in Hebrew means that the thing remembered is to become the *defining operational reality* of life in the present. Every Israelite was to live their life as one who had been personally delivered from a life of slavery and servitude. They were to always remember the pit from which they were rescued. They were to live in a continual state of remembrance. Every Sabbath was a rehearsal and a remembrance of that deliverance. Every passover, each person was to consider themselves as personally coming out of Egypt, out of slavery.

Similarly for us as Christians, we must never forget what Christ has done for us through the cross. We must make our deliverance from our slavery to sin the *defining operational reality* of our lives. In inaugurating the Lord's Supper, Jesus said *"Do this in remembrance of me"* (Luke 22:19). I must never forget the pit from which I was freed. I was a sinner, destined for destruction and Jesus died for me, rescuing me from an eternity in hell. The discipline of remembrance means living life continually in the shadow of the cross. It is not that the cross was an event in the distant past that I occasionally think about and am grateful for. Rather I am to live my life daily remembering who I was, who I am now and what God had done for me. I am to consider myself co-crucified with Christ and continually raised in newness of life with Him. I no longer live, but Christ lives in me. The Apostle Paul expresses it well:

> *"I have been crucified with Christ. It is no longer I who live, but Christ who lives in me. And the life I now live in the flesh I live by faith in the Son of God, who loved me and gave himself for me." Galatians 2:20*

In order to make the discipline of remembrance a reality, I must find a practical way of living my life so as to never forget this. Because each one of us is different, we must develop some way of continually reminding ourselves of this. For some, it might be wearing a cross as a perpetual reminder. For others, it might be a daily prayer discipline. For some it might be a favorite worship song. Each of us ought to develop some "memorial stone" to remind us of the pit from which we were rescued. We must never allow ourselves to forget who we are and whose we are.

WORSHIP

The first commandment admonishes us: *"You shall have no other Gods before me" (Ex. 20:3).* This is the discipline of exclusive **worship.** To have other gods is to have divided loyalties. God will tolerate no rivals. We have a natural tendency to allow other things and people to displace our allegiance to God. We must replace this with a commitment to have God alone as the centerpiece of our lives. God ought to occupy such a prominent place in our consciousness that everything else pales in comparison. As an answer to a question about which was the most important commandment, Jesus said:

> *"You shall love the Lord your God with all your heart and with all your soul and with all your mind and with all your strength." Mark 12:30*

To love God with everything that is in us means that we will make deliberate choices about spending time with Him. Two lovers who are truly in love with one another will desire above all else to spend time together. It is inconceivable that I would love God with all of my heart, soul, mind and strength and go day after day without actually spending some quality time with Him. The reality is that most of us don't spend much time with God because we have other priorities. We can say that we love Him, but our calendars say otherwise. Like Martha we are distracted with much serving, because we have created our own gods and have left Jesus sitting in the drawing room alone (Luke 10:39-40).

To truly love God and worship means that God receives first place in my life. He should be the first thing I think of when I rise in the morning and the last thing on my mind as I retire. My entire being must revolve around Him and His desires for me. I must ask myself daily, is this really true of me? Do I love God with all of my heart, my mind, my soul and my strength? The discipline of exclusive worship is to prioritize time alone with God on a regular basis. Each day, I ought to have in my calendar an appointment with God. At least once a week, I should have several hours set aside to be alone with Him. I must find a place that allows me to concentrate on Him and give Him all my attention.

In my life, I have found that sailing offers me such an opportunity. In the summer, I often go out alone in my boat and find a quiet anchorage. Being alone in a confined space like a boat, allows me to spend time with God and to listen to His voice. The exercises in each study guide of this book are designed to be done in solitude. It is in these quiet times that God gets to know me as well as I get to know Him. He becomes my all in all. He recalibrates my attitude and sets my heart aright. In the winters I make time with God as I cross country ski in the woods behind my house. I also spend times alone with God in the sauna that I use frequently in the winter. Often, walking can give a great opportunity to spend time with God in worship. We allow our minds to focus on Him and we clear our thoughts to allow Him space. But, this is a discipline that must be practiced as a discipline. We must make it a priority and we must do it.

RENOUNCING IDOLS

The second commandment states:

> *"You shall not make for yourself a carved image, or any likeness of anything that is in heaven above, or that is in the earth beneath, or that is in the water under the earth. [5] You shall not bow down to them or serve them, for I the LORD your God am a jealous God, visiting the iniquity of the fathers on the children to the third and the fourth generation of those who hate me, [6]but showing steadfast love to thousands of those who love me and keep my commandments." Exodus 20:4-6*

This is the discipline of **renouncing idols.** There is implicit in fallen human nature a desire to infer or imagine God to be something other than what He is. We are spiritual beings and we yearn to be connected to a spiritual reality. But God is not subject to our imaginations or inferences. Any god inferred or imagined is an idol. For when Moses meets God face to face at Horeb, he sees a burning bush and he hears a voice, but he sees no form nor image. It is *the voice* that characterizes YHWH as God. The prohibition from making carved images is to show that God so transcends the created order that nothing on earth, above the earth or under the earth compares to Him. He is the transcendent One who cannot be imagined, inferred or depicted by human beings. To create an image or a statue and call it God is an abomination. Many people today are much too sophisticated to create images and bow down to them. However, while they do not make *metal images* of God, they do create *mental images* of God that are idols. People say things like "My God would never send anyone to hell". And indeed that is true, for such a god does not exist. It is a *mental* idol, a figment of a someone's mind.

The Hebrew word for idol literally means *a nothing*. The idols of the nations are nothings for they do not exist. However that does not mean that they are without power. It is the spirit that is behind the idol that captivates the heart. Satan and his demonic hordes love idolatry for it displaces God as the object of worship. I have spent considerable time in India and have visited Hindu temples where images of gods are worshipped. Priests burn incense and offer prayers and chants up to images and statues, which in fact are no gods at all. But there is a distinct demonic presence behind these idols. The power that they hold over the people is enormous. On my last visit to such a place, I felt so polluted by my time there, that soon after leaving that my co-visitors and I were led to spend an hour in prayer for cleansing and freedom for those who were under the demonic influence of these so called gods.

The discipline of renouncing idols means that I must continually check my own assumptions about God. I must replace idolatry with a life of discipleship and study to understand who He is and what He is really like. This means looking continually at Jesus Christ who is God incarnate. God in the flesh is the Person of Jesus Christ. When I encounter Him, I encounter God. When I remake Jesus according to my own preferences, I have created an idol.

Historically, the church has been guilty throughout history of recasting Jesus according to its own image. There is the socialist Jesus, the capitalist Jesus, the prosperous Jesus, the military Jesus, the Jesus of monasticism, the Jesus of the cathedrals, the evangelical Jesus, the Jesus of western imperialism and so on. The only way out of such idolatry is to embrace a Biblical Jesus who is deeply rooted in His identity as a Hebrew who came to fulfill and complete the Old Covenant and establish a New One, which would unite all of humanity both Jew and Gentile in Him. Biblical literacy is essential in maintaining a right perspective of who God is. Such perspective must stay faithful to the Apostolic witness to Christ contained in scripture. It is vital for both the church and the individual to be well grounded theologically. There must be a continual rechecking of our assumptions and a renouncing of our tendency to make Jesus in our own image.

Renouncing idols requires that I constantly check my own lifestyle. What things have I come to value more than God? For some this is money, for others privilege, power, pleasure, position, influence, family, prestige, reputation. Anything that I feel that I could not completely give up should God require it, is an idol. Certainly for those in the West who live as the wealthiest one percent of the population of the world, the question is crucial. We have become so materialist, consumerist and corporate in our values that we have equated our way of life as a right given to us by God. We consume an inordinate share of the world's resources and use our money for pleasure and privilege, while most of the world lives in abject poverty without the bare essentials of life. If Jesus were present on the face of the earth today, whom would He relate to? Who would He rebuke? How would He be living? I expect that it would be a lifestyle more like a Mother Teresa than that of a corporate CEO.

God calls us to a lifestyle of self-denial and bearing of one's cross. We are to model our lives after Jesus, the suffering servant who came to serve and to give His life a ransom for many. To embrace His way is to embrace the way of the cross and not the way of worldly glory. The discipline of renouncing all idols means that I must continually ask God to reveal to me what idols I have inadvertently accumulated in my life. The Apostle John says it simply in the closing of his first letter:

> *"Little children, keep yourself from idols." 1 John 5:21*

GUARDING MY TONGUE – BLESSING OTHERS

The third commandment is:

> *"You shall not take the name of the LORD your God in vain, for the LORD will not hold him guiltless who takes his name in vain." Exodus 20:7*

This is the discipline of **guarding my tongue and blessing others**. The name of God, YHHW, occurs 6,823 times in scripture and was considered a name too holy to utter. It is translated LORD in most Bibles and represents the personal name of God given to Moses, the "I AM WHO I AM" of Exodus 3:14. The nation Israel was to reverence God by esteeming His name. To misuse God's name was to display a lack of seriousness about His presence in Israel and His holiness, majesty and sovereignty. Rather God's name was to be honored, blessed, praised, celebrated and revered. God's name represents His nature, who He is and what He does. This prohibition of using God's name in an offhand, pointless, idle or wicked way applied not only to his personal name YHWH, but to all other names of God as well. God's name was not be to given to idols or used for selfish purposes or in rash vows or to suppress the truth. This applies not only to vows and idle swearing, but also to using God's name in bearing false witness and lying.

In stark contrast to ancient Israel, we today are most cavalier in the way we casually use God's name. Swearing, cursing and deliberately vile use of the precious name of Jesus Christ is rampant in our society. We ought not to be surprised by this among unbelievers, however, among professing Christians God's name is frequently abused. For believers, guarding our tongues ought to be an urgent issue of conduct and character. Jesus warned that we will be judged by every careless word we utter.

> *"I tell you, on the day of judgment people will give account for every careless word they speak, [37] for by your words you will be justified, and by your words you will be condemned." Matthew 12:36-37*

If we truly loved God and reverenced His name, we would be much more careful of our speech. I have observed that many vile words get spoken in anger and under the influence of alcohol. When we give vent to our *sinful self,* we denigrate ourselves and cover ourselves with shame on account of our words. The Apostle James warns believers in stark terms:

> *"So also the tongue is a small member, yet it boasts of great things. How great a forest is set ablaze by such a small fire! [6] And the tongue is a fire, a world of unrighteousness. The tongue is set among our members, staining the whole body, setting on fire the entire course of life, and set on fire by hell.........It is a restless evil, full of deadly poison. [9] With it we bless our Lord and Father, and with it we curse people who are made in the likeness of God. [10] From the same mouth come blessing and cursing. My brothers, these things ought not to be so". James 3:5-10*

It is wise therefore, for every one of us to develop the discipline of guarding our tongue. We ought to always be slow to speak and slow to anger. When provoked, we ought to remember who we are and take a few deep breaths and simply refrain from speaking for a few minutes. We must let our passions cool, for they are the source of anger, bitterness and guile which is not at all godly. We are instructed to "swear not at all" but to simply let our yes be yes and our no be no. (Matt. 5:33-37). To be faithful to the teachings of Jesus, we ought not to take oaths, other than a simple undertaking to tell the truth. We are to rather put a guard over our mouths and be very careful what we say.

This applies especially to expressing opinions about others to third parties. The sinful practice of gossip is relaying "juicy" information about someone else to a third party. Such talk is not edifying and it serves only to tear down and not build up. Once a derogatory word is spoken, it cannot be rescinded. It is as if someone took a pillow full of feathers to a rooftop and cut it open. The result is feathers floating in every direction. It is impossible to undo the damage and to try to gather the feathers back up again.

To successfully guard our tongues, we must use our speech to edify, build up and bless. This discipline of blessing others allows us to use God's name in a way that is uplifting, encouraging and a manifestation of love. It trains us to speak positively or not at all. If difficult situations need to be discussed, the circle of discussion should involve only those who might have a role in restoring the situation and making it right. This does not mean that we hide wrongdoing, but rather it means that we exercise discernment and good judgment in dealing with difficult situations. We must always ask ourselves if the Lord Himself would engage with us in such conversation.

REST

The fourth commandment is:

> *"Remember the Sabbath day, to keep it holy. [9] Six days you shall labor, and do all your work, [10] but the seventh day is a Sabbath to the LORD your God. On it you shall not do any work, you, or your son, or your daughter, your male servant, or your female servant, or your livestock, or the sojourner who is within your gates. [11] For in six days the LORD made heaven and earth, the sea, and all that is in them, and rested the seventh day. Therefore the LORD blessed the Sabbath day and made it holy." Exodus 20:8-11*

This is the discipline of **rest.** Human beings were not designed to work seven days a week. Rather, we require a cycle of rest and restoration, ideally once every seven days. This commandment to Israel was modeled after God's own creative work in making the universe. Just as God rested on the seventh day, so too Israel was to cease from their everyday labor and observe a Sabbath day of rest. This rest would allow servants and slaves and masters alike an opportunity to cease from work and remember YHWH who had redeemed them from slavery, where there was no rest.

The Hebrew Sabbath rest also has a strong connotation of restoration. Just as one day in seven was designed for rest and restoration of the body, so the Sabbatical year cycle was to provide release of debts for those who had fallen into poverty (Deut. 15:1-2). Once every seven years all debts were to be released as a way of restoration. This made Israel a society where poverty was to be mitigated by the systemic mercy of the wealthy. Similarly, cultivated land was to lie fallow once every seven years (Ex. 23:11). This was not only to allow the land to rest but to allow the poor and the wild animals to eat whatever grew naturally. One can easily see the principles of rest, restoration, release and mercy in the observance of the Sabbath.

In addition, this day was to be holy to YHWH. It was to be set aside as a day of reflection, contemplation and worship. It was not to be used for personal pleasure or for idle pursuits, but rather as a holy day of delight consecrated to YHWH (Is. 58:13-14). Hence the Sabbatical commandment was closely tied to the commandment to love and worship YHWH alone. It was a sign of the covenant made at Sinai between God and the people and was to distinguish God's people from all the nations of the world.

Now, it is clear from the Apostolic teaching of the New Testament, that Christians today are not bound by the Sabbath law (Col. 2:16, Acts 15:28-29). Moreover, the Apostles also recognized that Jesus *Himself* was Lord of the Sabbath (Matt. 12:8). They taught that as we enter in Christ by faith, we enter into His rest. Just as Adam's first full day on earth was a day of rest, so too for a new creation in Christ, Jesus Himself is that rest. He restores those who trust in Him to that Sabbath rest relationship with the Father. The writer of Hebrews admonishes his readers to not miss entering into that rest.

> *" For we who have believed enter that rest, as he has said, "As I swore in my wrath, 'They shall not enter my rest,'" although his works were finished from the foundation of the world.......So then, there remains a Sabbath rest for the people of God, for whoever has entered God's rest has also*

rested from his works as God did from his." Hebrews 4:3-4, 9-10

It is interesting that in one of the first discipleship documents that we have from the early church, *The Didache* [lxxxviii], there is no mention at all of the necessity of keeping the Sabbath. That is because it was clear to the early church that Christians are no longer under Sabbath law. We are free to worship God on whatever day of the week we choose, for Christ Himself is our Sabbath rest. However, the Sabbath principle is an important one for believers to live by.

We are well advised to set aside one day a week as a day of worship, reflection and cessation from normal work, not as a legal requirement, but as a loving response to the Father to whom we are reconciled in Christ Jesus. It is pleasing to God when we do so for it shows that we take Him seriously. Everything written in the Old Testament was written for our instruction (1 Cor. 10:11). As we have shown in chapter five, we must apply diligence in interpreting the Old Testament, by extracting the principles from the law and applying those principles to our situation today.

In contemporary society, it is not always possible to cease work on a particular day of the week. Those who work in health care and essential services are required to work on weekends. However, each person and household would do well to set aside certain days in his or her calendar as rest days. Those days should be devoted to worship, reflection and recovery. It is important to resist the temptation to work seven days a week and, as a personal conviction, set aside one day each week as a personal day of rest. For most Christians, this day will be Sunday, however, when I served as a pastor in a large church, I found that Sunday was not really a day of rest for me. Consequently, I set aside each Monday as a day off and a day of rest, reflection and restoration. On that day, I would seek to spend time alone with God and with my family as we rested and renewed our spirits. God has redeemed us and claimed us as His own. All of our days belong to Him and, in one sense, every day is a day of worship. Yet it is wise and Biblical to observe a weekly cycle of rest. For those raising families, rest days will become some of your children's most precious memories. This is the discipline of rest.

"... I have calmed and quieted my soul, like a weaned child with its mother; like a weaned child is my soul within me." Psalm 131:2

GIVING HONOR

The fifth commandment is:

"Honor your father and your mother, that your days may be long in the land that the LORD your God is giving you." Exodus 20:12

This is the discipline of **giving honor**. The commandment is specific to children and is the first commandment with a promise, a promise of long life. The principle of honoring one's parents reflects God's heart for His people to honor those who are in authority. The first line of authority within the family unit is the parent. Consequently, the penalty in ancient Israel for dishonoring parents was severe. Those who cursed father or mother were to be put to death (Ex. 21:17). While this punishment sounds harsh to modern ears, we must remember that cursing a parent was an act of willful deliberate rebellion. It was not to be tolerated. Rebellion is equated in scripture with witchcraft (1 Sam 15:23). The penalty for rebellion was most often executed by God immediately as rebels perished by plague, earthquake or fire (Num 11:33, 16:25-34, Deut 11:6). The opposite of rebellion is submission to God and to God ordained authority. This principle is reflected throughout scripture. We are to honor those who are placed in authority over us, recognizing that God governs the affairs of nations and no authority exists other than that which God appoints. Only in the case where human authority deliberately violates God's express commands are we to resist, but even as we do so, we are to do so with honor. (Acts 5:29) We are to honor those to whom honor is due. That includes everyone, for all people are worthy of honor (1 Peter 2:17). Every person is made in the image of God. Even if that image is severely defaced, as in the case of a serial killer or mass murderer, we have no right to treat people with dishonor.

The discipline of giving honor is a reflection of the command to love our neighbor (Matt 22:37-39). Love of neighbor begins with honor. Those who dishonor others do not have the love of God in them. To truly honor another is to treat them in the same way in which one would like to be treated. This ultimately stems from seeing ourselves rightly. We are to consider others more significant than ourselves (Phil 2:3). True humility is always reflected in giving honor to the other person. We do so because we recognize our own sinfulness and operate out of an attitude of poverty of spirit and meekness.

Therefore each disciple of Christ must commit to honor everyone and give special honor to those to whom such honor is due. This means that my demeanor and attitude in addressing others must always be one of respect, courtesy and kindness. Nowhere is this more needed than in the home. Often familiarity and proximity result in a husband or a wife being curt and abrupt with one another. Often arguments break out in which the language used is what one might expect in a brawl in a back street bar. These things ought not to be, and we should become instantly ashamed of such language. Once again, that restless evil, our tongue gets us into trouble. Rather, each person in Christ ought to commit to the discipline of giving honor to all, especially to parents and to those in authority.

RENOUNCING ANGER – PRAYING FOR ABUSERS

The sixth commandment reads:

"You shall not murder" Exodus 20:13

Jesus took this commandment and intensified it in the Sermon on the Mount. He added that *"everyone who is angry with his brother will be liable to judgment; whoever insults his brother will be liable to the council; and whoever says, 'You fool!' will be liable to the hell of fire."* (Matt. 5:22). Here Jesus is describing a situation in which one is angry at someone else in a purely human way from purely human motives. Jesus is not prohibiting all anger. There are some things that ought to make us angry. Flagrant unrighteousness and diabolical evil ought to make us angry. Jesus was angry when He cleared the temple grounds. Those selling their wares and the leaders that endorsed it had turned the house of God into a marketplace. God's anger is also kindled when we deliberately sin. The difficulty is that because of our sinful nature, human anger is most often on account of our own passions. The Apostle James writes:

"You desire and do not have, so you murder. You covet and cannot obtain, so you fight and quarrel. You do not have,

because you do not ask. You ask and do not receive, because you ask wrongly, to spend it on your passions." James 4:2-3

Anger as a human response to not getting our own way is almost always sinful. The prophet Jonah was sent to the great city of Ninevah to preach. He hated the people of Ninevah for they were great sinners so he refused to go. Eventually he did go and preached repentance as God had commanded. When the people of Ninevah repented, God had mercy on them and relented of His plan to destroy the city. Jonah was not at all pleased and sat outside the city angry that God had not destroyed the very people who repented as a result of his preaching. Such anger does not reflect the righteousness of God, but rather reflects the depravity of the human heart. When I am angry at another person, it is seen by God as wanting them dead. It is equivalent to murder.

Such unrighteous anger must be replaced by the discipline of renouncing anger and prayer. Every time I feel anger welling up inside of me, I ought to renounce it, check my motives and pray for the situation. Why am I angry? Is my anger selfishly motivated because I have been prevented from getting my own way? If there is unrighteousness on the part of the other, am I willing to let God deal with it in an honorable way, or am I bent on taking vengeance into my own hands. If I find myself wanting to make the other person pay, then I am really on the track of a vengeful vendetta. The scriptures tell us that such a response is wrong.

"Know this, my beloved brothers: let every person be quick to hear, slow to speak, slow to anger; for the anger of man does not produce the righteousness that God requires." James 1:19-20

"Be angry, and do not sin; ponder in your own hearts on your beds, and be silent." Psalm 4:4

"Be angry and do not sin; do not let the sun go down on your anger, and give no opportunity to the devil." Ephesians 4:26-27

"Beloved, never avenge yourselves, but leave it to the wrath of God, for it is written, 'Vengeance is mine, I will repay', says the Lord." Romans 12:19

God calls us to release unrighteous anger and allow God to execute judgment at the proper time. That does not mean that we condone evil or allow it to proceed unfettered. We do what we can to oppose it and stop it. But our heart attitude must not be one of vengeance and anger. Rather, we are exhorted to pray for our enemies, for those who despitefully use and abuse us. (Matt 5:44). When we feel such anger rising up within us, we ought to immediately replace it with prayer. We ought to remember that we have done many things that have made other people angry. Just as God has forgiven us, we ought to release the abuser to God and pray for them. We are to do good to those who persecute and abuse us. We are to pray for the salvation of the sinner. Unrighteous anger must always be replaced by prayer and blessing.

TRAINING MY EYES - RENOUNCING LUST

The seventh commandment reads:

"You shall not commit adultery" Ex. 20:14

Once again Jesus intensified this commandment in saying: "*But I say to you that everyone who looks at a woman with lustful intent has already committed adultery with her in his heart." (Matthew 5:28)* Marriage is a covenant relationship whereby husband and wife become one. The physical union of husband and wife creates a "one flesh" unity that is the basis for stable family life. Adultery breaks the covenantal relationship and tears apart the union of husband and wife. YHWH would not tolerate adultery in the covenant community of Israel. So serious was this breech of faith that the prescribed penalty under the Old Covenant was death (Lev. 20:10). Jesus taught that adultery is not just an issue of the physical act but rather an issue of the heart. Faithlessness in marriage occurs when either partner lusts after another. To engage in such lust is to violate one's marriage vows and treat them as nothing. God's heart for His people is faithfulness in all things. If one cannot be faithful to a human relationship, how can one be faithful in a heavenly one? God often likened Israel's worship of the gods of the nations to adultery and prostitution (Jer. 3:9, Mal 2:11, Hos. 1:2). Israel had formed a covenant relationship with YHWH to worship Him alone. He alone was God, and He alone was to be worshipped. Breeching this covenant by lusting after other gods was spiritual adultery. The penalty under the old covenant was death.

To simply refrain from adultery is not enough. It requires the discipline of training my eyes and renouncing lust. Desiring another's husband or wife is covetousness. It is wanting that which God has placed off limits. It is also a breech of love, for to lust after someone else's spouse is to fail that person in love.

King David was walking on the rooftop of his house at a time when he should have been with his troops in battle (2 Sam. 11:1). His idleness allowed him to see a beautiful woman bathing in broad daylight on her own rooftop. The seeds of lust were easily sown. Rather than renouncing lust, David took the next steps and inquired after the woman and then sent for her. It turns out that the woman was the wife of Uriah the Hittite, one of David's own mighty men, his 30 personally appointed valiant warriors. He knew Uriah well.

David's subsequent adultery with Bathsheba was a failure of love toward his faithful servant Uriah. David recalled him from battle and tried to get him to sleep with his wife to cover up his own sin. Uriah's faithfulness to his fellow soldiers, as he refused, stands in stark contrast to David's own faithlessness. David then murdered Uriah by orchestrating his death in battle. Through Nathan the prophet, God rebuked this shocking breech of love and David did repent. However, his sin caused him great anguish in the years ahead as the consequences of that sin played out in his own family.

Too often, the entry portal for lust is the eyes. Had David not seen Bathsheba bathing, the incident would not have happened. Our eyes allow us to behold and appreciate beauty and there is nothing inherently wrong with that. However, our eyes must be controlled by our will. We must discern what we see and exercise self-control by not allowing our minds to dwell on that which our mind knows is forbidden. If we allow our eyes to have free rein, then our sinful self begins to covet that which we see and soon we begin to dwell on that which we ought not to dwell. The Apostle James describes it thus:

> *".... each person is tempted when he is lured and enticed by his own desire. 15 Then desire when it has conceived gives birth to sin, and sin when it is fully grown brings forth death". James 1:14-15*

Hence, we must approach this commandment by disciplining ourselves to train our eyes. I am not suggesting that our ears cannot also kindle desire as can any other sense. However, most commonly it is our eyes that see and desire what we should not. To train my eyes, I must develop convictions and place limits on what I will allow my eyes to see and my ears to hear. Men especially are aroused visually. If I know this, then I must refrain from putting myself in situations where this can happen. Women also should be aware of this and refrain from wearing suggestive dress that arouses desire in men. Moreover, I must exercise self-control by instantly taking all thoughts captive in Christ. Whatever I think, I must pass through the filter of the Holy Spirit who lives in me. Ungodly thoughts and impulses must be instantly renounced. Pornography must be absolutely shunned.

However, just putting unwholesome thoughts to death is not enough. To be victorious, I must replace these thoughts with their godly counterparts. In the area of sexual lust, the godly counterpart is to see the other person as a brother or sister for whom Christ died. My eyes must be trained to see people the way Jesus saw people. Jesus did not lust after women, but saw them as people who needed salvation. His love for them transcended the physical and moved to the spiritual. Ultimately, when we all get to heaven, there will be no male nor female, but we will all be like the angels (Matt. 22:30). Our gender specificity and our sexuality are confined to this life for a purpose. The person who has the mind of Christ sees all people in light of eternity. Rather than lusting, that person loves the other with the love of Christ. That person will pray for the other and bless them. The discipline of guarding my eyes means not allowing my sinful self exercising control over my senses. It means offering my body as a living sacrifice to the one who saved me and whose I am. The Apostle Paul makes this an appeal:

> *"I appeal to you therefore, brothers, by the mercies of God, to present your bodies as a living sacrifice, holy and acceptable to God, which is your spiritual worship." Romans 12:1*

INTEGRITY & WORKING HARD

The eighth commandment is:

"You shall not steal." Ex. 20:15

This is the discipline of **integrity**. Stealing destroys integrity for when I steal, I take something that is not rightfully mine. Stealing defrauds a neighbor and is a failure of love. When I steal, I put my own needs and desires above those of my neighbor. Many people will refrain from stealing when they know the person who will be injured, but have no qualms about stealing from governments, corporations or organizations. They rationalize their lack of integrity by depersonalizing the victim and magnify their perceived "rights". Stealing is always an expression of considering oneself more significant than others. Stealing is also an expression of lack of faith in God. God has promised to provide all of our needs (Phil 4:19). When I steal, I declare a lack of faith in God and insist on providing for myself by defrauding someone else.

Stealing is not only an active offense, as when I take something that is not rightfully mine, but can also be a passive offense. To fail to pay what I owe is also stealing. Many Christians refrain from active stealing, but see no problem in exaggerating their business expenses in order to reduce their taxes. They also may do work "under the table" for cash, that is undeclared. In so doing, they fail to pay what they rightfully owe and hence defraud the community on whose behalf the government collects taxes. Rather we are told that we are to pay everything that we owe.

> *"Pay to all what is owed to them: taxes to whom taxes are owed, revenue to whom revenue is owed, respect to whom respect is owed, honor to whom honor is owed. 8 Owe no one anything, except to love each other, for the one who loves another has fulfilled the law. Romans 13:7-8*

Integrity is an expression of the law of love. Just as is the case for all the commandments, these can only be kept through faith in Christ. If someone refrains from stealing, but does not have faith, they have violated God's law, for their keeping of the law does not proceed from a faith relationship with God. They have violated the first commandment and have become guilty of all.

The discipline of integrity means that I develop a conviction that I will accept only what I have earned or that which has been given me as a gift. I do this in faith that God will to supply all my needs. I do this because I love God with all my heart soul mind and strength. I do this because I love my neighbor as I love myself. I do this because I consider others to be more significant than myself (Phil 2:3). That means that if I am in a checkout line and the teller gives me more change than I am due, I instantly stand for what is right and point it out to her. At that moment, I must be so committed to integrity that the temptation to keep the extra change as a windfall must never even occur to me. Will I sell my integrity for pocket change?

The discipline of integrity means that I replace the temptation to steal with working hard to provide for my needs and in order to bless others. Believers are not to be idle or to live in expectation that someone else will provide for them, but rather they are to work to contribute to society. That does not mean that everyone must have a job and earn income. There are many ways of contributing to society apart from earning an income. However, note that the Apostle Paul chastises those who are lazy and refuse to work:

> *"For even when we were with you, we would give you this command: If anyone is not willing to work, let him not eat. For we hear that some among you walk in idleness, not busy at work, but busybodies. Now such persons we command and encourage in the Lord Jesus Christ to do their work quietly and to earn their own living." 2 Thessalonians 3:10-12*

TRUTHFULNESS

The ninth commandment reads:

> *"You shall not bear false witness against your neighbor." Ex. 20:16*

This is the discipline of **truthfulness**. To bear false witness against a neighbor is to fail to love that person. Spreading false reports about another is slander. Slander destroys another's reputation and does great harm. When I slander or lie, I align myself with Satan who is the father of all lies. (John 8:44) This is a serious offense. Many people justify lies calling them "white lies" for they perceive that they do no one any harm. However, lying lips are an abomination to the Lord and are one of the things that God hates. (Prov. 12:22).

Whenever I am under stress or in a difficult or embarrassing situation, I am tempted to lie as an easy way out. Such a temptation appeals to my sinful self, my inner corruption. If I have not developed a conviction to always tell the truth, then I can easily fall victim to the temptation. The way around this temptation is to develop an *a priori* conviction to always tell the truth. Lying must be replaced by truth telling. I can do this by the Holy Spirit who lives in me for He is the Spirit of Truth. As I live and move and have my being in Him, I will be characterized as one who always tells the truth.

The only exception permissible is an ethical one. If truth telling in the face of evil would result in the destruction of a neighbor, then I must choose to follow God's heart. Those who hid Jews during the Nazi era were often forced to lie in order to protect the lives of those they harbored. In such a situation, God is not honored by a strict moral adherence to truth telling. Those who lied to protect lives actually stood on the side of the Truth. In ethical dilemmas, much prayer is needed and God will guide those who seek to do what is right.

CONTENTMENT WITH THANKFULNESS

The tenth commandment reads:

> *"You shall not covet your neighbor's house; you shall not covet your neighbor's wife, or his male servant, or his female servant, or his ox, or his donkey, or anything that is your neighbor's." Exodus 20:17*

This is the discipline of **contentment with thankfulness**. To covet something that God has blessed someone else with is wrong. Covetousness goes beyond simply wishing for things that others have. It is a lustful desire for something that sets the mind working on ways to get what is not lawfully mine. The issue with covetousness is that it puts myself above God and neighbor. Covetousness turns the thing or person desired into an idol that displaces God. It shows a lack of contentment and a lack of thankfulness for the situation that God has placed me in. It also is an expression of hatred and disregard for the one whom I will injure to get what I covet.

The tenth commandment is the most damming of all for it convicts everyone of sin. Who is it on the face of the earth that has not coveted something or someone? Covetousness is the root of sin for it leads to lying, to cheating, to stealing, to adultery and murder. The only way to conquer covetousness is to replace it with its Godly counterpart. Covetousness must be replaced by gratitude and contentment.

Gratitude is a key virtue in the Christian life for it springs from an understanding of what I really deserve and what God has given me.

Today, we are frequently inundated with discussions on human rights and individual rights. Yet, a biblical understanding of rights shows us that the only right that we truly deserve is an eternity separated from God. Naturally, that is what we deserve and that is what we have coming to us. The amazing mercy and grace of God is that He saved us and redeemed us from condemnation, death and eternal destruction. Once we are thus saved, everything else is a bonus. Thus, no person can be a true Christian without a deep and abiding sense of gratitude. In my own life, I am one who should have died in a car accident in 1975. But God graciously let me live, and then saved me, blessed me with a wife, children, grandchildren and opportunity to live and work and study and minister to others. Absolutely everything about my life is a bonus. To continually remember this is to live a life of thanksgiving.

Thanksgiving for all things leads to a life of contentment. Contentment sees God as the most important possession for which I would willingly surrender all the things of this world. Contentment means that I desire absolutely nothing but God and what He has entrusted to me. Contentment means living life simply and holding all things lightly, being ever ready to surrender it all and to meet God face to face. *"There is great gain in godliness with contentment."* (1 Tim 6:6)

But this discipline, like all the others must be continually practiced. Practicing thankfulness means accepting all situations in gratitude for God has allowed them. It is a discipline because in stressful or painful situations, it is very hard to be grateful. However, if I set my mind on things above, where Christ is, I can practice gratitude even as I am facing death. Gratitude and contentment show the world that my life is not my own but belongs to God. They also show that I love and trust my faithful Savior who will soon return to take me home.

> *"Whom have I in heaven but you? And there is nothing on earth that I desire besides you. [26] My flesh and my heart may fail, but God is the strength of my heart and my portion forever." Psalm 73:25-26*

Love's Rule Discipline Chart

#	The Commandment (God's Heart)	The Discipline (My Love Response)
Pre	**Exodus 20: 1-2** I am the LORD your God, who brought you out of the land of Egypt, out of the house of slavery.	The discipline of **remembrance** – I must never forget the pit from which I was dug. I was dead in sins. Christ has given me life and has made me His. This is why I respond in love through the disciplines that follow: (Luke 22:19)
1	**Exodus 20:3** You shall have no other gods before me.	The discipline of **worship**. He alone is worthy of all honor and glory and I will put nothing above my devotion to Him. I will worship Him continually with all of my mind, my heart & my strength (Luke 4:8).
2	**Exodus 20:4-6** You shall not make for yourself a carved image, or any likeness of anything that is in heaven above, or that is in the earth beneath, or that is in the water under the earth. 5 You shall not bow down to them or serve them for I the LORD your God am a jealous God, visiting the iniquity of the fathers on the children to the third and the fourth generation of those who hate me, 6 but showing steadfast love to thousands[1] of those who love me and keep my commandments.	The discipline of **renouncing all idols.** What lifestyle have I bought into and come to value more that Christ? Whom am I really serving? While I recognize that I need to work to feed my family, I will not give my allegiance to anything other that Christ. I will practice **self denial** to break the world's hold on me (Matt. 16:24). The discipline of **loving God and doing His Word.** I will show my love for God by feeding on His word each day, and doing exactly what He says. He has given His Word for my good and I will delight in it and put it into practice (Deut. 8:3).
3	**Exodus 20:7** You shall not take the name of the LORD your God in vain, for the LORD will not hold him guiltless who takes His name in vain.	The discipline of **guarding my tongue.** I renounce all cursing and foul language and will use my voice only as an instrument of righteousness to praise God and to bless and build up others. I will use God's name only in reverence and worship (James 3:6, Ps. 34:1).
4	**Exodus 20:8-11** Remember the Sabbath day, to keep it holy. 9 Six days you shall labor, and do all your work, 10 but the seventh day is a Sabbath to the LORD your God. On it	The discipline of **rest.** I will resist the temptation to work seven days a week, and will schedule and take a full day (24 hours) each week to devote to rest and reflection, allowing God to recharge my

	you shall not do any work, you, or your son, or your daughter, your male servant, or your female servant, or your livestock, or the sojourner who is within your gates. [11] For in six days the LORD made heaven and earth, the sea, and all that is in them, and rested the seventh day. Therefore the LORD blessed the Sabbath day and made it holy.	spirit, so that I might keep Him the center of my world. I will use that time not just for pleasure, but for drawing closer to Him. I will slow myself down and enter into His rest (Matt. 11:28, Heb. 4:11).
5	**Exodus 20:12** Honor your father and your mother, that your days may be long in the land that the LORD your God is giving you.	The discipline of **giving honor**. I will be proactive in blessing my parents, and also those to whom honor is due. (1 Peter 2:17).
6	**Exodus 20:13** You shall not murder.	The discipline of **renouncing all anger.** I recognize that when I am angry at someone, it is the same as wanting them dead. Rather I will pray for those who hurt and abuse me, turning over all judgment to God forgiving every injustice as Christ forgave me (Matt. 5:22, James 4: 1-8).
7	**Exodus 20:14** You shall not commit adultery.	The discipline of **training my eyes** and **renouncing lust.** I renounce all impure thoughts, I will see all people as brothers or sisters, fathers or mothers seeking only their good (Matt. 5:28, 1 Tim. 5:1-2).
8	**Exodus 20:15** You shall not steal.	The discipline of **Integrity.** I will accept only what I have earned or purchased unless it has been given to me as a gift. I will work hard so as to be able to give generously to God and to others (Eph. 4:28).
9	**Exodus 20:16** You shall not bear false witness against your neighbor.	The discipline of **truthfulness.** I renounce all lying, slander and gossip. I will tell the truth in love. My yes will always mean yes and my no will mean no (John 8:44, Matt. 5:37)
10	**Exodus 20:17** "You shall not covet your neighbor's house; you shall not covet your neighbor's wife, or his male servant, or his female servant, or his ox, or his donkey, or anything that is your neighbor's.	The discipline of **contentment and thankfulness.** I will rejoice when God prospers others and will not begrudge others. I will give thanks to God for what He has entrusted to me (Col. 2:6-7, 1 Tim. 6:6).

Study Guide for Chapter Seven

A. Questions for Personal Reflection

- Record answers in your journal.

1. Have you personally experienced the tendency to want to add certain behavior to faith in Jesus Christ as the basis for salvation? Why do you think that we do this?

2. What do you see is the difference between religion and faith? (see page 170) Write this out in your own words. What is it that makes worship acceptable to God rather than a religious ritual? (see Rom. 12:1)

3. What are the four major functions of the law? (pages 172-174) How can the law be used wrongly?

4. Do you agree that the preamble to the Ten Commandments is a critical part? (see Ex. 20:1) If so, why? What is the difference between obeying out of fear of punishment and out of gratitude and love?

5. Which of the ten disciplines modeled after the Ten Commandments resonates with you the most? Why?

B. **Exercises** (Individual or Large Group)

1. Jesus often used the principle *"law to the proud – grace to the broken"*[lxxxix] in approaching people. Read the following passages and reflect on which approach you see. Why is it inappropriate to extend grace to the proud and law to the broken?

   Luke 18:18-24, Luke 18:35-43, John 8:1-11, Matthew 15:1-9

2. Jesus said: "Come to me all who labor and are heavy laden and I will give you rest" (Matt 11:28). Is this statement grace (gospel) or law? What is the

relationship between them? Why do we need both? How do they function together? Discuss

C. Small Group Breakout (2 or 3)

4. Read Leviticus 19. Take three of the many commandments listed and construct a principle and a corresponding conviction or discipline that reflects God's heart in the matter.

5. Take some time to share prayer requests and pray for one another.

D. Assignment for This Week

1. Continue to observe five devotional times in solitude this week. Use the breath prayer *Lord Jesus, I delight to do your will (*based on *Ps. 119:16)*. Begin with the ACTS formula. As you pray, remember what God has done for you and be thankful.

2. Each day select one the ten disciplines outlined in the chart at the end of the chapter. Write down a personal resolution for yourself that reflects your desire to please God out of gratitude and love.

3. Continue to take 10-15 minutes at the end of each day to do a Prayer of Examen (see pages 80-81).

4. Observe a purposeful fast for one or two meals this week.

5. Continue with your Bible reading plan.

6. Read chapter eight. Answer the Questions for Personal Reflection your journal.

8. Mission & Community – The Expressions of Love

"As the Father has sent me, even so I am sending you" John 20:21

Disciples of Jesus Christ are a sent people. In John's gospel, when Jesus appears to His astonished disciples after rising from the dead, He has four things to say to them. First, He says, *"Peace be with you"* (John 20:19b). This is *Shalom*[8], the peace of God. This peace is characterized by salvation, redemption, restoration, renewal and rest. For in the resurrection of Jesus, the consummation of all things and the end of the final ages has broken forth. Jesus has accomplished the work of redemption and He now declares peace to His disciples. The second thing that He says is a declaration of Divine intent "*As the Father has sent me, even so I am sending you"* (John 20:21). Jesus immediately commissions His disciples to be a sent people. They are not to sit comfortably in one place and call people to themselves, rather, they are to go and make disciples of all nations. Matthew records this commission as Jesus' last words of His gospel:

> *'And Jesus came and said to them, "All authority in heaven and on earth has been given to me. 19 Go therefore and make disciples of all nations, baptizing them in the name of the Father and of the Son and of the Holy Spirit, 20 teaching them to observe all that I have commanded you. And behold, I am with you always, to the end of the age."' Matthew 28:18-20*

The primary verb in this passage is "*make disciples"*. Going, baptizing and teaching are all subordinate participles that describe how this disciple making is to be done. All the verb forms are imperatives, which make them commands. According to Matthew, Jesus' last word to His disciples was a command to make disciples.

The third thing that Jesus says to His disciples in John's account is *"Receive the Holy Spirit..." (John 20:22b).* It would not be possible for the disciples to carry out this mission in their own strength.

---

[8] While the Greek word in the text is *eiraynay,* (peace) Jesus would have likely spoken Aramaic or Hebrew and used the classic Hebrew word *Shalom*

They must be empowered by the Holy Spirit. The Holy Spirit would teach them all things and bring to their remembrance everything that Jesus had said to them (John 14:26). The Holy Spirit would clothe them with power to perform healings and miracles in Jesus' name authenticating the gospel message. The Holy Spirit would inspire them to write scripture to establish and ground the church for all time.

The fourth statement that Jesus makes establishes the apostolic authority of the disciples over the Church. *"If you forgive the sins of anyone, they are forgiven; if your withhold forgiveness from anyone, it is withheld"* (John 20:23). Jesus was commissioning the apostles to be the instrument through which the gospel would be preached and through which forgiveness of sins was to be granted. It is not that the disciples could arbitrarily forgive sins or not, but rather through their ministry, the conditions of forgiveness would be proclaimed. They would be able to declare or withhold forgiveness based upon people's response to the gospel.

In reflecting on Jesus' last words and His commission to His disciples, we can see that mission is primary. They were to *"go and make disciples*." This was to start in Jerusalem, then proceed to Judea, Samaria and to the ends of the earth (Acts 1:8). God's heart is to reach all people with the gospel message and bring all whom He has appointed together in unity as His covenant people, a kingdom of priests and a holy nation. The community of disciples were to bear fruit, fruit that would remain in Christ as they themselves remained in Him (John 15:16).

Despite being told to "go", many of the disciples remained in Jerusalem. It was not until persecution broke out that the church was scattered and the disciples forced to go outside of Jerusalem and Judea (Acts 8:1). It is always easier to remain in one place and settle with a community than it is to go out and speak to strangers. Church life tends to be inwardly focused. In most churches, the existing community comes first. Eighty to ninety-five percent of the budget is spent on the existing community of faith. Perhaps five to fifteen percent is spent on "Missions". Moreover "Missions" is often external to the community. Those who are not part of the community, whom the community "supports" to go and reach the unreached, are asked to do it. What has happened is that we have come to believe that it is the church that has a mission. We believe that Christ's main objective was to establish a church, which is to then settle, build buildings, hire personnel and call people to join. Mission is often seen as a subtask of being "the church".

Thus we tend to believe that Christology determines Ecclesiology, which in turn determines Missiology.

Christology → Ecclesiology → Missiology
Christ → Church → Mission

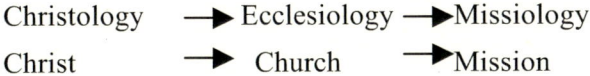

Allan Hirsch concludes, in *The Forgotten Ways,*[xc] that this is not Christ's intent. His intent was that sending be primary. We are to first go and make disciples. That is pure mission. Then as disciples are made, they will naturally gather in community, but that community must never displace the Mission. The correct sequence is:

Christology → Missiology → Ecclesiology
Christ → Mission → Church

We have largely forgotten that we are all to consider ourselves to be a *sent people.* That means that we as God's people must be aware of who it is that Christ is sending us to. It means that I, as a disciple must continually ask: *"Where and to whom is God sending me?"* To be a disciple is to be a missionary for we are collectively a sent people.

This is rarely the culture of most churches. Most churches have developed an institutional, attractional mindset. In the west, many leaders adopt modern marketing methods and a corporate structure to appeal to a consumerist culture. They establish popular programs, engaging worship and an alluring message. They present themselves as an appealing community and expect their people to go out and bring in their neighbors and coworkers so that the church will grow. A common temptation is to make the Christian life attractive. In the process, the gospel is often distorted. The Christian message can easily become *"Come to Jesus and He will give you a wonderful life full of peace, prosperity and happiness".* There is often little talk of sin. There is little talk of repentance, of dying, of taking up one's cross and self-denial. There is little talk of suffering for the sake of Christ and the gospel.

Jesus did not call us to a life of ease, pleasure and self-absorption. He did not call us to join a Christian country club. Rather He called us each to take up our own cross, which He Himself has appointed, and follow Him. We are to deny ourselves, and live *for Him.* The Apostle Paul reminds the believers in Corinth of exactly that when he says:

> *"...he died for all, that those who live might no longer live for themselves but for him who for their sake died and was raised." 2 Corinthians 5:15*

We are to live *for Him and in Him and through Him.* It is precisely when we surrender ourselves to do that that we experience our greatest joy. But exactly how exactly do we do that? Many people today are dissatisfied with the Christian life of ease, but do not know what to do. It is not just a matter of sincerity, of doing our best. We must know what to do.

Laborers in The Harvest.

In looking at the Great Commission, we must start with asking ourselves why did Jesus command us to go and make disciples. Having arrived at this point, we should now understand that what God desires is a real living thriving relationship with each one of us. He wants us to participate in the *Shalom* of God, the redemption of the world, the renewal of all things and the restoration of justice and righteousness. He wants us to announce and manifest His presence as the King, whose Kingdom is now coming, but is still not fully yet. It is here now, to eyes of faith, and ultimately will be indisputable when revealed to all. Meanwhile, we are collectively His bride and the Day is fast approaching. The wedding will soon be consummated and He wants us to know Him, love Him and act for Him. And He wants others to join us as His body, His bride to be. He desires that the full number of His people be gathered for that great wedding day. His heart is the salvation of a people that He has redeemed from every ethnic group, language, tribe and nation to be a people who will reflect His glory and give it expression through the manifestation of His own unbridled love. Many of these people are in the world today but most of them are enslaved to sin and in bondage to the things of this world. They need to be brought into the Kingdom. They need to become part of His eternal bride, God's own people.

Jesus Himself displays this profoundly evangelistic fervor. In the fourth chapter of John's gospel, Jesus is passing through Samaria and comes upon a woman at Jacob's well. The disciples go into town to buy food while Jesus engages the woman in a conversation, which leads her to faith and results in the entire village being saved. From the disciples' perspectives, Jesus is wasting His time. They do not want to be in Samaria. As Jews, they are culturally antagonistic toward Samaritans and especially women, and an adulteress at that. Jesus admonishes them telling them to lift up their eyes *"for the fields are white for harvest"* (John 4:35). The point is that the harvest is wherever we are. We just have to look. It is likely to be found in the most unexpected places. We are not likely to find it sitting in our churches and calling passers by to come in. In the words of Steve Hill *"That is like the farmer standing in his barn calling out, asking the harvest to come on in."* [xci]

The problem is never with the harvest. The fields all around us are white. God has people in every city, town and village who are waiting for someone to befriend them and introduce them to Jesus. The problem is always with the laborers. Either there are not enough of them, or they don't know what to do, or they are just plain lazy. We are those laborers.

In Luke chapter 10, Jesus commissions seventy-two others and sends them out two by two into the villages where He was about to go. Now, these seventy-two were not the twelve disciples who traveled everywhere with Jesus. They were from the larger group that surrounded Him. Jesus tells them that *"the harvest is plentiful, but the laborers are few."* (Luke 10:2) He then asks them to pray to the Lord of the harvest to send out laborers into His harvest. But Jesus was sending *them* out. They were the laborers. And so are we.

THE LUKE TEN PATTERN

It is interesting that in Jesus' instructions to these laborers, we find a pattern of evangelism that is much different to what we have been conditioned to think. Steve Hill in *The Luke 10 Manual*[xcii] comments extensively on this. He notes first that Jesus sends them out as *"lambs in the midst of wolves"* (Luke 10:3). In other words, there is danger inherent in such labor. They are being sent into unknown, possibly antagonistic territory. They are leaving the comfort of their own surroundings and going into other peoples' villages, into other peoples' homes. Yet they are told to take nothing for the journey (Luke 10:4). They are to rely on God to provide for them. They are to maintain a singleness of purpose and not get distracted along the way (vs. 4).

Next, Jesus gives them four specific instructions as to what to do. The **first instruction** is that they are to declare to every house that they enter *"Peace be to this house"* (vs. 5). Travelers would often find lodging in private homes. As they enter a house they are to declare peace to that household. This peace is the *Shalom* of God. It encapsulates God's favor, blessing, redemption, restoration and rest. In declaring "peace", they are declaring that God wishes to bless and redeem, give favor, restoration and freedom. They are declaring that the work of the devil is now being destroyed. They are telling people the full extent of God's love for them. They are announcing that He desires to redeem and rescue them from a life of futility and bondage and to usher them into a new life of reconciliation to God, to one another and to creation itself.

In declaring this message of peace, people would have likely responded by either being appreciative and inquisitive or by perhaps by being antagonistic and offhand. Jesus continues to say that if a *son of peace* is there, then the disciples' peace will rest upon him. If there is no son of peace, then that peace will return to them (vs 6).

It is very interesting that the first task of the disciple laboring in the harvest is to bless people and declare a message of peace. There is no religious dogma here. It is simply declaring a blessing upon each house. We can conclude that our first duty as laborers in the harvest is to bless people, to declare the peace of God, to testify to the love of God and His heart for healing, redemption and restoration. Those who hear us and respond by affirming that peace are "sons of peace". It is among them that we should spend our energy. Once we find a son of peace, we should stay there, putting our energies into that household ("*Do not go from house to house."* vs 7b)

The **second instruction** is that the disciples should remain in that same house, eating and drinking whatever is set before them. This instruction is repeated twice in verse 7 and 8. It should be noted that in Eastern cultures, eating and drinking as a guest is a sign of acceptance and honor of the hosts. The Jews, whom Jesus sent would have been trained by their own culture to be very careful as to what they ate and whom they ate with. They had elaborate rituals for washing of hands and cleansing of cups. They had strict dietary laws. But Jesus issues no such instructions. He tells them to eat and drink *whatever is set before them* (vs 8). They are to accept the hospitality of their hosts and accept them as they are. This is countercultural to us as well. We tend to eat and drink only with those who believe as we do and belong to the same social circle as we do. But Jesus instructs us to accept others and their hospitality first. He also points out that the laborer deserves his wages (vs.7). A true "son of peace" will not begrudge sharing food and provision with one who is God's ambassador. That is not to say that we should take advantage of people, but it does mean that those who hear the word should share good things with those who bring it.

In applying this second point to our situation, we should note that when we come into strange situations and different groups of people; we are to simply accept their hospitality without becoming judgmental, aloof or haughty. Often we are tempted to judge people because they drink or smoke or eat different food than we do. Such an attitude will always become a barrier to friendship and mission.

The **third instruction** given is that those sent should heal the sick. Jesus empowers His disciples to heal. It is interesting to note that one of the purposes of the healings and miracles of Jesus was to authenticate who He was and the message that He spoke. A second purpose was to show the heart and compassion of the Father. It is also interesting to note that such healings continued to occur after Jesus had been raised from the dead and ascended into heaven. The book of Acts is replete with healings, miracles and even people being raised from the dead (Acts 9:40). All over the world, miraculous healings occur in Jesus' name as people of God pray. A friend of mine recently returned from two weeks in India where he was ministering in a church that is in the slums of Vijayawada. He personally witnessed over one hundred healings in all day services as people lined up waiting their turn to be prayed for.

Praying for healing is something that any disciple can do. I was once in Goa, India, with a friend, when we decided to check on some transportation that we had arranged earlier. As we walked into Sweet Mama's restaurant we were greeted with many hellos. One lady looked at my friend who had injured his head that morning, telling him that he needed some spirits to ease the pain. My friend answered light heartedly that he already had the Holy Spirit and that that was all that he needed. Immediately, Sweet Mama herself got up from the table and asked us: *"Are you men of God?"* We answered: "Yes". She immediately asked us if we would come with her down the street and pray for her sister who was dying of cancer. So, off we went. The entire household gathered to hear us pray. We were able to bless this woman, anoint her with oil and commend her to Christ. We had to leave Goa that day, so we never learned how she made out, but we left with great joy knowing that we had prayed for healing and proclaimed the Kingdom of God.

The point is that this is something so simple that anyone can do it. If you come across someone who is sick, all you have to do is ask him or her if they would mind if you prayed for them. When you pray, you can invoke God's peace and redemption on them and pray for their physical healing. Who knows what God might do? Praying for them also allows the person to hear first hand the reality of your relationship with Christ. It can be an amazing source of blessing for you and for the other person. I have often done this and found that it opens the door to all kinds of conversations about God. It also shows people that you truly do care for them. I am astonished that so many believers miss opportunities to pray for others just because they are shy and shrink back.

The **fourth instruction** that Jesus gives is to say to them that *"the kingdom of God has come near you"* (Luke 10:9). It is interesting to note that this last proclamation, which is the heart of the gospel, is the last step in the process. Only after we have declared peace, enjoyed hospitality and prayed for healing are we to proclaim the Kingdom. How counter intuitive! Normally, we would want to reverse the order. We would want to proclaim the gospel first then, if they accept it, pray for healing, then enjoy their hospitality and then bless their house.

The pattern that Jesus inaugurates here requires that we move out of our comfort zones and go out into our community where the unbelievers are. This is not what we like to do. We prefer to stay in our own homes and churches and have people come to us. When people come to us, we are in control. We are the master of our own domain. We love to be in control and we love being masters. But when we go out and meet others in their homes or contexts, we are not master. We are not in control. Rather we come to them as servants. We bless them, pray for them and proclaim truth to them. We are not on our own turf and we are not comfortable. But that is exactly where Jesus wants us. His power is made perfect in our weakness (2 Cor 12:9).

We ought to pray earnestly that God will send us out of our comfort zone. We ought also to ask Him specifically where He wants to send us. In the Luke 10 narrative, Jesus sends His disciples into the villages where He Himself was about to go. We need to ask God in prayer where He is about to go in our own context. We all move in many different worlds at work, in neighborhoods, in our sports and leisure activities, in schools, clubs and places where we volunteer, places where we shop. If we find that we have too few such worlds, then we should prayerfully consider getting involved in activities where our world would be expanded. Every daily activity that we are a part of provides opportunities for us to be a sent person, declaring the peace of God, enjoying hospitality, praying for the sick and proclaiming the Kingdom. If this is our mindset, we will find ourselves living in an incarnational attitude, going into every setting in order to be a sent person to incarnate Christ among the people there.

NORTH STREET

One of the best examples of this in my own life is my involvement in a community we call North Street. Several years ago, I was hosting a discipleship group in my home. One of our members Nino had a heart for blessing people by cooking for them. Nino volunteered at the local Salvation Army soup kitchen and wanted to do more. One day, he gave one of the patrons a ride home to a large rooming complex on North Street. This was a very rough neighborhood and this particular building was well known as a crack house in Barrie. Many tenants were drug dealers, prostitutes, and the some of the poorest of the poor in Barrie.

Nevertheless, Nino felt God tapping him on the shoulder and saying: "Why don't you cook for these people?" Nino initially struggled with this. He could barely stand to go into the front door, for the smell and filth made him very uncomfortable. However, he persisted in obedience and began to cook up huge pots of food bringing them into the building, knocking on doors and telling people that there was free food in the kitchen. Before long Nino got to know almost everyone in the building. He worked in a grocery store and he would buy meat at discount prices and distribute it to people as they needed. When people asked him why he was doing this, he would simply say that Jesus had changed his life. Nino was once a drug addict and a veteran of three extensive rehab programs, none of which were successful. Finally, someone introduced him to Christ and he was instantly cured of his addiction.

As Nino became well known in the building, he suggested starting up a Bible study. When Nino asked me if I would lead the Bible study at North Street, I agreed. Some other members of our group also volunteered to help, some buying Bibles, some donating food, others supplying chairs. The first few evenings we were there was way beyond my comfort zone. As we met in the common kitchen we had fights breaking out in the hallways around us, much yelling and cursing, people smoking, some coming in drunk. It was a crazy environment. But it was also exciting. We were like sheep among wolves. In one of our meetings, two police cruisers pulled up and took out one of the men who was in our Bible study. We prayed for him before he went down into the police car for questioning. In a few minutes he came back much relieved. They only wanted some information.

In our Bible study, we worked chapter by chapter through the book of John. It was highly participative with people asking questions at will and asking for prayer for themselves and others. Soon we added some worship music and before long we had an active church service at North Street. The owner of the building gave us a room in the building to store our supplies and we soon began midweek Bible studies, community barbeques and film nights. By the time, we finished the book of John, we had baptized two people in a portable hot tub. Others reaffirmed a faith lost years ago. We now had a community of believers. Shortly thereafter one of the residents was found dead in a wooded ravine. He had died of a massive heart attack. Our group conducted two memorial services for him, one at North Street and one at the drop in center downtown where he was well known. To this day, I continue to be involved in the community at North Street.

Now this church would never have started had Nino simply stayed in his comfort zone. I would not have been blessed to be a part of it had I stayed in my comfort zone. The ironic thing was that for months before Nino asked me to lead the bible study, he had been trying to get people from one of the local churches to pick up some people from North Street and bring them to their church. Some did go, but never really connected. They simply did not feel at home there. But as soon as we went to them, the situation changed entirely. As sent people, we were there solely to serve them. We were there to bless that house, to eat and drink with them, to pray for the sick and to proclaim the Kingdom. It was exactly what Jesus asked His disciples to do in Luke chapter 10. And it gave me a fresh understanding of my role as one who is sent.

The question for you as you read this is: To whom is God is sending you? Who are the people around you that God wants to bless and bring to Himself? You ought to consider neighbors, work associates, those at leisure activities and places where you do volunteer work. Perhaps you should start some new activities to enlarge your friendships. You should also consider how much "hanging around time" you have. It does not help to have many acquaintances if you are always rushing off to one thing or another. You need some "hang out" time. I have found that most Christians are so absorbed with the activities of their church that they have no time to reach out and befriend people around them. My son, his wife and five kids attended a very large church for several years. Between the two of them and the kids, they were at the church four to five nights a week. They also lived in a poor Hispanic area of the city and desperately wanted to reach out to people around them but found that all they could do was wave to them as they drove off to the suburbs to go to church activities. Finally, they decided to change their worship lifestyle and free up most weeknights. Soon, they were having Hispanic kids from the neighborhood in their backyard and were beginning to make real friendships. They were able to volunteer as a family in a downtown soup kitchen. They made blankets for the homeless as a family. They ran a backyard Bible camp for neighborhood kids. They began to have a keen idea of where God was sending them. They are currently planning a family mission trip to Mexico with some other families to experience first hand the background of their neighbors.

Reflecting on their experience and my own as well, I have to ask myself which lifestyle God desires for us. A household that worships God daily and continually reaches out to others or the church-centered life that only interacts with other Christians? I believe that church leaders need to reflect on these principles and consider where it is that they and their people are being sent.

Moreover, we understand from the life of Jesus that He had a heart for the poor, the destitute, the sick and the demon possessed. Jesus spent most of His time with these sorts of people. He took much criticism for the religious elite believed that these people were being punished for past sins. They accused Him of eating and drinking with "sinners". Yet Jesus pointed out that it is precisely those who are sick who need a physician. If we are to model our personal ministry after that of the Savior, we must have a heart of compassion towards the poor of our society. A compassionate heart is one sign of a true follower of Christ (Isaiah 58, James 1:27).

When we read scripture, we quickly see that God's heart is one of compassion for the poor, the lonely, the destitute. Jesus made this abundantly clear when He spoke of His return at the end of the age. At that time He will separate the sheep from the goats. The characteristic of the sheep is that they were compassionate and actively generous to those who were hungry, sick, in prison and in distress. In loving and serving them, they were loving and serving Jesus Himself. These are the ones who will inherit the Kingdom. On the contrary, the goats are those who refused to have compassion. These will be cast into eternal punishment.

> *"For I was hungry and you gave me no food, I was thirsty and you gave me no drink, I was a stranger and you did not welcome me, naked and you did not clothe me, sick and in prison and you did not visit me.' Then they also will answer, saying, 'Lord, when did we see you hungry or thirsty or a stranger or naked or sick or in prison, and did not minister to you?' Then he will answer them, saying, 'Truly, I say to you, as you did not do it to one of the least of these, you did not do it to me.' And these will go away into eternal punishment, but the righteous into eternal life.". Matthew 25:42-46*

One cannot be a disciple of Jesus and ignore the needs of the poor. As long as there is a hungry human being on the face of the planet, we have work to do. We must carefully consider how we use the resources that God has given us. Are we spending our excess on ourselves or on human needs in desperate situations?

APPROACHING PEOPLE

People are often leery and suspicious of attempts to woo them into our churches. They mistrust our motives sensing that we want to "capture" them and make them carbon copies of ourselves. We need to examine the image that we project to the secular world. Are we really the type of follower that Christ desires? If not, reproducing ourselves in others may not be God's heart. It is more likely that God wants people to be unique and individual expressions of His love, sent out into the world. He wants a personal relationship with them where He is their

Lord, not the church, nor Christian culture. As people come to faith they ought to be released to become what Christ wants them to be.

Therefore our motivation for reaching people must be love alone. We love people because even the worst of them is made in God's image and bears the divine imprint. Loving one's neighbor sincerely from the heart is an expression of our love for God. The Apostle John writes *"for he who does not love his brother whom he has seen cannot love God whom he has not seen."* 1 John 4:20.

Love does not look down on a person who is unsaved. That stance comes from pride and not love. Love rather descends into the world of the beloved and relates to people at their level. When we go into their world, we must become a servant and not a master. We are there to love them and tell them about God's love for them. We are to declare the *Shalom* of God, pray for their sick and tell them about the love of Jesus, the King whose kingdom has come, is ever coming and will come again.

SHARING YOUR FAITH

While believers find it easy enough to bless people and even pray for healing, they often stop short of actually speaking the gospel message and the name of Jesus Christ. I have found that in my own life, even though I have been a Christian for many years, I have found it awkward to speak of Christ because, in the secular realm, I could find no context in which to do so. Religion and politics are often seen as taboo subjects. Yet, as a pastor I was charged with the responsibility of proclaiming the gospel and training lay people to do the same. As I was developing an evangelism-training program for our church, I had an opportunity to research a number of different approaches[xciii] to encourage people to share their faith. What I was looking for was a way in which people, through the everyday course of their lives, could engage people in conversation in a way that had left them thankful for that conversation yet at the same time actually did declare the good news of Christ. I found that the best model for evangelism was Jesus Himself.

If we look at how Jesus approached people, He never approached them by telling them up front that He was the Messiah and that they needed to put their faith in Him. Rather, He would engage them in conversation, move the discussion to things of God, and then bring up the issue of their sinfulness and their need for salvation. For example, in meeting the Samaritan woman at the well in John 4:7-42,

Jesus starts by engaging in every day conversation, asking the woman for a drink. Then He swings the discussion to things of God by commenting that if the woman knew who He was she would have asked Him for *"living water"* which would become a *"spring of water welling up to eternal life"* (John 4:14). As the woman asks for such water, Jesus tells her to go bring her husband and come back. In doing so, He puts His finger on one aspect of her life that highlights her sinfulness and need. She denies having a husband and Jesus commends her for telling the truth and points out that she has had five husbands and that the man that she now has is not her husband. She is astounded and convicted. She attempts to swing the conversation to issues of worship. Only when she expresses a belief in the coming Messiah does Jesus reveal that He is that Messiah. She rushes off to the village and excitedly reports her conversation. The whole village comes out to hear. As Jesus presents Himself and the gospel, the entire village comes to faith.

Jesus' approach was motivated out of a deep love for people. He did not come at them like a bulldozer but rather engaged them in conversation at whatever level they were at. Even though He was God, He relied upon the Holy Spirit's work in the person's heart. He would start up a conversation, move it into a discussion of the things of God, get the person's attention regarding their sinfulness and need for salvation and present Himself as Savior.

Likewise, whenever we approach people, we need to be motivated by love. We must see the other person as one for whom Christ died. We engage them in conversation and sensitively move the discussion to things of God. We must rely on the Holy Spirit to give us clues and promptings as to where to take the conversation. If we follow Jesus' own model, we will then bring up the subject of life and death, righteousness and judgment. Once we sense that a person is convicted or concerned we tell them about God's provision of salvation in Christ Jesus. This pattern is universally applicable. It has three simple steps.

Step 1: Swing the discussion to things of God

Engage people in conversation about everyday things. Ask them questions about their background. People generally love to talk about themselves. Then move the conversation to things of God. Ask a question like: *"Do you have a Christian background?*" or "*Do you have a faith"?* or *"What do you think life is about?"* or *"Do you ever think about God?*

Step 2: Bring up the subject of death, heaven, hell and judgment. Does it concern them?

In getting a person to face up to his or her need for salvation, there is no way of avoiding the universal human dilemma. We will all die and after that comes the judgment (Heb. 9:27). You might ask a person: *"Have you ever thought about death?"* or *"What do you think happens when you die?"* or *"Have you ever had someone close to you die?"* Most people will tell you what they think about death and some will be uncomfortable talking about it. You can personalize the discussion by asking: *"If you were to die today, do you think that you would go to heaven or to hell?* Most people will express a hope that they would go to heaven. Some might say that they don't believe in heaven or hell. The fact that they don't believe in it shouldn't dissuade you. Many people believed for thousands of years that the earth was flat, but their belief did not make it so. Regardless of what they say, you can move to the next questions, which focus on righteousness.

As this step progresses, you will have to be direct. You can ask *"Do you consider yourself a good person?"*[xciv] Most people will answer yes, because they can always think of people who are worse than they are. Unfortunately, God's standard is not other people but absolute righteousness. So you can ask simply *"Have you ever lied?"* If the person is honest, they will admit that yes of course they have lied. You can then express that you too have told a lie, after all who hasn't? What you are doing here is bringing them to an admission that according to God's standard (the Ten Commandments), that they fall short and are sinners. You can then repeat the process by asking: *"Have you ever stolen?"* or "*Have you ever used God's name as curse word?"* By their own admission they are forced to admit that they are a liar, a thief and a blasphemer.

You can also ask if they have ever looked with lust at another person? Jesus said that whoever has looked with lust at another has already committed adultery with them in his heart? So too they would be admitting that they are an adulterer at heart. The important part of this line of questioning is that your attitude *not be judgmental* but *empathetic*. You are trying to lead them to admit that they have fallen short of God's standard of moral perfection, as has every other human being. The Bible is clear that no liar, thief or adulterer (Gal. 5:20-21, Rev. 21:8) will inherit the Kingdom of God, so this sets up the next question.

Ask: *"When you stand before God on judgment day, will you be innocent or guilty?* (Rev. 20:13) Most people will admit that they are guilty of transgressing God's moral law as contained in the Ten Commandments.

Then ask again "*So would you end up in heaven or hell?"* Here most people will say heaven, for universalism is a popular heresy. You can ask them on what basis? If they are guilty of violating God's law, would they not be punished? Many believe that because God is a forgiving God, they will go to heaven, however you can point out that God is also a just God. So murderers, rapists and thieves will not be allowed into heaven. Here, you can also use the analogy of a courtroom scene. If a person was standing before a judge and they were guilty of a crime, the judge would have to punish them accordingly. If the judge were to just let the person go free, then justice would not be served. Eventually, they will admit the truth that, based on what they have done, they would likely go to hell and not heaven.[9]

Finally ask *"Are you concerned about your eternal destiny?"* If a person has been truly honest, they should be convicted at this point and should express a concern. At this point you will need to be very compassionate and sympathetic. Remember that you too were once without Christ and in danger of hell.

Step 3: Tell them about the Savior – What God has done for them

Ask: "*Do you know what God has done for you so that you can escape being sent to hell?"* Whatever they answer, tell them the good news that Jesus Christ is the Son of God and that He came to die on the cross for the sins of all humanity. All of us have sinned, but Jesus took our punishment upon Himself. He could do this for He was fully human and fully God. But in order to benefit from this, you have to confess your sins, repent (that is turn away from sin) and trust in Jesus Christ alone for your salvation. When you do that by expressing that to Him in prayer, then He forgives your sins, and cleanses you from unrighteousness. He also gives you a new heart and His Holy Spirit to live inside you so that you can be empowered to love God and others and to live for Him.

---

[9] This line of questioning has been adapted from *The Way of the Master* Series, Comfort and Cameron, (Genesis Publishing Group, 2006) see www.livingwaters.com for their training products.

Encourage them to have a prayer conversation with God, expressing their sorrow for sin and accepting what Jesus has done on their behalf. This does not have to be done on the spot. You could suggest that they find a quiet time to be alone and have a heart to heart meeting with God. Remember that it is the Holy Spirit that converts a person, so leave it to God. Encourage them also to get a Bible and read it and fellowship with some other believers.

At this point, you may want to get some personal information so that you can stay in contact with them to encourage or answer any questions. Also commit to praying for them. If you feel comfortable, you could even pray for them on the spot. If you do so, they will hear first hand of your own relationship with God. Continue in prayer for them as God brings them to mind.

This entire process should not be done mechanically, but from an understanding that the function of the law is to convict people of sin. Once convicted, the gospel is there to show them God's amazing grace. However, people are not prepared for grace if they have no concept of their own sinfulness. We must bring them to an understanding of their sinfulness with compassion and humility, recognizing that we share in that sinfulness. If our hearts are in the right place this will be an easy process for it is wrapped in love and truth. People can sense genuine love. The truth will set them free. God has called us all to be agents of reconciliation, helping people to be reconciled to God (2 Cor. 5:20).

Sharing our faith with others can be an unsettling process for it takes us out of our comfort zone. We risk being rejected by others and mocked for our own faith. Yet, we must always remember that we too were once estranged from Christ. Where would we be today if no one had ever shared the gospel with us? We ought not be ashamed of the gospel for *"it is the power of salvation for those who believe"*. (Rom 1:16) As we step out in faith the Holy Spirit will embolden us more and more.

Christ's call to us is to go and make disciples. Bringing people to a saving knowledge of Christ is only the beginning. We must then take the responsibility of teaching and mentoring new believers so that they grow in their faith. Babies cannot be left to themselves but must be nurtured, cared for and taught. This book and study guide is designed to be an aid to such a discipleship process. Leading someone through it would be an excellent start.

Community – Together in Christ

As people come to faith in Christ, they are added to that immense community of faith that is the Church Universal. Hence the Church of Jesus Christ is never shrinking, it only grows. Moreover, when any community of faith gathers it does not gather alone but gathers with that "*great cloud of witnesses*" (Heb. 12:1) that surrounds us. We do not often think of this, but those in Christ who have gone before us are part of us. We are never alone. In addition, we are called together into physical communities of faith as we gather together to worship, to pray, to study and to work together. These communities are an expression of our love for God and our love for one another. They can be as small as families and house churches or as large as mega churches and large denominations. Wherever Christians gather, Christ is present (Matt. 18:20).

A number of metaphors are used in scripture to describe the Church. It is the bride of Christ (Rev. 19:7). It is God's family of faith (1 Tim. 5). It is a spiritual house (1 Pet. 2:5). It is the flock of the Good Shepherd (John 10). It is a branch of the true vine (John 15). Yet the most frequently used metaphor is that of a body (1 Cor. 12).

> *For in one Spirit we were all baptized into one body- Jews or Greeks, slaves or free- and all were made to drink of one Spirit. For the body does not consist of one member but of many.* 1 Corinthians 12:13-14

This scripture emphasizes both the unity *"one body"* and the diversity *"many members"* of the church. It is the Holy Spirit in us and Christ's presence among us that gives life to this body. Yet God has placed this body in a world that is ruled by Satan and hostile to Christ. Sometimes it appears as if the forces of history and the forces of evil are like a huge ocean that assaults a tiny ship. Yet the ship is never lost for it is anchored spiritually to Christ, its living head. In evil times it may have to take different forms, go underground and meet in secret but it is never non-existent. God calls and sustains His people.

Dietrich Bonhoeffer was a German pastor and theologian who ran afoul of the Nazi's when he refused to be a part of the official German church, which had succumbed to Nazification. Bonhoeffer, together with others like Herman Maas founded the Confessing Church, which was forced underground by the Gestapo. During that time Bonhoeffer lead a clandestine "illegal" seminary in Pomerania to train pastors for the Confessing Church. During those days he wrote a tiny book *"Life Together"*[xcv] in which he described his convictions about life in community. This book has become a classic of discipleship. Some key concepts are worth exploring here.

Bonhoeffer begins by pointing out that *"it is not to be taken for granted that the Christian has the privilege of living among other Christians".* [xcvi] Jesus lived among His enemies. The early church was a scattered people living in a hostile environment. They were commanded to *"go and make disciples"* not to rest in ease and comfort. The reason for this scattering was so that they might be like seeds into *"all the Kingdoms of the earth"* (Isa. 37:20). At the same time, the church is a gathered people for God has promise to gather the remnant of His people together (Zech. 10:8-9). That has happened spiritually as in Jesus Christ. We are all gathered together into the body of Christ, and it will also happen visibly at the end of the age when Jesus Christ returns *"to gather together his elect from the four winds, from one end of heaven to the other."* (John 11:52)

Thus, the church lives in constant danger and in constant hope. Because we are all called to suffer for the sake of Jesus Christ (Phil 1:29), *"the physical presence of Christians is a source of incomparable joy and strength to the believer"*[xcvii]. There is a bond between believers that is thicker than blood. Because I am in Christ and you are in Christ, we share a spiritual unity that will transcend time and space. Even after the world has long been destroyed, we will still be brothers and sisters together in Him. Moreover, we are all together one Bride with Him, members of the family of God, one household in faith, one flock of the Good Shepherd.

The fact that we are all in Christ means that we all need one another because of Christ. We need each other to speak the truth of God's word into one another's heart. We need each other to declare forgiveness of sin and absolution in the name of Christ. We also need one another to stir one another up to devotion to Christ and to deeds of righteousness. We also need one another for rebuke when we sin. It is only because we are in Christ that we can do so blamelessly, for only in Christ are we delivered from our own ego.

We also come to one another because of Christ. In Christ we have been chosen, accepted and united with Him and one another. Hence I can have peace with a brother or sister only because of Christ. I can relate to a brother or sister only through Christ. That is because, as Bonhoeffer says: *"The Christian no longer lives of himself, by his own claims and his own justification. He lives wholly by God's Word pronounced upon him."* [xcviii] As such, believers meet one another as agents of the message of salvation to a lost world. Without Christ there is discord and hostility between every person and God, and between person and person. But as agents of reconciliation, we have both a common mission and a common destiny. We are called to go into the world and we are called to be together in the world and into eternity. Therefore, I need you, I can relate to you, and I belong to you, only in and through Jesus Christ.

Bonhoeffer goes on to say that the community we call church is not an ideal, but a Divine reality.[xcix] We are not to descend into wishful thinking and dreams of what such an ideal community might look like. *"He who loves his dream of community more that the Christian community itself becomes the destroyer of the latter, even though his intentions may be ever so honest and earnest and sacrificial".* [c] He who dreams of creating his own perfect community soon becomes proud and pretentious. His lofty ambitions consume him. He comes to think of the community as his own. When that dream fails he first accuses others, then accuses God and finally accuses himself.

Rather, Bonhoeffer says, the church is that community already created by God and founded upon Christ, which we must simply receive in gratitude and humility. *"We enter into that common life not as demanders but as thankful recipients."* [ci] We are the ones grafted into that which God has already created. Hence our primary response should be one of great thankfulness. Unfortunately, many Christian communities are characterized not by thankfulness but by a judgmental attitude, spiritual pride, a critical attitude and a quest for personal preferences. This is wrong and sinful. Complaining and criticism are sinful and must be replaced by thankfulness and love. Love is the one virtue that covers a multitude of sins (1 Pet. 4:8). Here we must differentiate between human love, which is often self-seeking and self-serving and Divine love which is life giving and releasing. Bonhoeffer goes on to describe in detail the difference between these two kinds of love.[cii] I have summarized these differences in the table that follows.

HUMAN LOVE	**DIVINE LOVE**
Has little regard for Truth	Is based on Truth – The Word
Desires the other	Desires Christ for the other
Seeks to captivate	Seeks to release
Constructs own image of the other	Recognizes the true image that Christ gives the other
Seeks to interfere/manipulate	Seeks no dominion but Christ's
Is ruled by desires – comes from below	Is ruled by Christ – comes from above
Cannot love an enemy	Loves an enemy
Speaks to a brother about a brother (gossip, slander)	Speaks to Christ about a brother (prayer)
Cultivates its own ideal	Cultivates what God is building
Believes the worst	Believes the best
Ultimately self-focused	Ultimately other focused
Glorifies self	Glorifies God
Ends in death	Lives forever

The type of love described in the right hand column is from above. It is a supernatural love that comes from outside of us. It is ours because we are Christ's. It is the bond of our unity with Christ and with one another. Because we are all under such love, we can embrace the role of being a brother or sister in Christ to a brother or sister in Christ. Only one who is under the cross of Christ can fulfill such a role. Only one who has experienced and confessed sin, has known the forgiveness of the cross and embraced the Savior as his or her own can be a brother or sister to another. Only then can one speak the Word of Truth to a brother in humility and love. Mutual encouragement and edification is one goal of such a relationship. The many "one another" passages in scripture give us insight into other such roles.

The "One Another" Passages
Be at peace with each other (Mk. 9:50)
Love one another (Jn 13:34)
Be connected to one another (Ro 12:5)
Be devoted to one another (Ro 12:10)
Honor one another (Ro 12:10)
Rejoice with one another (Ro 12:15)
Weep with one another (Ro 12:15)
Live harmoniously with another (Ro 12:16)
Accept one another (Ro 15:7)
Counsel one another (Ro 15:14)
Greet one another (Ro 16:16)
Agree with one another (1 Co 1:10)
Wait for one another (1 Co 11:33)
Care for one another (1 Co 12:35)
Serve one another (Gal 5:13)
Carry one another's burdens (Gal 6:2)
Be kind to one another (Eph 4:32)
Forgive one another (Eph 4:32)
Submit to one another (Eph 5:21)
Bear with one another (Col 3:13)
Teach, admonish one another (Col 3:16)
Encourage one another (1 The 5:11)
Build up one another (1 The 5:11)
Stir up one another for good (Heb 10:24)
Be hospitable to one another (1 Pe 4:9)
Use your gifts to serve one another (1 Pe 4:10)
Be humble to one another (1 Pe 5:5)
Confess sins to one another (Jas 5:16)
Fellowship with one another (1 Jn 1:7)

Another role of a brother or sister in Christ is mutual accountability. Each believer should have someone of the same gender with whom they have a relationship of accountability. This also provides an avenue for the confession of sin. This person must also be a believer for only someone who is under the cross is a brother or sister who can hear a confession of sin. A regular meeting schedule for sharing one's faith journey provides an avenue for mutual encouragement, counsel and confession. In addition, such a brother or sister is in a position to ask some of the hard accountability questions that we all need to have asked. These questions can be generic accountability questions or can be based upon our own particular weaknesses. For example, someone who has had a gambling addiction should have an accountability partner who is comfortable asking them if they have refrained from gambling since they last met. Some common general accountability questions are:

1. What is the quality and frequency of your devotional times with God and His Word?
2. Have you violated any of God's moral commandments? (lying, stealing, coveting, lusting, dishonoring, etc)

3. Have you been with a man/woman in a way that was inappropriate and might lead to something sinful?
4. Do you have anyone that you need to forgive?
5. Have you shown love and respect to your spouse?
6. Is there anything that you should have done that you did not do?
7. Have you just lied to me?

Although, these questions may seem very personal, it is exactly this sort of relationship that is needed to keep us free from sin. If we feel that we can handle it on our own strength, we will soon be in for a rude awakening. Accountability is crucial in the Christian life.

Another crucial role of Christian community is worship. While we are called to worship God continually, there is a need for us to gather as a community and raise our voices together in praise, in prayer and in confession. The author of Hebrews tells us that we should not neglect meeting together (Heb 10:25). We must gather together regularly to remember Christ's death and resurrection and to celebrate His presence with us in the fellowship of the Lord's table.

It is at the Lord's table that we are nourished by the bread of eternal life, Christ Himself. It is there that we drink symbolically of His blood poured out for us (John 6:53). As we do so we are reminded that He is the one that provides our daily bread. He is the one who provides us with life and breath and everything. It is in Him that we live and move and have our being. Secondly, it is as we feast on Him that we know Him. The two disciples on the road to Emmaus following the crucifixion were dejected because they believed that their hopes for Israel and the Kingdom had been dashed by Jesus' crucifixion. Even after hearing of the empty tomb from the women, they still did not understand. Suddenly Jesus, unrecognized, walks beside them and begins to inquire about their sadness. As the conversation goes on, their hearts burn within them, but they still do not know Him. It is finally as they sit at supper and *Jesus takes the bread and breaks it that they know Him*. It is in the breaking of bread that their eyes were opened and they recognized Him. (Luke 24:31). So it is with us as we partake in the Lord's Table. It is through the breaking of bread that we also recognize Him. His presence with us at the communion table is a deep and profound mystery. It is also an assurance of that table fellowship to come in the Kingdom of God. As we partake of bread and wine we proclaim His death and resurrection until He appears again. At that time, He will be marveled at by saints and angels alike.

On that day, the marriage supper of the Lamb will be consummated. We all know how much excitement a royal wedding generates. The wedding of Prince Charles to Diana and the wedding of Prince William, and his lovely bride Catherine Middleton created a global stir. For each of these weddings, the United Kingdom declared the day a national holiday. Much as those weddings were spectacular, majestic and utterly romantic, they pale in comparison to that final great wedding where the bride of Christ, His universal church, made up of believers from every age and people group, will walk the heavenly aisle to be united forever with Him.

It is there that the ultimate love story will be consummated. God's love for His people will be displayed across time and space into eternity. Together we, who belong to Him, will take our places alongside the King of the universe as that divinely appointed royal bride to the King of kings. Until that day, we continue to live in that bitter-sweet tension between the sin soaked world and glory of heaven. But we do so in a community of faith that is called to be the perfect expression of His love. Together, we continue to prepare for His coming. We set our minds on things above. We long for Him above all else.

> *"If then you have been raised with Christ, seek the things that are above, where Christ is, seated at the right hand of God. Set your minds on things that are above, not on things that are on earth. For you have died, and your life is hidden with Christ in God. When Christ who is your life appears, then you also will appear with him in glory." Colossians 3:1-4*

For He is, and forever will be, our greatest joy. He is Love's greatest joy.

Study Guide for Chapter Eight

A. Questions for Personal Reflection

Record answers in your journal.

1. To what extent does this idea of being a "sent person" commissioned by Jesus change your view of the Christian life?

2. Read 2 Cor. 5:14-19. According to this passage what is the reason that Jesus died? How is the ministry entrusted to us described? What attitude would normally characterize someone who was sent on a "mission of reconciliation". Who is being reconciled to whom?

3. In your Christian life, how much of your energy has gone into your church community as opposed to reaching out to those who are outside the faith? Do you think this proportion is correct? Why or why not?

4. In the sharing your faith approach described on pages 215-219, how is the law used (see Rom. 3:20)? If someone is not concerned that they have broken God's law, is there any benefit to telling them about what Jesus has done for them?

5. Look at the chart comparing human love and God's love on page 223. How would you rate the way that you have loved in the past based on this polarity? What changes do you need to make in how you love?

B. Exercises (Individual or Large Group)

1. Read Acts 17:16-34. What did Paul use as an entry point to swing the discussion to things of God? Once he got their attention, what was the message that he delivered (see vs. 29-31)? What was the response?

Relate this to the suggestions for sharing your faith on pages 215-219. How can you apply these yourself?

2. This week commit to sharing your faith with someone. Start by asking people if they can help you complete an assignment for a course you are taking. You do not have to get all the way through the questions. Go as far as you feel the Holy Spirit is leading you.

C. Small Group Breakout (2 or 3)

1. Read Luke 18:18-25. How did Jesus correct the ruler's understanding of the word "good"? Why do you think Jesus pointed him to the commandments? Why did Jesus allow him to walk away? What does this tell us about how we ought to present the gospel?

2. Take some time to share prayer requests and pray for one another.

D. Assignment for This Week

1. Continue to observe five devotional times in solitude this week. Use the breath prayer *"Lord Jesus, here I am send me"* (Isa. 6:8) . Begin with the ACTS formula (see page 127-128). As you pray, ask God to show you where and to whom He wants to send you.

2. Begin to prayerfully reflect upon your own lifestyle as one sent and in community. Fast for one or two meals or for a full day. Ask God to show you His will for you as a member of His body.

3. Spend some time reflecting on how you will continue with your devotional times now that you have finished this study.

Epilogue

As part of the research for this book and study guide, I had the privilege of leading two groups of participants through it. They have had much input into the content of the material and I am extremely grateful for their partnership with me through this journey. If you are anything like them, you probably need to take a deep breath right now. This has likely been an intensely personal experience with the God of all grace.

The question that you, like them, may now have on your mind is, "Now what? Where do I go from here?" The answer to these questions is simple. Continue to work on your personal relationship with Jesus Christ. Nurture your love for Him. Spend time with Him. Honor Him by keeping His commandments. Love your neighbor as yourself. Express that love by doing good to all.

If you have been participating in the spiritual exercises that accompanied the chapters, you will have been exposed to a number of spiritual ways of experiencing God. Some of these will have resonated with you and some will likely not. Keep experimenting and build on what you have been doing. Be diligent to carve out time each day to spend with God.

If you only read the chapters, then go back and use the study guides to give shape to your personal devotions over the next eight weeks. Of the nineteen participants who field-tested this study, many indicated that their time alone with God doing the exercises had the greatest impact on them. So don't miss out. Perhaps you can gather a group of people and go through the book and exercises together. A summary video of each chapter will soon be available on-line at *www.lovesgreatestjoy.com.* These videos can be used to summarize the chapters each week as your group gathers.

The God who is love longs for you to draw close with Him, to deepen your relationship and to share that relationship with others. As you draw nearer to Him, you will draw closer to one another. You will become united in spirit with that great cloud of witnesses who have gone before us and surround us.

In chapter 11 of the book of Hebrews, the Apostle testifies to the amazing faith of those who believed the promises of God. They saw these from afar and persevered in their walk, even though they had not received in their earthly life what was promised (Heb. 11:39). What they longed for was not available on earth. They dreamed of a better country, a heavenly one. So it is true of us. What we long for, we can only see from afar. Citing their example, the Apostle exhorts his readers to get serious about their quest for this heavenly prize. He writes:

> *"Therefore, since we are surrounded by so great a cloud of witnesses, let us also lay aside every weight, and sin which clings so closely, and let us run with endurance the race that is set before us, looking to Jesus, the founder and perfecter of our faith, who for the joy that was set before him endured the cross, despising the shame, and is seated at the right hand of the throne of God." Hebrews 12:1-2*

We are not just walking with God, but we are running a race. The Greek word for race in this passage is *agon* from which we get our word agony. This is not just a short dash that is being described. This is a serious race, a marathon. God has set this race before us and we are to run with endurance. This Greek word is *hupomone,* which means steadfast determination to keep going, no matter what. Whether the sun is shining or we are running in soaking rain, sleet or snow, we plow on, determined to finish.

Such is the Christian life. We run as one who will get the prize. There is no abandoning the race, no sitting it out. We press on to the mark for the high calling of Christ. We are to do so by casting aside every weight. No one runs a marathon with a backpack full of stuff. We cast things aside, which slow us down. We also rid ourselves of the sin that clings so closely. We cast off our sinful self and run in the power of the Holy Spirit, looking to Jesus, *"the founder and perfector of our faith".* We keep our eyes on Him, for He runs with us, just ahead of us. The race that we are called to run, He has already run. And He runs with us. He is the Architect of our faith and will bring it to completion. For the joy that was set before Him, He endured the cross, despising its shame. So too, He calls us to run, ignoring the derision heaped upon us by people who are not in the race and beckon us to quit and sit. But there can be no quitting or sitting. We are in it to finish. And by the grace of God we will. There is laid up for us a joyful crown of righteousness, which God will give to us all who have loved His appearing (2 Tim. 4:8). Until that day, may God strengthen and equip you for the race.

> *"Now to him who is able to keep you from stumbling and to present you blameless before the presence of his glory with great joy, to the only God, our Savior, through Jesus Christ our Lord, be glory, majesty, dominion, and authority, before all time and now and forever."* Jude 1:24-25

Amen.

Notes

Chapter 1

[i] Victor A Shepherd, *Systematic Theology I* (Toronto, ON: Tyndale University College & Seminary, 2005).

[ii] Harley A Swiggum and Adult Christian Education Foundation, *The Bethel Series: A New Format in Adult Biblical Studies* (Madison, Wisc.: The Foundation, 1960), Lesson 2, p 15.

[iii] This line of questioning is taken from: Ray Comfort and Kirk Cameron, *The Way of the Master Basic Training Course: Study Guide*, Stg. (Genesis Publishing Group, 2006).

[iv] Frank Viola, *From Eternity to Here* (David C. Cook, 2009).

[v] David Sherbino, *Re:connect: Spiritual Exercises to Develop Intimacy with God* ([Toronto] Canada: Salt Creative Group, 2008), 17.

Chapter 2

[vi] J. Alec Motyer, *The Prophecy of Isaiah: An Introduction & Commentary* (IVP Academic, 1998), 77.

[vii] Victor A Shepherd, *Systematic Theology I* (Toronto, ON: Tyndale University College & Seminary, 2005), Lecture 7 - The Doctrine of Sin.

[viii] Gerhard O Forde, *On Being a Theologian of the Cross: Reflections on Luther's Heidelberg Disputation, 1518* (Grand Rapids, MI: W.B. Eerdmans, 1997), 51.

[ix] James Edwin Loder, *The Transforming Moment: Understanding Convictional Experiences* (San Francisco, CA: Harper & Row, 1981).

[x] Shepherd, *Systematic Theology I.*

[xi] Loder, *The Transforming Moment*, 31.

[xii] Ibid., 32.

[xiii] Ibid.

[xiv] Ibid.

[xv] Ibid., 35.

[xvi] Ibid., 83.

[xvii] Ibid., 79.

[xviii] Ibid.

[xix] Dietrich Bonhoeffer, *The Cost of Discipleship*, Touchstone ed. (New York ; London ; Toronto :Simon & Schusster, 1995), 89.

[xx] Martin Luther, *Luther's Primary Works: Together with His Shorter and Larger Catechisms ; Translated with English* (London: Hodder and Stoughton, 1896).

[xxi] Henri J. M Nouwen, *Spiritual Formation: Following the Movements of the Spirit* (New York: Harper One, 2010), 105.

Chapter 3

[xxii] Jean Calvin, *Institutes of the Christian Religion* (Philadephia, PA: Westminister Press, 1960), 3.11.1.

[xxiii] Martin Luther, *Luther's Primary Works: Together with His Shorter and Larger Catechisms ; Translated with English* (London: Hodder and Stoughton, 1896).

[xxiv] Wayne A. Grudem, *Systematic theology* (Zondervan, 1994), 828.

[xxv] Peter Nelson, *Spiritual Formation: Ever Forming, Never Formed* (Biblica, 2010), 47.

[xxvi] Harold Ewing Burchett, *Spiritual Life Studies* ([S.l.]: H.E. Burchett, 1980), 132.

[xxvii] Ibid.

[xxviii] John Owen, *The Works of John Owen* (London: Banner of Truth Trust, 1965), vol. 6, 168.

[xxix] Ibid., Vol 6. 168.

[xxx] Ibid., Vol 6, P. 227.

[xxxi] Calvin, *Institutes of the Christian Religion*, 3.3.11.

[xxxii] Dietrich Bonhoeffer, *Life Together* (HarperSanFrancisco, 1993), 19.

[xxxiii] Owen, *The Works of John Owen*, vol. 6, 43-76.

[xxxiv] Ibid., Vol. 6, 59.

[xxxv] Ibid., Vol 6, 61.

[xxxvi] Ibid., vol 6, 62.

[xxxvii] David Sherbino, *Re:connect: Spiritual Exercises to Develop Intimacy with God* ([Toronto] Canada: Salt Creative Group, 2008), 54.

Chapter 4

[xxxviii] Brother Lawrence, *The Practice of the Presence of God* (Health Research Books, 1996).

[xxxix] I am indebted to Victor Shepherd's lectures that emphasize this concept: Victor A Shepherd, *Hans Urs Von Balthasar's Prayer a Theological Investigation* (Vancouver,

BC Canada: Regent College, 2001). Lecture 1.
Also: Martin Buber, *I and Thou*, 2nd ed. (New York: Charles Scribner, 1958).

[xl] Victor A Shepherd, *Theology of the Human Person* (Vancouver, B.C: Regent College, 2004), Lecture: Two Kinds of Knowing.

[xli] Henri J. M Nouwen, *Spiritual Formation: Following the Movements of the Spirit* (New York: HarperOne, 2010), 11.

[xlii] Shepherd, *Theology of the Human Person.*

[xliii] Buber, *I and Thou.*

[xliv] Shepherd, *Hans Urs Von Balthasar's Prayer a Theological Investigation*, disk 1.

[xlv] Ibid.

[xlvi] Henri J. M. Nouwen, *The wounded healer* (Random House of Canada, 1979), 83.

[xlvii] Ibid., 84.

[xlviii] Lawrence Crabb, *Inside out* (Colorado Springs Colo.: NavPress, 1988), 71.

[xlix] Ibid., 87.

[l] Ibid., 88.

[li] Ibid., 90.

[lii] Victor A Shepherd, *Systematic Theology I* (Toronto, ON: Tyndale University College & Seminary, 2005), Sovereignty of God lecture.

[liii] Dietrich Bonhoeffer, *The Cost of Discipleship*, Touchstone ed. (New York ; London ; Toronto :Simon & Schusster, 1995), 43.

[liv] Nouwen, *The wounded healer.*

[lv] Nouwen, *Spiritual Formation*, 9.

[lvi] Ibid.

[lvii] Jean Pierre de Caussade, *The sacrament of the present moment* (Harper & Row, 1982), 26.

[lviii] Ibid., 25.

[lix] Aaron Milavec, *The Didache: Text, Translation, Analysis, and Commentary* (Collegeville, Minn: Liturgical Press, 2003). 52

[lx] Jean Calvin, *Institutes of the Christian Religion* (Philadephia, PA: Westminister Press, 1960), 2.

[lxi] Mark Nysewander, *The Fasting Key: How You Can Unlock Doors to Spiritual Blessing* (Sovereign World, 2002).

[lxii] John Wesley, "Sermons on Several Occasions" (Weslyan Conference Office. London, 1868), Vol. 3, Sermon 116, Section 14, P. 276.

Chapter 5

[lxiii] Victor A Shepherd, *Hans Urs Von Balthasar's Prayer a Theological Investigation* (Vancouver, BC Canada: Regent College, 2001), lecture 1.

[lxiv] Ibid., lecture 1.

[lxv] Victor Harold Matthews, *Old Testament Parallels: Laws and Stories from the Ancient Near East* (New York: Paulist Press, 1991), 7.

[lxvi] Dietrich Bonhoeffer, *Letters and papers from prison* (Simon & Schuster Inc, 1997), 199.

[lxvii] J C 1816 Ryle, *Practical Religion. Being Plain Papers on the Daily Duties, Experience, Dangers and Privileges of Professing Christians* (Nabu Press, 2010), 10.

[lxviii] Stanley J. Grenz, *Prayer: The Cry for the Kingdom*, Revised. (Wm. B. Eerdmans Publishing Company, 2005), 25.

[lxix] Ibid., 27.

[lxx] Robert Webber, *The Renewal of Sunday Worship* (Hendrickson Publishers, 1993), 25.

[lxxi] Dietrich Bonhoeffer, *Life Together* (HarperSanFrancisco, 1993), 44.

[lxxii] Paul J. Achtemeier, *HarperCollins Bible Dictionary*, Rev Upd. (HarperOne, 1996), 81.

[lxxiii] Patrick J. Geary, *Readings in Medieval History, 4th Edition* (University of Toronto Press, 2010), 242.

[lxxiv] Dennis Ngien, *Gifted Response: The Triune God as the Causative Agency of Our Responsive Worship* (Paternoster, 2008).

[lxxv] Robert Webber, *The worship phenomenon* (Star Song Pub Co, 1994), 33.

Chapter 6

[lxxvi] Victor A Shepherd, *Systematic Theology I* (Toronto, ON: Tyndale University College & Seminary, 2005), Lecture, The Primacy of Scripture.

[lxxvii] Eugene H. Peterson, *The Message: The Bible in Contemporary Language* (Navpress Publishing Group, 2002).

[lxxviii] Gordon D. Fee, "Exegesis and Spirituality : Reflections on Completing the Exegetical Circle.," *Crux* 31, no. 4 (December 1, 1995): 1.

[lxxix] Ibid., 4.

[lxxx] J. Scott Duvall, *Grasping God's Word: A Hands-on Approach to Reading, Interpreting, and Applying the Bible / Hays, J. Daniel,; 1953-* (Grand Rapids, Mich.: Zondervan, 2001), 21.

[lxxxi] Ibid.

[lxxxii] Ibid., 22.

[lxxxiii] Ibid.

[lxxxiv] Ibid., 24.

[lxxxv] Haddon W Robinson, *Biblical Preaching: The Development and Delivery of Expository Messages*, 2nd ed. (Grand Rapids, MI: Baker Academic, 2001), 39.

[lxxxvi] Duvall, *Grasping God's Word*, 29.

[lxxxvii] Victor A Shepherd, *Systematic Theology I* (Toronto, ON: Tyndale University College & Seminary, 2005), lecture "The Work of Christ".

Chapter 7

[lxxxviii] Aaron Milavec, *The Didache: Text, Translation, Analysis, and Commentary* (Collegeville, Minn: Liturgical Press, 2003).

[lxxxix] Ray Comfort and Kirk Cameron, *The Way of the Master Basic Training Course: Study Guide*, Stg. (Genesis Publishing Group, 2006), 22.

Chapter 8

[xc] Alan Hirsch and Leonard Sweet, *The Forgotten Ways* (Brazos Press, 2007), 143.

[xci] Steve Hill, *The Luke 10 Manual: Mission as Modelled & Mandated by Jesus* (Lulu.com, 2010), 18.

[xcii] Hill, *The Luke 10 Manual: Mission as Modelled & Mandated by Jesus*.

[xciii] Ray Comfort and Kirk Cameron, *The Way of the Master Basic Training Course: Study Guide*, Stg. (Genesis Publishing Group, 2006).

[xciv] Ibid., 44.

[xcv] Dietrich Bonhoeffer, *Life Together* (HarperSanFrancisco, 1993), 10.

[xcvi] Ibid., 17.

[xcvii] Ibid., 19.

[xcviii] Ibid., 22.

[xcix] Ibid., 26.

[c] Ibid., 27.

[ci] Ibid., 28.

[cii] Ibid., 34.